A W A K E N

T H E   S L U M B E R I N G

G O D D E S S

**The Latent code of the Hindu
goddess archetypes**

by
Ashok Bedi, M.D.
Additional Research by Ami Bedi

ISBN: 1-4196-7260-6
ISBN-13: 9781419672606
Library of Congress Control Number:

Visit www.booksurge.com to order additional copies.

Contents

As clinicians, we are well aware that patients bring to us encoded behavioral communications that are non-verbal. These are often presented to us in their transference, or as part of their character pathology, or in their symptomatology. Our task, is to help them break the code, and to "translate" these symptoms into words, so that they can be understood and processed.

In this, his most groundbreaking work as yet, Dr. Bedi proposes that the soul itself conveys it's message, via the "latent code of timeless wisdom templates that have crystallized in human consciousness over several millennia". Defining our limited outer consciousness as the ego, and our deeper consciousness as the soul, Dr. Bedi points out that it is only when the ego and the soul are connected, that we can bridge the gap. This allows our destiny to blossom, and reach its true potential.

Dr. Bedi's book itself is a bridge that takes us on a fascinating journey -- a journey that enables us to connect our outward consciousness with the deeper wisdom of our unconscious psyche. This wisdom is born of the cumulative wealth of human experience through the ages.

Equally at home with clarifying Jungian theory, and explaining the Vedas and Hindu spirituality in all it's glory, Dr. Bedi gives us a masterful analysis of human distress as a manifestation of the ego's disconnection from the soul (the source of innate wisdom).

He explains, step-by-step, with vivid personnel and clinical examples, how to identify clues that are made available to us by the latent code of our soul. He likens this to DNA; just as DNA analysis in these modern times can sometimes set a prisoner free, so can the identification of this code release us to reconnect with the timeless wisdom of the ages. Such an analysis may at last free us from the tyranny of psychological distress and reaffirm us in our larger purpose in the universe. Perhaps this is what John Newton, in the hymn Amazing Grace, meant when he wrote the words "I once was lost but now am found was blind and now I can see".

The overall design of the book, like a fine Persian

carpet, is interwoven with stories of Dr. Bedi's fascinating encounters with the latent code in his own life and in the lives of his patients.

Using dreams, synchronistic events, and symptoms, he produces a kaleidoscope of fascinating patterns. As these patterns flash before the clinician's eye, they evoke images of patients who could make important discoveries in their selves, and increase their creativity, if only they were able to tolerate what they experience as a "void", and listen to the whisperings of the latent code from their souls.

In a particularly illuminating chapter on the city of Bombay, Dr. Bedi describes the dream that helped to establish the Mahalakshmi temple, and to bridge the separate islands together into a cohesive city.

And in the end, Dr. Bedi warns how important it is to be aware of this spiritual code and dimension, without being possessed by it to the extent that all analytical objectivity is lost. Thereby we can avoid the present state of affairs that seem to exist, in terms of one extreme or the other, in both the East and the West.

I must stress, that although this book is full of fascinating clinical insights, Dr. Bedi's mastery of the subject, as well as his language, make it a must for any individual who is searching for enlightenment.

Once again, Dr. Bedi points out for us the path to regain our "sight" and sense of purpose, by letting the words expressed by our unconscious guide our egos into safe harbor.

Dinshah D. Gagrat, M.D.
Director, Adult Psychiatric Services
Aurora Psychiatric Hospital

In Dr. Bedi's book, he elegantly provides a template to translate Hindu mythology into dynamic clinical psychology in ways that not only inform but also provide a paradigm and a guide to personal growth. Dr. Bedi presents

and integrates his understanding of Eastern spirituality, *vii*
including the archetypes of the Hindu Goddesses, as a
powerful metaphor in achieving balance, harmony, and
healing in our own psyche as well as in our relationships
with others. His discussion of the importance of reflection
and insights into ones "latent code" is especially helpful.
Finally, this book, in addition to Dr. Bedi's presentation
of clinical vignettes of his psychotherapy with patients,
describes examples in his own personal life experiences
which illustrate how these insights are able to contribute
to the development of an individual's personal narrative
that is coherent and sustaining.

Irving H. Raffe, MSSW
Clinical Professor, Department of
Psychiatry and Behavioral Medicine,
Medical College of Wisconsin

Why are so many people depressed? Why do so many
people chase after one stimulating experience after another?
Why does "the pursuit of happiness" sound more and more
like a cruel joke, or an unattainable state of being?

In *Awaken the Slumbering Goddess - The Latent Code* of
the Hindu Goddess Archetypes, Ashok Bedi, M.D., offers
both an answer to these questions as well as a method
for restoring our personal and our collective sense of
meaning and purpose: Our consciousness is rootless, and
consequently starved for the nourishment that only the
objective psyche—the "collective unconscious"—can offer.
We are more like hydropontically-grown plants, subsisting
on slurry of artificially compounded nutrients flushed into
the sterile gravel where our hungry roots seek real food.

Through an insightful exploration of many of the great
Hindu goddesses, those images of the archetypal feminine
in their Indian cultural manifestations, Dr. Bedi reminds
us with myths and clinical vignettes how discovering and
connecting with the archetypal feminine aspect of the

objective psyche offer us the possibility of meaning and purpose, not just brute survival. Meaning and purpose arise through dialogue, that (often non-verbal) "conversation" in which we come to know and interact with real forces and personalities—goddesses—whose existence is invisible but palpable.

Perhaps we first encounter the goddess as Kali, "the dark goddess . . . [who] incarnates in our life to destroy the darkness of the personality to make room for a new consciousness to emerge." As C.G. Jung pointed out many years ago, often we must first dismantle our habitual conscious attitudes to make room for the new attitude that makes fruitful life possible. After Kali has cleared away the dead old growth, we may lie fallow, like the garden in winter. This is the realm and our experience of Aditi, the goddess and "energy of the void—the sacred space that is essential to make room for new creation." Kali and Aditi are often the first two goddesses to appear in the transformative process of renewal.

Dr. Bedi does not stop there, for the experience of renewal is more than the first two phases, imaged in these goddesses. Many of the people who come to us with their depression, anxiety, sense of futility and entrapment—and the many other symptoms we all have heard about or suffered ourselves—have felt Kali's presence in their flesh and bones. Many feel stranded in Aditi's realm—the void—neither knowing they are in the presence of a goddess, nor having any idea what might lie beyond. But there are more aspects to the Great Goddess than these two, and Dr. Bedi presents them in vivid hews.

Dr. Bedi's sure guidance may well help you, the reader, rediscover your "latent code" and sink your roots in the fertile, nourishing soil of the source and sustainer of all life.

Boris Matthews, Ph.D.
Jungian Psychoanalyst
Madison, WI
25 June 2007

CH 1
Introduction

Whenever sacred duty decays
And chaos prevails
Then, I create
Myself Arjuna
Bhagwad Gita: Chapter 4, Para 7

A patient recently reported this dream in his first session.

I have forgotten the combination code for my safe deposit box. I am desperately trying to remember it.

This is a classic dream that highlights the dilemma of every individual. What is the combination to open the safety deposit box of our unconscious to harvest the treasures in our psyche? This combination code is the latent code of our souls. Each one of us has a unique code that unlocks the mystery of our potential and well being. This book will explore the workings of this latent code and how each one of us can remember the code to engage the riches of our inner potential.

Life rarely works out as we planned. It is my hypothesis, based on my extensive clinical experience as a psychiatrist and a psychoanalyst, that when we live life out of the outer fringes of our psyche, or our Ego, it often works out worse than we hoped for. When we live life out of the deeper center of our psyche – our Soul – it plays out much better than we anticipated. Life that is lived out of our Ego— the center of our outer, conscious personality— is lived on the outer fringes of our potential. Life lived in tune with the Soul, the center of our deepest personality and the pacemaker of our destiny, usually blossoms to its fullest potential. The soul conveys its message via the latent code of archetypes, or timeless wisdom templates that have crystallized in human consciousness over several millions of years of collective experience as a species. This latent code lives in the rich myths, fables and legends of each culture. In this book, I have presented one such group of stories or wisdom templates. This is the latent code of Shakti, the life force that energizes and guides us on our life course. These are the stories of the powerful and mysterious goddesses of Hindu culture, collectively called Shakti, the spiritual energy that can help us live out of our soul. Welcome to the realm of Shakti, the inner goddess in every man and every woman.

Whenever we are dealing with a personal crisis, transition, a traumatic event, a relationship tangle, a major life decision, some spiritual or psychological crossroad, this latent code is activated by our soul to guide us. This helps us to make an informed decision consistent with our life purpose and spiritual calling. When there is a big split between our outer life and our spiritual path, the soul creates a symbol that aligns our outer consciousness with our soul's purpose. The latent code may send us a symbol embedded in our medical or psychiatric problem, our relationship difficulty, our hang ups, a significant dream, a synchronistic event, or an accident to guide us on our path. For each specific life problem there is a corresponding aspect of the latent code that spurs us onto our path.

To prepare for a new endeavor the latent code of the goddess of arts and academics, Saraswati, steps in; to attain peace and prosperity the code of Laxmi guides our path. When we walk the line between self assertion and mutuality, the code of Parvati guides us. When we are struggling to tame the dark side of our personality, the code of Kali helps us trim our shadow. Life transitions often call for a period of void and inner emptiness before new life structures can be created. The code of Aditi presides over the inner void and new creations. When we are trying to reconcile the opposites in our nature, the latent code of the archetype of the sacred marriage – the dance of the masculine Shiva and the eternal feminine Shakti – provides a useful template.

In my work as a psychotherapist as well in my personal quest, I have found that invoking the guidance of this latent code is essential and invaluable in attending to the process of healing the suffering of the mind and the body. This latent code guides us to destroy old dysfunctional attitudes. This is guided by Kali, the dark goddess of destruction of the old order. This then leads to the creation of a void in our lives. The code of the goddess Aditi then invokes new creation by holding us in the void. Often this sacred space in the psyche is perceived as depression, and the human tendency is to fill it in with habitual diversions like addictions and compulsions. If an individual can honor the void as discussed later in this book, the goddess can guide us in making new beginnings. The codes of the goddess trinity of Saraswati (the goddess of knowledge), Laxmi (the goddess of worldly success) and Shakti (the goddess of enlightenment) preside over this act of new creation in the psyche. Once the new consciousness is created, the latent code of the sacred marriage helps us unite the masculine and the feminine aspects of the psyche. This is the process of the sacred marriage of the divergent aspects of the psyche. The latent code embedded in the myth of the union of Shiva (masculine aspects of our psyche) and Shakti (feminine aspects of our psyche) in its numerous manifestations guides us in attending to this sacred union. This helps us to achieve wholeness and health of the mind, body and the soul.

In the Hindu spiritual and healing tradition, this latent code has a masculine and a feminine component. The masculine god images provide the structure or form to mediate the process of healing and change, while the goddess codes provide the energy and the psychological navigation to make the necessary changes in the healing process. This book focuses on the feminine aspect of this latent code, which leads to healing the rift between the conscious and the unconscious. When a bridge is established across this rift, our ego connects with the infinite and timeless wisdom of our soul, and we then live out of our totality. In such a state of totality, the timeless, cumulative collective wisdom of humanity is now available in the form of the myriad myths to guide the individual to deal with life and its problems. Mundane life is now informed and guided by the sacred dimension of the soul and its source, the Spirit.

In the Hindu tradition, the Spirit is like the great ocean and the individual soul is like a bucket of water from this great ocean. Each one of us is entrusted with our own small fractal of this great ocean. What we do with this gift that is in our temporary custody is up to us. Will we live life in a way worthy of the trust of the universe or will we betray it? Will we muddy up the world by mucking up our soul or will we leave this world a slightly better place than we found it? This choice is ours. The latent code can guide us in living a spiritually informed life and leave this world minutely better than it was.

Archetypal Activation of the Latent Code

Whenever the individual or culture becomes lopsided in its orientation, the spiritual consciousness is activated to compensate for this distortion and re-establish a homeostatic balance and wholeness. This is the phenomenon of archetypal activation in order to restore the integrity and wholeness of individuals and cultures. In my personal and clinical observation, the contemporary culture is dominated by a patriarchal, masculine, materialistic value system. While not without its merits, the current system is nevertheless lopsided and limited in its orientation. Conditions are ripe for activation of the latent code of the goddess archetype to begin healing and restoring the balance and wholeness of our civilization.

The present civilization is best characterized as materialistic and patriarchal, dominated by Western values. Figuratively, the West seems to represent masculine energy and the East to represent feminine energy. The pendulum is presently at the materialistic extreme, and the West is undoubtedly the leader in this enterprise. But whenever the individual or the collective psyche is at one extreme of values, the latent code activates the opposite energy to balance it. This process is what Carl Jung conceptualized as the phenomenon called *enantiodromia* [1]. Enantiodromia means 'running counter to' and designates the play of opposites in the course of events, the view that everything that exists turns in the course of time into its opposite. From the living comes death, and from death, life; from youth comes old age, and from the old, youth; from waking, sleep, and from sleep, waking. The stream of generation and decay never stands still. Construction and destruction, destruction and construction -- this is the principal which governs all the cycles of life, from the smallest to the greatest. Just as the cosmos itself arose from chaos, so must it return once more into the same, a dual process running its measured course through vast periods of time, a drama eternally re-enacted.

Conditions are now ripe for the Latent Code to activate the forces of enantiodromia. Our contemporary culture, dominated by materialism and Western values and technologies, is primed to move back toward its opposite. We have already seen this trend emerging in our present deepening interest in spirituality and Eastern values. However, the danger in enantiodromia is a total reversal and hence lopsided pendulum swing to the polar opposite, in our case to a naïve spiritual tourism and archaic "easternization" such as we saw in the sixties hippie movement and present so-called New Age thought. What is needed is not a complete enantiodromia but rather a creative integration of the East with the West, the material with the spiritual, mature masculinity with sacred femininity. Otherwise, we may move from one tyranny to another, from a one-sided archetypal masculine dominance to an equally one-sided archetypal feminine dominance.

When such a compensatory force becomes active, it is important to honor the collective movement of the human psyche by systematically studying the emerging trends, in this instance the eastern spiritual systems, and integrating these trends into the currently dominant western and material templates. An integration of Western thoughts and values with Eastern spirituality can yield a creative blend and produce a generative symbiosis for the each and every one of us to guide us through life's problems. On the other hand, if we disregard this enantiodromian swing toward spiritual and Eastern thought, it will be relegated to the shadow side of humanity and could erupt in destructive movements: for example the emergence of various extremist groups and cults in the United States and around the world.

The Latent Code of Shakti – the Inner Goddess

The term "Shakti" originates from the root *sak* which means "to do" or "to act." Thus Shakti worship is the worship of energy that is personified as female and is generally conceived of as the all-pervading Mother Goddess. She is regarded as the Supreme Creator, Sustainer, and Destroyer of the Universe. One who worships Her is known as a Sakta. While in India there are formal devotees of Shakti, most of us encounter Shakti in our life in more subtle ways. We may encounter her in dreams or synchronistic events. In her relational aspect Shakti guides our significant relationships; as Parvati she helps us get into relationships; in her Laxmi aspect she guides us to maintain our relational matrix; in her Saraswati aspect she helps us incubate new learning to tackle developmental tasks. Whenever life gets lopsided and the shadow aspects of personality gain ascendancy, Shakti incarnates in our inner life in her Kali manifestation and may destroy a certain dysfunctional aspect of our inner or outer life. When the old order is destroyed and the shadow aspects of personality have been assimilated into the personality, she may constellate in a significant dream or synchronistic event in her Aditi aspect and usher in new beginnings. When the masculine and feminine aspects of our personality are in optimal balance, Shakti engages in a dance with Shiva, her masculine consort, to establish the mandala (circle) of wholeness in the personality.

These various profiles in the latent code of the goddess are differentiated renderings of the archetype of the great goddess archetype. She may appear in these different relational manifestations as consort of the three gods of the Hindu Trinity. In her Parvati profile she is the consort of Shiva, the god who destroys the old order. She helps him to discern what is to be destroyed and what must be salvaged. In her Saraswati profile she is the consort of Brahma, the god of new creations. She facilitates new creation by guiding necessary preparations to make new creation possible. In her Laxmi profile, she is the consort of Vishnu and helps him maintain the Dharma or Spiritual order.

In her non-relational aspects, the latent code of Shakti constellates as Kali to tame the shadow aspects of the personality. In her Aditi profile, Shakti helps us honor the void and then inspires us to entertain new beginnings. Once Shakti has refined various facets of personality, she then helps unite it with her opposite masculine counterpart, her Shiva potential, to establish conscious wholeness of personality. At this point, different and opposite aspects of personality are conscious and in optimal balance which promotes the welfare of the individual and the culture. This dance of Shiva and Shakti aspects of personality continue in harmony until a new inner or outer crisis, or a developmental challenge, calls for a new adaptation. The necessary aspect of Latent Code is then activated anew to guide adaptation of personality to the new challenge and grow from it.

The story of contemporary Western civilization is one of material, masculine enterprise. While the fruits of this masculine orientation are many – in terms of mastery of certain aspects of nature, it has also alienated us from the deeper, healing wisdom of nature and created an imbalance in our consciousness. Whenever culture falls out of balance, the compensating archetypal forces in the Latent Code are activated to re-establish the homeostasis of the consciousness. It is my hypothesis that now, the early 21ˢᵗ century, is the time for us to rediscover the feminine dimension of our latent code, so that it may guide us to restore wholeness of our individual personality and collective culture. Such feminine consciousness is ushered in by the healing wisdom of the goddess archetype. If we honor the emergence of our feminine psyche and goddess wisdom, it may heal the crisis of the material world by anchoring us back to our spiritual foundation. This will restore the health of every individual and our contemporary human civilization.

Biotechnology and the Spiritual Dimension

Another parallel trend in the world of medicine and the life sciences is the pendulum swing towards scientific, biological, psychological, sociological, and medical models of treatment. This biomedical trend in health care is fueled by profound yet seductive new discoveries in the chemistry and the structure of the body, the nervous system and the brain, the mapping out of the human genome and the emerging frontiers of stem cell research.

The spiritual dimension is marked by its absence in the modern biopsychosocial health care model. While promising new antidepressants like Prozac[2] may restore the neurochemistry of the central nervous system, what is to heal the wounded soul? What are often missing in treatment are the relational and spiritual components necessary to restore the ailing soul. The biotechnological interventions put the fire out but may not attend to the gas leaks in the psyche that keep rekindling the fire of illness, disease and relationship tangles.

In this context, it is my hypothesis that in the next few decades, we will see a move towards a restoration of balance through the activation of the latent code and spirituality will emerge as a major determinant in contemporary treatment and healing methods.

Integration of the Mature Masculine and the Sacred Feminine aspects of our Latent Code

In addition to the leadership of Western and material values, another important trend that is crucial to mention is that contemporary civilization is male-dominated. The principal of enantiodromia (return to the opposite pole) would indicate that in the evolving civilization there would be ascendancy of the power of the feminine, affirmation of feminine values, and the era of the return of the goddess archetype. At this critical point in our cultural evolution, the danger is that there may be an archaic enantiodromia from the masculine to a feminine consciousness. The stereotypical devouring feminine could replace the dominance of the patriarchy. The goal of the latent code and its cultural consciousness is not to replace one extreme with another, but rather to integrate and balance the mature masculine and sacred feminine in the healing of the individual and collective human consciousness.

We are in an era of genocide when power-driven men rape hundreds and thousands of women in order to dominate other ethnic and racial groups. In many parts of the world, greed drives people to plunder the environment and defile the earth by carelessly dumping toxic chemicals and radioactive wastes. Some of these sites may take several decades to start cleaning up. In the Midwestern United States, the Great Lakes, which are the largest bodies of fresh water on the planet, swimming or fishing is unsafe at times because of toxic contamination. It is paradoxical that as we continue to wound the great Mother, She returns to heal us and redeem us, sometimes with a vengeance as the dark Kali, but more often in the form of the Healing Goddess. If we attend to the Latent Code and honor it, we can tune into its timeless wisdom to heal ourselves and our civilization.

How the Latent Code guided this book

I was pondering several topics for my book based on my experiences as a psychiatrist and a psychoanalyst, when, synchronistically, an invisible guidance of the latent code appeared to help me with this decision. My daughter decided to join me on the trip to India in February/March of 1999. When I told her about the various book topics I was entertaining, she suggested to me that since my interface with the feminine (and with her of late) had been turbulent, I might gain deeper insight into my own personal growth by undertaking the Latent Code project. She offered to facilitate it by assisting me in the India visit part of the project. She spoke with deep love and wisdom, and I was moved by her wish to collaborate with me, in spite of me! Was the latent code in its Shakti dimension whispering via her voice? Actually that turned out to be the case. One of the greatest soul dividends of our collaboration was a subtle deepening of our relationship and in the process my encounter with the inner daughter (my budding feeling function) and with the latent code of the Shakti archetype (the Healing aspects of my inner feminine).

The trip to India involved managing cumbersome photographic gadgetry to take photographs at the temple sites in Mumbai, Varanasi, Ahmedabad and Khajurao. This was a great challenge to my low sensate (difficulty in attending to small details) inferior function. This is based on Jung's theory of psychological types, which posits that we have a superior function, in my case intuition; a secondary auxiliary function, in my case thinking; tertiary auxiliary function, mine feeling; and finally an inferior function, mine sensate as aforementioned. These functions are pairs of opposites and form a typological mandala. They are discussed in detail in volume 6 of C.G. Jung's Collected Works. My daughter, Ami, is a patient person and a capable photographer and rather than take over my rather archaic attempts to photograph the Goddess images, she assisted me in managing the ordeal on my own and attaining a certain level of mastery of my own accord. I took most of the photographs in this book, and Ami took some. The degree of mastery of my sensate function was a valuable dividend of this endeavor, perhaps a gift reaped

due to the attention I was finally giving to the Shakti
archetype's role in my life.

Blessing of the goddess

As I took up the project of revising the original manuscript, I had the following dream, which confirmed to me that I must continue my work on the latent code project. The dream follows:

> *I am working in my garden shed. My daughter Ami, my son Siddhartha, and my grandson Signe are playing inside the shed. The door is flimsy but functional. I peek outside the loosely closed door and see a lioness lounging in the garden with her cub. Initially I am afraid for the safety of my children, but the lioness and her cub seem relaxed and not in any mood to attack anyone. I am reassured and continue to admire the lion mother and her son in amazement.*

This dream had a profound impact on me. A lioness is the mount of the great goddess Amba, my patron goddess, and she is one of the manifestations of Kali (or Durga in my home state of Gujarat in India). It felt to me that as I undertook the revision of my manuscript, the great goddess appeared in my dream to bless me and reassure me that I may continue my project under her auspices without any danger of being professionally or publicly misunderstood. Initially I had been skeptical of writing this book for the fear that my medical, psychiatric and Jungian peers might think that I am advocating some mumbo jumbo goddess spirituality and have gone off the deep end in my spiritual research. There are some real blind spots in the latent code of the Eastern spirituality. My favorite author Gita Mehta eloquently and humorously discusses these in her book *Karma Cola.*[3] She describes how thousands of Westerners travel to India in the belief that they will find holy men able to free them from their existential despair and disenchantment with the material world. What they find instead is traumatic exploitation. They confuse the banal for the profound in their attempts to levitate above the harsh realities of life. Additionally, in the dream, the goddess appeared with her cub, her divine child, an offspring of the goddess. Perhaps my book would be a cub of the goddess, inspired and blessed by her grace.

The Latent Code of Personal Spirituality and Religion

I want to take one brief moment to clarify that the trend I see in our present culture is from material to spiritual, not from material to religious. This is a unique phenomenon in our contemporary civilization. While some may seek the spiritual destination via the religious route, many people in our present civilization are starting to make a clear distinction between spirituality and religion. Religion—as participation in an organized institution and adherence to a creed and doctrine—is but one road on the spiritual quest to decode the latent code. The goal of the latent code and spirituality is to help an individual establish a bridge to one's soul and the soul's connection with the divine Spirit or Universal consciousness. Many roads lead us from our outer ego consciousness to our Soul and the Soul's connection with the Spirit. It is as if the spring flows into the river, and the river flows into the great ocean. A spiritual attitude as well as religious traditions provides a framework to attend to this goal. Many individuals confuse the road with the destination, which is to achieve their fullest spiritual potential, their dharma. Spirituality is personal religion, and religion is collective spirituality. Either connects us to the spirit. The choice is whether one chooses a collective or individual path. Sometimes a collective path may not attend to the specific needs of an individual who needs a more personalized spiritual focus than the religion may offer.

The question of defining and establishing personal spirituality is one of the most frequent problems that come up in my psychoanalytic work with individuals grappling with the challenges of contemporary life. The watershed issue for most of them comes down to discerning personal spirituality from institutional spirituality, i.e. Religion. I have seen modern men and women struggle with their emerging personal spirituality within the tenants of their faith or religion. They find that concepts from many different faiths and traditions help them build the mosaic of their personal spirituality, which helps them discern the latent code. They struggle with how to reconcile this with their religious tradition.

The solution that emerges for most of them is an ecumenical framework that honors Universal Spirituality or a belief that all paths lead to the same destination. The language and the rituals of different religions may differ, but the goal and the destination is the same: to connect individual soul with the divine Spirit. Whether we subscribe to Hinduism, Christianity, Buddhism, Islamic or Judaic tradition, all roads lead to connection with the realm of the divine universal Spirit. They use different languages, but the message is the same. If I say "I love you" in Hindi, English, Chinese or German, it is still love, as far as we honor and understand each others language. This concept is embodied in the Hindu scriptures of Rig Veda.

As expressed in the *Rig Veda* verse:
Ekam sat vipr bahudh vadanti
Truth is one, but sages call it by many names
Rig Veda 1:164:46.

I am not a theologian, clergyman or an expert on either spirituality or religions. As a psychiatrist, psychoanalyst and physician, I have had to struggle with the latent code and the concept of spirituality to help me understand and help my patients. The framework that emerges in my work is often an empirical resolution to a much larger question that we will have to dialogue about and struggle with collectively. So I will briefly discuss this concept of personal spirituality as it has crystallized over time to help my patients deepen their soul work and healing. I always encourage individuals to honor and follow their own religious path and use their personal spirituality to amplify their inner work.

In my working model, spirituality is an individual's effort to understand and assimilate the presence of one's deeper center of consciousness, the soul, and its connection with higher consciousness – what I call the Spirit. To make a connection with one's soul and the Spirit, an individual may use all available psychological and pragmatic methods and paradigms which help one identify their personal symbols and healing myths. Such a personal system constitutes our personal spirituality.

Such a personal Spirituality may certainly employ one's religious orientation. As far as the religious system facilitates understanding our personal symbols and myths, it becomes a component of our Spirituality. However, in establishing a framework of Spirituality, many informed contemporary individuals may use more than one religious system to weave a personal matrix of spirituality. My own background and upbringing is as a devout but not rigid Hindu in my personal life. However, my Spiritual life is often guided, amplified and enriched by Christian symbols and myths. Perhaps, this is why nature gave us two eyes. Two eyes give us a bigger horizon and a three dimensional perception. Carl Jung advised his students to learn one religion other than their own tradition to deepen their sense of their own religion by comparative context. I have often heard the term "Cafeteria Catholic or Hindu." I think this may be a compliment rather than a criticism, provided one chooses the essence of one's religious guidance. However, this choice must be made out of personal spiritual conviction, not convenience.

John and the Healing Symbol of the Two Elephants

In my work with my patients, I am amazed that many of the medical or emotional problems that beset us eventually turn out to be a spiritual problem. For instance, when individuals present with manic depressive illness, they need stabilization of their mood swings with the help of medications. However, the medication puts the fire out, but the gas leak in the psyche persists. When we dig deeper into the problem, it often turns out to be a spiritual issue. Many of these individuals are caught in the oscillation between earth (depression) and sky (manic) modes of adaptation.

Consider the case of my patient John. He had a dream that there were two elephants playing, one with the trunk up pointing to the sky and the other with the trunk down, pointing to the earth. John had learned to adapt to his life problems through a manic, heroic output of rushing to the sky to solve the problem. Then he would burn out and fall to the earth and crash into a depressive episode. This was a repetitive cycle for him.

The elephant image in his dream was activated by his latent code and provided the necessary symbol for his healing. The elephant is firmly grounded on earth but has the capacity to raise his trunk to the sky or earth as needed. He learned over time to stay solidly grounded in his daily life and in his precious relationships with his loving wife and children, as he dealt with challenges of his life. Our analytic work focused on helping him establish a sense of his own ground out of which he could operate rather than to fly into the skies or crash to the ground. I feel that the symbol of the elephant in John's dream was also meant to guide me as his analyst. Elephant is the symbol of the elephant headed god Ganesha in Hindu mythology – he is a god of sacrifice of the head or the old attitude and auspicious new beginnings. John had to sacrifice his heroic attitude of rushing into things and make a new beginning by learning to stay grounded. Interestingly, this pattern also has the mythological motif of Icarus, the hero who had wax wings. When he flew close to the Sun, his wings melted and he crashed and drowned in the ocean below. John had learned to honor the symbols that emerged in his dreams to guide him in his life. This attention to personal symbols is facilitated by cultivation of personal spirituality and a reflective attitude to life. This helps us tune into the latent code. Our soul and the Spirit are constantly trying to guide us on our path, if we pause and listen to these whispers of our soul.

Many of the relationship problems of modern men and women are spiritual problems in disguise. For instance, when a man presents with the dilemma of involvement in an extramarital affair, even when the marriage is on solid ground, I have found in my clinical practice that on closer assessment this is a spiritual issue. The man has lost connection with his anima, or the unconscious inner feminine. The analytic task is to help the patient move from the literal to the symbolic meaning of this affair and help him claim a relationship with his inner, creative, feminine potential. The attention to the latent code of the goddess archetypes are extremely helpful in helping men and women enter the sacred precinct of these inner potentials and are the subject matter of this book.

In understanding and healing human suffering and the human condition, we need the help and support of the rich and varied symbols from all the religions of the world. When we display religious and cultural tolerance, it does more than serve human rights; it enhances the chances of survival of the human race and what is human about our race.

CH 2
Deciphering the Latent Code
of the Slumbering Goddesses

The Latent Code is the program of our Soul to align our outer conscious life with our unconscious psychological and Spiritual life. Our Soul's latent code aligns us with our life's purpose, meaning, spiritual calling, and destiny. It aligns our limited outer consciousness with the intention of the Universe in a way that is unique to each individual. When we live out of our Latent Code, we honor our innate and unique talents and potential, optimally attend to our family and relationships, play an altruistic role in the fabric of our community and fulfill the instructions of the Primal Spirit in this lifetime. Such a spiritually engaged life feels vital, robust, and meaningful and is not only healthful and soulful to the individual but makes a crucial contribution to the wellbeing of our family and our community. Such an individual leaves this world a little bit better place than they found it.

The Latent Code is like the genetic code of our psyche. It contains the information which our Soul can access from the deeper layers of the human psyche and from the universe in a focused and systematic way. This helps us to attend to the crucial needs of our life in the present moment and directs us to our spiritual destiny. Our Soul is the central agency that activates this latent code, our ego is the implementer of this code, and the archetypal matrix in the universe is the ground source of this latent code.

The genetic code is a set of rules that maps DNA sequences to build proteins in the living cell and is employed in the process of protein synthesis. The genetic information carried by an organism – its genome – is inscribed in one or more DNA molecules. Each functional portion of a DNA molecule is referred to as a gene. Each gene is transcribed into a short template molecule of the related polymer RNA, which is better suited for protein synthesis. This in turn is translated by mediation of a machinery consisting of ribosomes and a set of transfer RNAs and associated enzymes into an amino acid chain (polypeptide), which will then be folded into a protein.

Like the genetic code, the latent code has several coordinates that must be aligned to activate the latent code and reassemble it in a way that is relevant to the individual's circumstances. The DNA of the human psyche is the Soul. It takes the archetypal sequences in the universe and the collective human consciousness and translates them into unconscious templates and subsequent consciousness, personality structures, life experiences, attitudes and relationships that are essential for our personal growth.

The Ego or the center of our conscious personality is like the RNA, which takes its cue from the soul and embodies them into life experiences. The third coordinate is the archetypal matrix of the universe that holds the timeless wisdom templates that the Soul can draw upon to deal with the ego's dilemma and the demands of the life situation. It is akin to the Genome or the total archetypal wisdom matrix available to the Soul to draw upon to fulfill its task in this lifetime. The Soul then chooses the appropriate archetypal program to deal with the life situation and finds an appropriate symbol to communicate this to the ego. Ego must now implement the guidance of the Soul and the archetypes. This activation of our latent code redirects our life journey onto its spiritual trajectory. If we consciously implement the prescription of the latent code, we live a happy, healthy and wholesome life and have robust relationships. If we ignore the latent code, we do so at our own peril to our physical and mental health and relationship problems.

The Soul is the genetic material of the psyche like the DNA is in our genes. It carries information about our life's purpose and the program from our ancestral and past life matrix. The DNA-like function of our Soul controls the synthesis of the archetypal information in a way that is relevant to our life problems. The Soul assesses the ego's need in the present life situation and matches them with the available archetypal possibilities in the universe and synthesizes an appropriate response to the situation. In Bhagwad Gita, this is symbolically described as the reincarnation of God Vishnu to deal with the individual or collective crisis.

> *Whenever sacred duty decays*
> *And chaos prevails*
> *Then I create*
> *Myself Arjuna,*
> *To protect men of virtue*
> *And destroy men who do evil*
> *To set the standard of sacred duty*
> *I appear in age after age.*

Ref: Bhagwad Gita, Chapter 4, Para 7-8

Soul –The Global Positioning System to Decipher the Latent Code

The central structure in deciphering the Latent Code is the archetype of the soul. Our soul synthesizes all the relevant archetypes that are pertinent in our specific journey and activates them in precise order. The archetype of the soul is the conductor of the symphony orchestra of archetypes as it relates to our individual life journey. The archetype of the soul is like a "Global positioning system." It orients us in the bigger picture of life and the cosmos. It helps us find our place in the Spirit's plans.

My patient David was a Resident in Medicine, who was struggling with recovery from depression, conflict in his marriage, pressure of parenting young children, moonlighting to make ends meet and trying to decide on the future course of specialization in his medical training. His decision for further specialization was a few years away. Yet he found himself obsessing about his future plans, sometimes as a defense against his present life pressures, and at other times as a reality issue. In this context he had a dream, part of which is presented here.

I am lost in the forest. However, I discover that I have a global positioning system in my car. This reassures me. I relax and enjoy the ride.

This dream had a profound and soothing impact on David. The archetype of the soul came in his dream to reassure him that he may attend to his present life in the here and now and that he will get guidance from a higher source to find his destination and navigate his journey in due course. This bore out in the next several years. He got timely instructions from his dreams, synchronistic events and certain other circumstances that gradually guided his way to make relevant choices in the personal and professional sectors of his life in accord with his soul's calling. He was able to choose a professional course of action that was consistent with his soul's calling, his passions. He and his wife negotiated and made compromises so that they could both grow together. The global positioning system in this pivotal dream was the symbol of his archetype of the soul.

One of the most critical tasks in our life path is to identify where the soul is pointing in deciphering the latent code that guides us. This central archetype of the soul orients us continuously towards the Spirit. The soul may metamorphose as needed to keep our ego in synch with the Spirit.

In my own journey, I have had to confront the task of recognizing and working with my latent code. For instance, at one point I was struggling with the optimal way to integrate the East and the West, the medical and the spiritual aspects of my life and work. When I worked with my medical peers, I had to be cautious how I presented my spiritual thoughts. When I was with my Jungian analytic peers, I had to be understated in terms of expressing my medical views. As I struggled to be authentic in integrating this split in my psyche and my world, I had a dream.

I am carrying a big stone in my two hands and I am not

permitted to put it down. I feel overburdened. In the dream I pray for help. Suddenly, the stone becomes light, and it becomes a small child. The child is baby Lord Krishna, and he is playing his flute.

Initially I was puzzled but eventually I was ecstatic about this dream. I knew intuitively that Krishna, or the divine trickster, was my personal guiding myth at this time. Krishna is like Hermes, the messenger, trickster god, who connects different worlds. Lord Krishna had appeared in my dream to instruct me in the art of communication, the realm of the fifth or the throat chakra. I knew that, like Krishna, I must hold the tension of the opposites, east and west, medical and spiritual, and let the Latent code guide me in carrying my burden. It is interesting that just after this dream, my grandson Signe was born. Perhaps he is the incarnation of Krishna in my life! I have been guided by this image and the divine tricksters Hermes and Krishna as I attempt to fulfill my dharma, my soul work to be one brick in the bridge between the East and the West, between medical and spiritual dimensions of healing.

The Archetypes – the substrate of the Latent Code

The third and the most mysterious of the three coordinates of the Latent Code are the Archetypes. These archetypes are timeless wisdom templates that have crystallized in the human psyche over million of years of human experience to guide us through transitions and turmoil in our life. They are the default modes of our unconscious adaptation that have evolved over several million years of human existence. They are activated to deal with important life events and changes like birth, death, marriage, leaving home, illness and recovery, crisis and trauma. It is the task of our consciousness to modify these default unconscious templates in ways that are consistent with our personality attributes and personal circumstances. In this book, we are going to explore the

22 archetype of the healing goddess as a crucial substrate of a larger body of the latent code. A new born child is not a spiritual blank slate but carries the timeless archetypal imprints of cumulative wisdom of countless long gone generations. In the course of development, the individual fills out and reanimates the vestiges of the experiences of our ancestors.[4] German biologist Ernst Haeckel[5] proposed that individual development, or Ontogeny, recapitulates species development, or Phylogeny, and the archetypes are the ontogenetic manifestation of the Phylogenetic memory of our human race.

First, let me define the terms archetype and their healing impact on our lives. Archetypes are well defined in classical Jungian literature. My take on the archetypes: Archetypes are the cumulative wisdom of the human psyche that are activated in each human being to help us navigate our spiritual development, help us with personal growth, help us with initiations and transitions in life, guide us during time of crisis, and adapt to the inner and the outer reality and future possibilities. Archetypes may be transmitted via genetic material, mediated by the nervous system and are embodied in the stories, fairy tales, myths, art and artifacts of every culture.

Archetypes have several facets or manifestations. They have instincts at the core; for example, sexual instinct in the lover archetype, generative instinct in the father archetype, nurturing instinct in the mother archetype, adventurous instincts in the warrior archetype, diplomatic instinct in the trickster archetype, altruistic instinct in the leader archetype and the mentoring instinct in the Guru/Guide/ Sophia archetype. They provoke images or fantasies that reflect the instinct and the purpose of the archetype. They have a tendency to provoke projections. For instance, if we are caught in the mother archetype, we may project the unconscious image and expectations of mother onto a corresponding maternal individual who may be available to receive this projection. We may start behaving with our boss or with our spouse or therapist as if they were our mothers. Archetypes are embodied in our dreams and fantasies, in the daydreams and creative process of the genius and the hallucinations and delusions of the mentally ill, embodied in the art and culture, and transmitted in the fairy tales, legends and myths of our civilization. Serious study of these manifestations of the archetypal substrate of the latent code is crucial if we are to decode these and harvest their potential for personal growth and collective welfare. This soil of the latent code embodied in myths is the partial subject matter of this book.

How the Latent Code Heals Us

Let me now define the term healing. Each one of us lives in a limited outer consciousness and has a deeper center of consciousness. The center of the outer consciousness is defined as the ego, and the center of the deeper consciousness is defined as the soul. When the ego and soul are connected, we bridge the gap between these two aspects of our psyche and can proceed to live out of a broader and deeper base. This connection between our limited outer ego consciousness and our deeper, ancient soul consciousness is what heals us by connecting us with the sacred wisdom of our soul (Figure 3-Ego and the Soul).

All human disease and distress is in part a manifestation of our ego's disconnection from the soul. When we reconnect with the soul consciously, we heal, become whole and live in harmony between the inner and outer world. The latent code of the soul informs and facilitates this connection. Our mundane life is perfused with the mystery of the soul, its program for our life, and the unique contribution we must make to this world in this lifetime, however small or large. A life without connection with the latent code of the soul is like a driver driving his car aimlessly with no destination in mind. A life lived in accord with the latent code of the soul is like a driver navigating with the help of the latest global positioning satellite system. A brief case example may illustrate this point.

A patient of mine once reported that he had a dream. In this dream, he was flying a small plane and the plane was in distress. He was trying to make an emergency landing in some field or clear patch of land. However, to his dismay, each time he tried hard to control and maneuver his plane, it got more out of control and starting bobbing on treetops. He is a trained pilot and was making all the right moves under the circumstances. Something was terribly wrong with the situation. Then he took a deep breath and scanned his horizon once again. To his utter surprise he found that he was not in a plane at all but a small glider and his glider was tethered to a bigger plane ahead of him. Immediately, he understood what was wrong with his attempts. Now the strategy was clear. He relaxed and let the big plane direct him safely out of trouble. He let the big plane take the lead, and he gently caught a nice, smooth wind current and rose above the trees and in a few minutes he was over a clear patch of land and the big plane cut him loose and he made an easy, safe landing near the Milwaukee river.

This patient's dream is a paradigm for the relationship between the ego and the soul. Each one of us is the pilot of our small glider, our ego. However, most of us live in the illusion that we can independently navigate our glider. This leads to numerous difficulties, since we struggle with our soul rather than dance with it. When we relinquish control and let the big plane we are tethered to lead us, when we let the soul guide us, we ride the gentle waves of the contours of our destiny. When the small plane aligns itself with big plane, when our individual life is lived by the program and intentions of the soul, we eventually land safely near the great river of life, near the water, the source of renewal by the unconscious. Water is the symbol of the unconscious where the Spirit resides. It is the source of renewal and rebirth of our psyche. In Christian tradition the baptismal water is source of new birth. Carl Jung has reported that in the dreams and fantasies of his patients the sea or the large expanse of water signifies the unconscious.[6] Jung further asserts that the water symbolizes the maternal nature of the unconscious, a source of renewal and rebirth.

The Latent Code in Action

So how does the latent code work? What are the triggers for the activation of the code? How does the latent code reorganize our consciousness? What are psychological operations that are carried out by the latent code to help us with creating a new consciousness to deal with life's challenges and opportunities? What aspect of the archetypal substrate does the latent code glean from to fulfill its mandate to help us with transitions and initiations, development and change, health and illness, new beginnings and necessary endings? These facets of the latent code are the subject matter of this book and are explored in each chapter in the context of specific archetypes and myths that are activated by our soul to engage our life and its long, winding and tortuous path.

The Triggers for the Latent Code

The latent code is activated in several contexts in our life. Most commonly, it is triggered when we are making a developmental transition from one life stage to another. For instance, when we leave the parental home to strike out on our own in the outer world, we need the archetype of the warrior to stake out new ground. When we embark on a new course of study, our soul activates the Saraswati's code to incubate new learning. So for each developmental transition, there is a challenge of letting go of the old attitude and adaptation to a new life stage. This transition often involves sacrificing the old attitude to make room for the new. This sacrifice is medicated by the latent code of the goddess Kali. Kali is also the emergency back up adaptation when ego consciousness fails (Crisis or Trauma).

The latent code also compensates for lopsided orientation of the ego. When we are flying high, the latent code helps us get close to the ground. The myth of Icarus is a good example. The Icarus myth has been activated time and again in the lives of my manic depressive patients. This protects them from flying too high away from mother earth, from their secure base of nurturance and safety.

Finally, the archetypes propel our teleological destiny, our life's purpose in this incarnation of our soul. Our Soul is constantly reaching out to the Spirit like a river rushing to unite with the ocean. The Spirit is the great attractor of the Soul. In our life journey, our Soul is constantly in the process of purification, maturation and refinement to be worthy of union with the Spirit. The latent code via the archetypes is the mediator which helps with the maturation process of the Soul. The most crucial aspect of the maturation of the Soul is the act of the Soul becoming conscious of its spiritual quest or connection. The archetypes mediate this process of creating consciousness of our spiritual origins and spiritual destiny.

How Does the Latent Code Reorganize our Consciousness?

Firstly, the soul decides that the latent code needs to be activated to deal with ego's situation, crisis, needs, lopsidedness, transition, initiation and change. The next task of the soul is to choose the relevant archetype from the collective consciousness to deal with the agenda at hand. In this book we will explore the substrate of the goddess Shakti in her various manifestations to guide the working of the latent code.

Using the substrate of the goddess Shakti archetype, our soul reworks our consciousness to create a new personality paradigm, which balances our ego's needs with our spiritual destiny. The latent code acts on the consciousness to reassemble the masculine and the feminine aspects of our psyche in ways which help us adapt to life's challenges and potentials. This is discussed in detail below.

Next the latent code of the goddess archetype gives us a new typological lens to look at ourselves, our world, others and the future, which is more appropriate to the total situation. This may give us a new look at the situation and open up new possibilities for adaptation and growth. This new typology may be congruent with our own typology or

be at odds with it. These divergences must be reconciled
by our ego.

The Promise and the Perils of the Latent Code

While the purpose of the latent code is to guide us through the labyrinth of our life journey, it may not always be experienced as a positive or nurturing encounter by our limited ego consciousness. Each archetype has a positive or negative impact in terms of its impact on being facilitative or prohibitive in our journey. Even when it feels prohibitive or negative, this is an experience of our ego consciousness, not the soul's archetypal intent. The purpose of an apparently negative archetypal experience may be to protect us like a good set of brakes in a very fast car. However, if we don't recognize the duality of the latent code, its promise and its perils, we may hinder the natural incarnation of the latent code in our life and get stuck in a complex, an illness, a relationship problem or an accident. Each chapter will discuss ways to balance the promise and the peril of each subset of the latent code and its archetypes. For instance, during the unfolding of the latent code of goddess Aditi, we may confuse the necessary transitional sacred void with emptiness and depression and try to fill it up with an affair, an addiction, or unhealthy distractions, rather than honoring the void as a prerequisite for creation of new life structures.

How the Latent Code establishes a new marriage between the Masculine and Feminine Aspects of our consciousness

Noted Jungian analyst Gareth Hill's[7] fundamental premise is that there are four basic patterns which underlie all human activity. These patterns are revealed in behavior, motivations, dreams, fantasies, and other aspects of psychic functioning. They operate in family and social systems and underlie basic cultural patterns. The masculine and feminine energies are best understood as a basic set of opposites, each with their "static" and "dynamic" and positive and negative attributes. This creates a system of eight templates (See Table 1). The four patterns are static feminine, dynamic feminine, static masculine and dynamic masculine, each with a positive and negative polarity. The patterns describe intrapsychic modes of consciousness in the individual. At the collective level, they describe patterns that we can identify in social groups or entire cultures. The contemporary Western culture may be conceptualized as in static masculine consciousness. The static masculine implies order, organization for its own sake, complacency, rigid expectations, dehumanizing righteousness, a Saturn guided culture. When consciousness is stuck in this static masculine mode, the psyche activates compensatory mechanisms to balance this. The feminine archetypes are then activated to balance this static masculine into dynamic feminine consciousness. The dynamic feminine archetypes are characterized by transformational energies, chaos, despair, destruction and new beginnings.

This initiation into the realm of the feminine is called the watery initiation as it dissolves the static masculine consciousness when individual or collective consciousness is stuck in the feminine mode. The compensatory masculine archetypes are activated in the form of a fiery initiation that vaporizes the excessive feminine orientation. Feminine water consciousness is balanced by fiery masculine energies. These are the natural rhythms of the unconscious.

Our present culture is in the watery initiation mode in which the feminine consciousness balances the fiery masculine adaptation. Fire is balanced by water. The goddess archetypes usher in this feminine balance to the present masculine structure of our culture. These goddess archetypes are the subject matter of the present book.

Transition from the dynamic feminine into the static masculine mode is a fiery initiation. The fiery initiation is an imposition of the structure of consciousness over the instinctual energies, impulses and drives. This involves sacrifice of the fiery hot effects of frustrated individualism.[8] The fiery initiations foster socialization and social hierarchy in service of the development of civilization. These initiations are fiery both because the initiate must go through the "fiery hoops" of the trials set for him or her and because the fiery hot effects of frustrated individualism have to be swallowed and suffered within rather than enacted. The individual must be given over to the will of the group. In contrast, the watery initiation is the dissolution of the conscious ego structures in service of soul work. Such an initiation presides over the transition from static masculine to the dynamic feminine realm of consciousness.

In Hill's terms, our "soul making" flows from the myriad movements of consciousness through the masculine and feminine consciousness in a repetitive continuous pattern throughout development. These transitions of consciousness inspire new initiatives like a hero's emergence (dynamic masculine). Gradually, this new consciousness or potential matures through the trials of life and consolidates into new personality structures in an individual (static masculine). Eventually these structures, while initially adaptive, become redundant over time. The former rebel hero now becomes the standard bearer of the establishment. Eventually some inner or outer crisis gives way to new disorientation of the established order under the auspices of some dynamic feminine experience. This may emerge in the form of new values, e.g. from focus on work to play, profit to people, material to spiritual values, etc. The dynamic feminine or the anima or yen experience now guides the way to dissolving the old system and a new paradigm of managing life emerges. In time this new value system is accepted as a baseline. This is now a return to the source of renewal of the soul (static feminine). This constant dynamism is evident in large and small manifestations throughout our lives -- the movement from a state of being into goal-directed exploration to discover new structures in our soul work. These structures eventually form a new baseline of the personality, only to disintegrate before the unexpected and spontaneous ebb and flow of experience. Eventually this transforms our personality into a more soulful state.[9] The young immature soul becomes a wise old soul, worthy of merger with the Spirit.

Throughout this book, some of these templates of the archetypal masculine and feminine patterns will form a backdrop for conceptualizing the latent code in action. These archetypal patterns of the goddess can be understood as having been activated to compensate for and to transform the Western, patriarchal, static-masculine consciousness into its higher spiritual potential. For several thousand years, the East has carried the torch of Spirituality. The torch has now been passed onto the West as the East grapples with issues of survival and security at the material level of existence. The West has achieved material and technological superiority and now has the opportunity and responsibility to invoke Spiritual leadership for the human race. The goddess archetype may help the West accomplish this mammoth task via dynamic feminine watery initiation by dissolving material values into a spiritual matrix. This initially may feel like the experience of chaos of the existing material values but has the potential to put the culture in touch with its potential for Spiritual ascendancy and wholeness. In astrological circles, it is postulated that we are moving from the age of Pisces to the Age of Aquarius, characterized by the renewal of Spiritual life in the present and future generations.

How the Latent Code Offers a New Lens for a Balanced Typological World-view

When Carl Jung and Sigmund Freud parted ways, it was an extremely traumatic event in Carl Jung's life. He went into a deep depression and went through a period of introspection between 1914 through 1918. He called this period the encounters with the unconscious. Some of his insights during this phase set the ground work for many of his later discoveries. The question of why he and Freud broke up remained a crucial question in his mind.

To make sense of this inner chaos, he came up with his theory of psychological types. It was his hypothesis that he and Freud had different psychological types and this may have led to many of the mismatches in their world views.

According to Jung,[10] all individuals may essentially be construed to fall into four basic personality orientations. These are pair of opposites and include the feeling or thinking type and intuitive or sensate (detail oriented) types. Usually one of these four functions is considered our superior function, e.g. intuition in my case, and its opposite sensate is the inferior or the least developed function. The other pair of opposites constitutes one's auxiliary and tertiary functions. Whenever we adapt to our inner or outer world, we scan it via the lenses of our typological makeup. In my case, my first scan of the inner or outer world is by using my intuition. When this is exhausted, I use my auxiliary function, which is thinking in my matrix. When this fails, I get additional information and data by using my tertiary feeling function. When all else fails, I may reluctantly use my inferior function. In my case this is sensate function. Only after I have broken the computer do I look at the manual for details of how to set it up!

When Jung constructed his typology, he shifted from polarity between individuals to the typological polarity within the individual. Typological wholeness then became a useful and necessary tool furthering personality development. However, I have found clinically that individuals rarely operate out of their superior function alone. Rather, they perceive their inner and outer world from a composite lens of their superior and first auxiliary functions.

Osmond et al.[11] have elegantly formulated four pairs of superior and first auxiliary functions that they call "typological Umwelts" or worldviews. People with dominant intuitive-thinking are *ethereals*; the intuitive-feeling types are *oceanic*; the thinking-sensate types are *structural*; and the feeling-sensate are *experials*. (See Table 2 and Figures 1 and 2)

It is my clinical observation that the Masculine and Western World-views are primarily ethereal and structural. The goddess consciousness brings us in contact with the oceanic and experial World-views and may help us establish wholeness and balance in the typological mandala of collective Western consciousness. Where possible, I will emphasize the impact of the latent code of Shakti on the typological world view.

Personally, I am an intuitive-thinking type and am most comfortable in the ethereal world-view. In my work with patients, I have observed over time that at critical moments of intervention, my intuition and thinking betray me and I seem to respond out of my feeling and sensate functions, my experial World-view.[12] This can lead me to spontaneous expression of feeling in spite of my stodgy, deliberate, and aloof, orientation.

For example, once a patient in the third year of analysis came to her session prior to her graduation. She brought her graduation tassel to show me, and she was beaming with joy and pride at the successful completion of her undergraduate studies in her mid-forties after having suspended college in her early twenties, mostly under the influence of critical and harsh parental complexes. I felt like a proud parent, and in spite of myself shared my fantasy that I wanted to photograph her in her graduation tassel (like I had done on the day of my daughter's graduation). We shared a moment of grace in the session. As she was leaving the session, my patient invited me to take a Polaroid picture of her with her graduation tassel. (She knew I had a Polaroid camera, which I had used to take photographs of her sand tray images.) Rather than analyze her request, I took two pictures, one for her and one for my files.

After ruminating for weeks about my "counter transference acting out" -- that is, my gratifying her wish for good parents -- I understood my behavior a bit better. My counter transference "error" was an avoidance of analyzing her parental complexes. In the following session, I acknowledged my error to my patient, and we were able to explore the matter further in a reflective mode.

However, even to this day a part of me feels that there was something authentic and not defensive about my behaving contrary to accepted theory and my own traditional way of functioning. Was my latent code activated in the shared moment of grace in the therapeutic vessel? Was the goddess present in the room, and was it she who guided me to act in a manner contrary to established theory and my conscious nature? Was such an act perhaps necessary to honor my patient's success and let the Great Mother archetype bless her soul work? Was I acting as a Hindu rather than a Judeo/Christian healer in that critical moment? I am still not certain but share my confusion with you for your consideration.

However, I do feel that when there are critical crossroads in my analytic work, my conscious orientation and typological World-view may fail me. It is then that I may respond out of a deeper part of my soul, my latent code. My hope is that my interventions did more good and less harm to my patient's healing than theory might predict.

Yantra – an activator of the Latent Code of the Soul

Yantra is an instrument, apparatus, talisman or mystical diagram through which the latent code is activated to support the rekindling of our life. The Sacred Geometry of the Yantras work via balancing several dimensions of our personality including the mind, body, soul and our connection with the Spirit. It realigns the five basic elements of Nature (Earth, Water, Fire, Air and Sky) in our body and psyche by recitation of certain Mantras. The Jungian alchemic tradition has explored this balance of elements in our personality in great detail, and the interested reader may refer to my favorite book, *Anatomy of the Psyche*[13] by Edward Edinger. The Sanskrit word 'Yantra' derives from the root 'yam,' meaning to sustain or hold. Hence in metaphysical terms a Yantra is visualized as a receptacle of the spiritual essence of our latent code.

Meditation on a Yantra helps us balance our personality under the archetypal guidance of the latent code that is relevant to our life situation. It balances the elements in our personality, for example balancing excess fire nature with the soothing waters of our personality potentials. A Yantra helps symbolically rebalance our masculine and feminine energies in necessary proportion to attend to the present life situation and developmental demands. The concept of the masculine and feminine in analytical psychology is different than in lay use of these terms. These are not gender based attributes but rather descriptors of the attributes of our personality which apply to both men and women. Both genders have so called masculine and feminine attributes in varying proportions unique to each individual. Carl Jung tried to get around this gender bias by coining the terms "Anima" for feminine psyche and "Animus" for masculine psyche. For lay purposes, masculine would involve a sense of initiative and enterprise in men and women, and feminine would be a sense of value and feeling about any given matter in both men and women. For instance, to deal with the challenges of professional enterprise we may need masculine initiative and feminine value judgment about what priorities are in the optimal balance.

A Yantra is a symbolic representation of the human body and psyche. Most Yantras are enclosed in a square outer form with four gates. The square represents the ego consciousness, while a circle represents the unconscious. Whenever something unconscious becomes conscious, it is symbolized by the circle or the round becoming a square or a cube. The square outer layer of a Yantra represents an act of entering the circle or the unconscious via our consciousness. The dream on the other hand involves the unconscious entering into consciousness. The goal of the latent code is to establish a bridge between the square and the circle, between the conscious and the unconscious, between the ego and the latent code of the soul. This eternal dance that involves the squaring of the circle and circling the square is essential for our consciousness to tune into the guidance of the latent code of the soul and tap into the wisdom of the Universe.

This balance of the masculine and feminine is represented in each Yantra. In the Saraswati Yantra, the patron goddess of academic and artistic pursuits, we need the feminine feeling about what we value as a subject of academic pursuit and the masculine drive of initiative and enterprise to pursue it. This balance of the masculine and feminine is represented in the Saraswati Yantra by one upward and one downward facing triangle. To deal with our power shadow we may need the guidance of the Kali Yantra, which moves the psychic energy from excessive male drive towards a feminine perspective. This is symbolized in the Kali Yantra by feminine or downward pointed triangles. A Yantra also helps us rebalance our typological imbalance to deal with life tasks. For example, if we are caught in a fluffy feeling intuitive realm, the Kali Yantra emphasizes a no-nonsense thinking sensate orientation. When we have done our inner work to honor the latent code, we activate the Yantra of The Sri Yantra. Sri Yantra is a symbol of wholeness where all aspects of our psyche are in perfect balance and our individual nature is centered in the Bindu point in a mandala circle. The Bindu represents the Soul, and in the Yantra it aligns the soul with the energies and the intentions of the Universe.

The latent code of every goddess archetype is activated by a specific Yantra and is like a password that opens up the immense energies and possibilities inherent in each archetype (Figure 4). By meditating on the Yantra on a regular basis, one can tune into the latent code of the corresponding archetype. This focuses the healing energies of the relevant archetype in our psyche and fosters personal growth.

A circle represents the unconscious aspects of our personality and must be squared or made conscious. The consciousness represented by the square has four doors open to four functions, four elements, and four seasons to comprehend the outer world. This permits the Lotus within (the soul) to blossom into wholeness (individuation) with eight petals. At the core of this constant dance between the square and the circle is a process of cooperation, mutuality and engagement between our consciousness and our unconscious to unfold the immense potential of our latent code. It is an attempt to integrate the opposite tendencies in our psyche to express their symbiotic expression. This involves integration of our masculine and feminine, ego and shadow, thinking with feeling, intuition with attention to details, consciousness with unconscious, personal fulfillment with community welfare, soul with the Spirit, human enterprise with the wisdom of the Universe. The squaring of the circle and the square retuning to the circle, to the great round, informs our personal psyche with the energy, wisdom and the purpose of the universe.

The center point, or Bindu, is symbolic of the point of super consciousness. The Bindu represents our outer personality's experience of its depths or the soul. In analytical language, the Bindu represents our ego's experience of our soul. It is the alchemic gold of the soul work, where light and shadow, ego and the complexes, superior and inferior functions, ego and the contra sexual archetypes are made conscious, balanced and integrated into the soul informed personality, tempered by sacrifice and reoriented by the latent code in realizing its potential through new beginnings.

The triangles in the Yantra represent the masculine and the feminine energies.[14] Passing to Yantric symbols, the male power-holder Shiva is represented by a triangle standing on its base. A triangle is selected as being the only geometric figure which represents Trinity in Unity -- the many Triads such as Willing, Knowing, and Acting in which the one Consciousness *(Cit)* displays itself. Power, or the feminine principle, or Shakti is necessarily represented by the same figure, for Power and the Power-Holder are one. The Triangle, however, is shown reversed -- that is, standing on its apex. Students of ancient symbolism are aware of the physical significance of this symbol. The number of masculine and feminine triangles may represent relative preponderance of masculine and feminine energies necessary to construct different Yantras. For example, the Kali Yantra has feminine reverse triangles only indicating the need to focus on feminine aspects of our psyche to compensate for the overly masculine orientation in a given individual.

During the process of meditating on the Yantra, the aspirant must try and project different aspects of their personality onto the symbols of the Yantra. Where is the earth, water, fire, and air aspect of my nature located in my present personality? What are the representations of my masculine and feminine potentials in the circle? Do I have a feeling for my Bindu, center or soul? Does my present life situation feel black, white, green, golden or red? This makes the Yantra a living embodiment of our soul. In as much as our present nature is at variance from the prescription of the Yantra, it is an opportunity to realign it to the prescription of the latent code embedded in the sacred geometry of the Yantra.

A Yantra can be a living embodiment of your latent code if you meditate upon it with focus, respect, patience and skill. The Yantra contains all the representations of the latent code. The square entrance to the Yantra represents the ego consciousness of the seeker, the circle represents the unconscious, the skyward facing triangle represents the masculine, the earthward triangle represents the feminine, the colors represent the alchemy of our nature, the flower or lotus represents the soul, and the Bindu or center point represents the soul's alignment with the Spirit and the wisdom of the Universe. The guiding myth or the Yantra represents the archetype that we need to guide us at the present moment in our life.

Putting it together

For those of you called upon by your soul to engage the mystery of your latent code to guide your manifest life, here is a brief summary of the deciphering process, as you engage the rest of this book. There are three big pieces of the jigsaw puzzle to decipher the latent code of your soul. The archetypes provide the substrate from which the latent code is derived. This makes it crucial for seekers to familiarize themselves with the archetypal matrix using their own cultural, spiritual, analytical and theoretical lens. This book explores one such framework of archetypal substrate using the goddess templates as a frame of reference.

The second piece of the jigsaw puzzle of the deciphering process is the archetype of the Soul. The soul is the psychic agency that does an unconscious assessment of life journey, our developmental needs, our strengths and liabilities, our ancestral gifts and curses,[15] our complexes and relationship tangles, and our spiritual destination. Based on these coordinates, it draws upon the archetypal substrate to create a symbol to reveal to us our latent code. This symbol is generated by our soul to signal to our ego the intentions of the universe for our life. It draws upon the energy of the relevant archetype to instruct our ego to take appropriate action to implement this intention. This symbol may manifest as dream, a fantasy, a complex, a medical or psychiatric symptom, a relationship problem, an accident or synchronistic event, a fascination or antipathy with a person, event, fairy tale, art work, movie or one of the many myriad ways that are intelligible to the ego, if only it is open to receiving the message.

The third piece of the jigsaw puzzle to decipher the latent code is the actual act of implementing it. This is the task of our ego or consciousness. It must make room to receive the symbol from the soul that carries the latent code, decipher it in context of the relevant archetype, make necessary sacrifice in the present life matrix to make room for a new beginning (chapter on Kali), honor the transitional void while the new code is gestated in the psyche (chapter on Aditi), and finally display the courage to make a new beginning under the auspices of the guiding wisdom of the latent code by integrating the old and the new, and holding the tensions of the opposites in our psyche for a new synthesis of our personality to emerge (chapter on Shiva and Shakti). Meditation on the appropriate Yantra can facilitate the process. The decoding and implementation of the latent code will be discussed in detail in the chapter on "Attending to the Latent Code."[16]

The next chapter explores my personal experience of the activation of my latent code. It emerged in a significant dream I had at the peak of my mid-life crisis when the symbol of the latent code in form of the goddess Shakti appeared and guided me through the minefield of mid-life transition. I came to understand this dream as a manifestation of my latent code to guide me through the turbulent course at the threshold of new beginnings. Join me now in encountering the three relational aspects of the latent code in the archetypal soil of the goddess Shakti: *Parvati* - the consort of Shiva and invoker of new creation, *Saraswati* - the consort of Brahma and the incubator of the creativity, *Laxmi*-the consort of Vishnu and the usher of peace and prosperity.

Table 1- Masculine and Feminine Archetypes			
Feminine static positive	Feminine static negative	Feminine dynamic positive	Feminine dynamic negative
• Organic, undifferentiated wholeness • Uterus, nature-in-the-round • Being and self-acceptance • The Great Mother	• Smothering entanglement • Inertia • Ensnaring and devouring routine. • Stuporousness, mere existence • The Devouring Mother	• Transformation • Inspiration • Flexibility and openness to new ideas and possibilities • Imagination and play • The Muses	• Transformations • Altered states leading to chaos, • Emptiness, despair, & death, • Depression, alcohol & drug intoxication, • Hysteria • Identity diffusion • The Madwoman
Masculine, positive static	Masculine, negative static	Masculine, positive dynamic	Masculine, negative dynamic
• Business as usual • Rules and regulations • Systems of meaning • Hierarchies of values • Standards • The Great Father	• Order • Organization for its own sake • Complacency • Rigid expectations • Dehumanizing righteousness • Pettiness	• Initiative • Innovation • Goal-directedness • Linearity • Technology • The Dragon-Slaying Hero	• Inflation • Willfulness • Rape, directed violence • Life-taking technologies • Disregard for nature and ecology • The Despot • The Eternal Revolutionary
Adapted from Gareth S. Hill. Masculine and Feminine: The Natural Flow of Opposites in the Psyche: Boston: Shambala Publications Inc. (1992), pp. 45-46.			

Table 2- Typological World-views

Ethereal World-view

- Composite of Thinking and Intuition as Superior and first Auxiliary Function & vice verse
- Psyche is experienced as synonymous with the mind, & limitless possibilities
- Psyche derives its reality from images, ideas, principles, theories
- Perceived by others as verbal, brilliant, imaginative, playful, or detached, nutty, impractical, visionary
- Examples: Carl Jung, Einstein, John Kennedy

Oceanic World-view

- Composite of Feeling and Intuition as Superior and first Auxiliary Function & vice verse
- Experience life as seamless whole: get personally involved
- Perceived by others as receptive, flexible, non-judgmental, romantic, mystical, inspiring, helpless, moody, unpredictable,
- Create confusion by disrupting existing order
- Examples: Gandhi, Churchill, Queen Victoria

Structural World-view

- Composite of Thinking and Intuition as Superior and first Auxiliary Function & vice verse
- Psyche is experienced as synonymous with the mind, & limitless possibilities
- Psyche derives its reality from images, ideas, principles, theories
- Perceived by others as verbal, brilliant, imaginative, playful, or detached, nutty, impractical, visionary
- Examples: Carl Jung, Einstein, John Kennedy

Experial World-view

- Composite of Feeling and Sensate as Superior and first Auxiliary Function & vice verse
- Reality is concrete, direct, personal, have difficulty in detaching from environment, have here and now orientation
- Ideal culture bearers, provide social glue, play a vital role in public affairs, and interested in ideas that can be built from experiences
- Perceived by others as socially adept, warm & sensitive in relationships, practical dependable, moral: also conventional, unimaginative, stubborn
- e.g. Eleanor Roosevelt, Sam Erwin

(Fall Adapted from Humphrey Osmond, Miriam Siegler, and Richard Smoke, " Typology Revisited: A New Perspective." Psychological Perspectives, 1977), pp. 206-219

Fig. 1 Four Functions

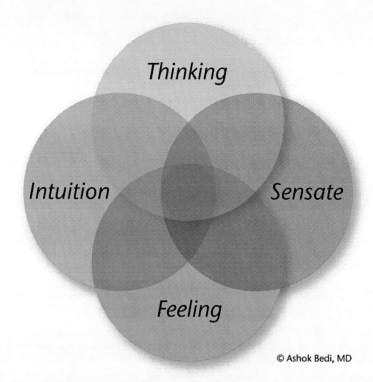

© Ashok Bedi, MD

Fig. 2 Typological Umwelts

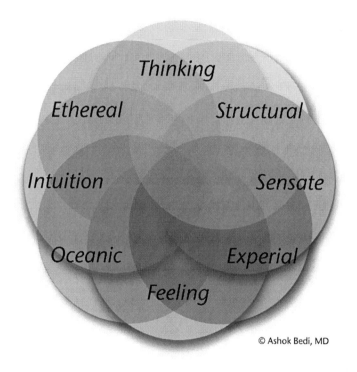

© Ashok Bedi, MD

Fig. 3 Ego and the Soul

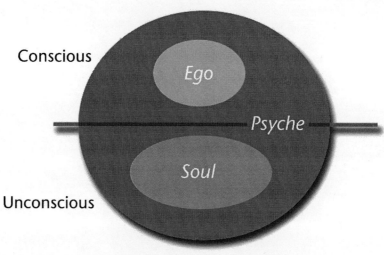

Structure of the Psyche

© Ashok Bedi, MD

Ganesha Yantra[17]

The Ganesh Yantra will be discussed in detail in the chapter of the latent Code of the Goddess Parvati

trimurti

brahma
the
CREATOR

shiva
the
DESTROY

vishnu
the
PRESERVER

CH 3

My Personal Encounter with My Latent Code

At the cross roads of my midlife crisis, when I was struggling to make important decisions about my personal and professional life, I got crucial and soul restoring guidance from the latent code in the form of a dream depicting my three Jesuit mentors/fathers. On deeper exploration it was apparent that this was a symbol of both the Christian and Hindu Trinity that was activated to guide me through the mine field of my midlife transition.

In the mid eighties and culminating in the early nineties, I ran into the crossroad of my midlife transition. In the previous fifteen years, I had established my psychiatric practice as an immigrant in a new country, rose through the ranks to a be a clinical director at a local psychiatric hospital, tended to my young children, tended to my ailing parents back in India, and endured the grind of managed care invasion. I needed to balance my personal and professional life – it was taking its toll, and I was feeling burned out. At this point, I was at a crossroad: to immerse myself in the tide of managed care and establish a comfortable professional life or to heed the call of my soul that I felt to be my private psychotherapy practice.

I made the latter choice, but it seemed very risky at the time. I relinquished my position as a clinical director at a local psychiatric hospital. It seemed that I gave up the trappings of external power and prestige, the big fish in a small pond syndrome. In this journey into the dark night of the soul, I had a dream, which had a significant impact on my life.

A guiding dream

I dream that I am back at my Alma Mater, St. Xavier's College, in India, having supper in the college cafeteria with my mentors, Father Valles and two other Jesuit fathers. Later we go to the college chapel and pray together.

The dream had a profoundly peaceful impact on me. Initially I thought that in my dark hour of distress my three father-mentors had appeared to reassure me. On deeper reflection, however, the image of my Grandmother came to mind. Whatever story she told, it always had a unique answer to my unstated question. For some of the biggest questions about the broader issues of the world at large, she told me the story of the *Trimurti*, the Hindu Trinity composed of Brahma, Vishnu, and Shiva. My Jesuit education resonated with the image of Trimurti with the Holy Trinity of the Christian tradition.

I heard my grandmother telling me that the Gods often present themselves to us in human form. I realized that these three Jesuits fathers could be understood as manifestations of the holiest Hindu Trinity: One of the three fathers, Father Ottega, was like Brahma, the god of creation; Father Valles reminded me of Vishnu, the god of sacred duty who maintains peace; and Father D'Soza reminded me of Shiva, the god of destruction of dysfunction and paving the way for the new order. The holiest Hindu Trinity had appeared in my dream to reassure and guide me. Their message was that although I might feel alone in Milwaukee, I was not abandoned. This dream and its message reaffirmed me in my work and spurred me on the path to the soul. This dream spurred me to follow my inner voice and follow the path less traveled. The god Shiva helped me destroy my dysfunctional attitude to my work and its emphasis on managed care and short term symptomatic treatment rather than attending to the deeper issues involved in an individual's life. I also had to challenge my dysfunctional attitude towards women in general and my wife in particular. Rather than seeing males as professional and women as the supporting cast, I gradually learned to heal this split and made more room for my wife's professional aspirations. Now she and my daughter are more successful than I am and run a chic and successful Indian restaurant in Milwaukee. I needed the guidance of Brahma and Saraswati to make creative new beginnings in my life. I undertook a program to train as a Jungian psychoanalyst, and with the help of my mentors and an intensive course of studies I learned a new language to attend to the mysteries of the Soul. These efforts have helped me establish a slightly better balance in my professional life (medical and Spiritual), in my inner life (balance thinking with feeling) and my relationships, especially my marriage (respect for my wife and daughter's creative and enterprising spirit). This new balance was established under the auspices of Laxmi and Vishnu, the archetypal couple that help us with a spiritually balanced order in our life. While I still have a long way to go on my own path to the soul, I am glad at my new beginnings. Continuing attention to my inner life, my dreams and symbols, synchronistic events and working on my hang ups gradually deepened my deeper acceptance and understanding of my path.

In my life and work over the next several years, it emerged that the gods were to function as a channel for me to access the energy and guidance of Shakti, the archetypal feminine, as manifested in images of the three consort goddesses. The god images provide the form and the structure, but the goddess or Shakti templates are the power and the energy that activate and propel these forms into their goals. Their story and account now follows.

My Early Encounters with the Latent Code of Trimurti

In my own soul work and in work with my patients, the image of Trimurti or the holy trinity of the three Hindu gods has played a significant role in guiding my path to the soul. As a child, whenever I would get lost in the complex problems of my life, I would go to my grandmother's consulting room (her kitchen table) and lay out these problems. Like a good therapist, she would not answer my question directly, but rather tell me some story, myth or fairy tale. Somehow, these stories always had an answer to the riddle that I was trying to untangle. The story of Trimurti (three images of god) always figured prominently.

These three gods and their consorts are the starting point of the journey into the mystery of the latent code.

The Trimurti: Mythology

The Trimurti, literally meaning three faces, is the Holy Trinity of the Hindu Gods— Shiva, Brahma and Vishnu— and their respective Goddess consorts— Parvati, Saraswati and Laxmi, who represent the power or energy of the god. The Trimurti god-goddess template is meant to guide us on the path to a soulful living and attend to our Spiritual calling. The multiplicity of gods and goddesses in Hinduism should not be thought of as polytheism. Although there are many images of deities, the seemingly limitless forms attempt to depict specific aspects of the One Essence. Thus the three-fold image of the Trimurti with their consort Goddesses represents the one Supreme Being, the total soul and its continuity with the unified spirit of the world.

The distinction between Gods and Goddesses in Hindu philosophy is not meant, nor should it be taken, as a gender role statement. Rather, God and Goddess are two sides of the same coin, two complementary aspects of the same archetypal pattern and force. Usually the male image is considered to be the form of the template (structure), while the female image depicts the kinetic energy and enterprise of the system necessary to guide the workings of the template.

Shiva –the Destroyer of Darkness

Shiva is known as the "Destroyer," the source of both good and evil. He is a god of contrasts, presiding over creation and destruction, fertility and asceticism, good and evil. Shiva is the original Lord of the Dance, whose dance creates our universe. He destroys the corrupt old order to make room for the new in conjunction with his consort, the Goddess Shakti.

The archetype of Shiva guides individuals who must

step onto the stage of world consciousness to combat and destroy the powers of the dark side to make room for new order and consciousness to prevail. One such individual is General Herbert Norman Schwarzkopf, Military Leader, born: August 22, 1934 in Trenton, New Jersey and Best Known as the U.S. General during the Persian Gulf War. A four-star general in the U.S. Army, H. Norman Schwarzkopf was Commander in Chief of the U.S. Central Command during the Persian Gulf War against Iraq (1990-91). He graduated from West Point in 1956 and spent most of his career in field assignments, including two tours of duty in Vietnam (1965-66 and 1969-70). Schwarzkopf served as deputy commander of U.S. forces in the invasion of Grenada (1983) and gained international recognition as the director of operations of Desert Shield and Desert Storm during the Gulf War, leading U.S. and Allied troops to a decisive victory against Iraq. Nicknamed "Stormin' Norman," Schwarzkopf achieved celebrity status for the way he handled himself during his frequent television press conferences. His father, H. Norman Schwarzkopf, was an army officer who served in World War I and World War II and the Superintendent of the New Jersey State Police during the Lindberg kidnapping case of the 1930s. General Schwarzkopf exemplifies the realm of the Shiva archetype. Like Shiva, he stayed out of the political fray and did not succumb to the desire for political power by staying out of the presidential race.

Shakti-the Goddess of Cosmic Welfare

Shakti helps Shiva tame his destructive instinct and domesticate it towards the goal of cosmic welfare. Clinically this may manifest as the feminine side of the male psyche, tempering it with feeling, relationality and wisdom. When men are caught in the goal directed mode of mastery in the outer material world, their inner feminine side guides them to balance this with attention to inner life, feelings, and wholeness. Work must be tempered by love.

Brahma-the Creator

Brahma is the name of God in his aspect as creator. Brahma's function is to bring multiplicity into being in place of the Primal Unity. Thus it is Brahma who creates the limited realities in which we actually live on earth. When we look at life in black or white terms, Brahma offers a prism which breaks down this black or white reality into a spectrum of many colors. Brahma offers us a glimpse into many renderings of an apparently linear reality. But to access the gifts of this creative potential, we need the help of Saraswati, the goddess of learning, who helps us perceive the complexity of reality.

The archetype of Brahma, the creator of new consciousness, guides the path of researchers, innovators and pioneers in the new frontiers of science, technology, medicine and all other areas of human enterprise. While the list of such an inspiring group of Brahma inspired individuals is long, I have chosen two contemporary individuals who exemplify the workings of Brahma. One such individual is George R. Stibitz (1904 - 1995).

George R. Stibitz is internationally recognized as the father of the modern digital computer. Stibitz's interest in computers arose from an assignment in 1937 to study magneto-mechanics of telephone relays; he turned his attention to the binary circuits controlled by the relays, to the arithmetic operations expressible in binary form, and, in November 1937, to the construction of a two-digit binary adder. The next year, with the help of S.B. Williams of Bell Labs, he developed a full-scale calculator for complex arithmetic. This computer was operational late in 1939 and was demonstrated in 1940 by remote control between Hanover, New Hampshire, and New York. Later, more sophisticated versions followed as the torch was passed to the new generation of researchers.

Another Brahma inspired individual is Leroy E. Hood, M.D., Ph.D., Professor and Chairman, Department of Molecular Biotechnology, University of Washington, Seattle. Leroy Hood was born October 10, 1938 in

Missoula, Montana. Dr. Hood's research interests focus on the study of molecular immunology and biotechnology. His laboratory has played a major role in developing automated micro chemical instrumentation that permits sequence analysis of proteins and DNA as well as the synthesis of peptides and gene fragments. Most recently, he has applied his laboratory's expertise in large-scale DNA mapping and sequencing to the analysis of human and mouse T-cell receptor loci. This represents important efforts of the Human Genome Project and the genomic analysis of the human immunodeficiency virus (HIV). Dr. Hood's laboratory is also interested in the study of autoimmune diseases and new approaches to cancer biology.

Such creative enterprise that inspires engagement of the new frontiers of consciousness for betterment of collective wisdom may be construed as inspired by the archetype of Brahma. Numerous individuals in exciting fields of science, medicine, genetics, informatics, biotechnology may be considered as operating out of the realm of Brahma consciousness.

Saraswati-the goddess of learning

Brahma's consort is Saraswati, the Goddess of the arts, learning, knowledge, and truth. Creative enterprise remains uninformed and ungrounded if Saraswati is not honored. Whenever we break new ground and strive for new creative possibilities, we must first prepare the soil by a course of learning. Saraswati is the patron goddess of new learning, arts and academic enterprise.

Vishnu-the preserver

Vishnu is called the "All Pervasive," "The Preserver," who represents the cohesive force that maintains the continuity of existence. Vishnu is the aspect of God maintaining the timeless order of nature that interconnects all that exists (*Dharma*). Periodically Vishnu reincarnates in one of his several forms (*avatars*) such as Krishna, Rama,

54 and the tortoise to reestablish order whenever necessary. Psychologically, we can say that whenever our life becomes lopsided, archetypes are activated to help us restore the balance and reestablish a new framework. If we are flighty, we get symbols that help us get grounded. We may have dreams that depict symbols like an elephant, turtle, tree, etc. that symbolize the need for reconnection with our ground.

This motif of archetypal activation in time of psychic turmoil and imbalance is well-stated in the sacred Hindu text – the Bhagwad Gita[18]:

"Whenever there appears on earth (Consciousness)
Decline of righteousness (disconnection from our Soul)
Uprising of Unrighteousness (medical and psychiatric illness)
I send Myself to birth (a dream or a symbol)

For protection of good (restoration of health and wholeness)
The wicked put to flight (challenging maladaptive life patterns)
I come into being age by age (archetypal activation)
Establishing the Right (Individuation or a
spiritually informed life)

Vishnu is the protector and preserver of the world and cosmic order. The individuals inspired by the Vishnu archetype are entrusted by the collective consciousness to uphold order and peaceful structure in our society to bolster peace, prosperity and growth. The individual who best exemplifies the Vishnu archetype in the present world matrix is Alan Greenspan (born March 6, 1926). He is an American economist and Chairman of the Board of Governors of the Federal Reserve of the United States. He is considered by many to be the leading authority and key participant concerning American domestic economic and monetary policy.

In 1987, Ronald Reagan nominated Alan Greenspan to succeed Paul Volcker. After the nomination, bond markets experienced their biggest one-day drop in 5 years.

Some feared that Greenspan would be a more political chairman. The senate confirmed Greenspan on August 11. Just two months after his confirmation, he was faced with his first crisis, the 1987 stockmarket crash. In the wake of the crash, markets around the world were put on restricted trading primarily because sorting out the orders that had come in was beyond the computer technology of the time. This also gave the Federal Reserve under the leadership of Mr. Greenspan, time to pump liquidity into the system to prevent a further downdraft. While pessimism reigned, the market bottomed on October 20, leading some to label Black Monday a "selling climax", where the excess value was squeezed out of the system. On May 18, 2004, he was nominated by President George W. Bush to serve for an unprecedented fifth term as Chairman of the Federal Reserve. He has been appointed to this post by U.S. Presidents Ronald Reagan, George H. W. Bush, and Bill Clinton. He married NBC journalist Andrea Mitchell in 1997.

Dr. Greenspan best examplifies the archetype of Vishnu in action. He has been the modulator of both the American and the global economic policies to preserve peaceful transitions in the monetory markets amidst crisis, strife, terrorism, internet bubles and crashes, among other things. Vishnu individuals best examplify the preservation of order, peace and prosperty.

Laxmi-the goddess of peace and prosperity

Vishnu's consort is Laxmi, the Goddess of prosperity and peace – the prerequisite for maintaining a just order in the world. For psychic wholeness and a spiritually informed life, we need outer prosperity and inner peace. Laxmi guides us to attain these by interventions like simplifying our life and attending to enterprise informed by spirituality. This will be discussed in the chapter on Laxmi.

The Trimurti represents the universal forces that create (Brahma), preserve the timeless order of nature (Vishnu), and destroy the corrupt old order to make room for the new (Shiva). There is an interesting parallel to the Trimurti archetype and the myth of the three fates in the Greek mythology.

Moirai[19] were the Fates, personification of the inescapable destiny of man. The Moirai assigned to every person his or her share in the scheme of things. Originally only one Moira was conceived; Zeus, as father of gods and men, weighed out the "fate" of individuals.

The three fates were Klotho, Atropos, and Lachesis. They were variously called daughters of Zeus. They were described sometimes as aged and formidable women, often lame to indicate the slow march of fate. Klotho spun the thread at the beginning of one's life (Brahma and Saraswati). Atropos wove the thread into the fabric of one's actions (Vishnu and Laxmi), and Lachesis snipped the thread at the conclusion of one's life (Shiva and Shakti). The process was absolutely unalterable, and gods as well as men and women had to submit to it.

Embedded in the myth of the Trimurti are two concepts: first, the timeless order of nature (*Dharma*), and second, the four-fold good, *chaturvarga*, which embraces *Artha* (pursuit of wealth), *Kama* (pursuit of pleasure and relationships), *Dharma* (sacred duty), and *Moksha* (freedom from opposites in our nature and subsequently freedom from the repetitive cycle of reincarnation and consequent union with the divine Spirit). These concepts are discussed in my earlier publication <u>Path to the Soul</u>.[20] How do these archetypal energies apply to our life, its problems, and ultimately contribute to the mystery of our individuation (Spiritually informed life)? In my situation, the activation of these archetypal energies unlocked the latent code that was essential to make a connection with my feminine, creative psyche, which I believe, guided me on my path to the soul. In the following chapters, we will explore the mysteries of the latent code specific to different stages of our life and how this code is specific to each individual's unique life situation and personality potential.

saraswati

THE ENERGY

TO GUIDE

NEW CREATION

CH 4
The Latent Code of Saraswati
The Code to Engage the Arts and Academic Pursuits

She sets in motion all the energies of
The soul and the intellect
She imparts deep knowledge
To all who are seekers of truth.

– Rig Veda 1.3.12

Before we plant the seed, we must prepare the soil. Outer enterprise and inner soul work call for serious groundwork and preparation. The Latent code of the goddess Saraswati presides over this process of preparing the soil for the seed of new beginnings. She helps us set up a system to undertake new ventures and creative enterprises. All serious projects need legwork, planning, research and study. The Saraswati archetype provides a template for such a preparation. She is the patron goddess of students and seekers and presides over the arts, science, knowledge, and written and spoken words. Her consort, Brahma, the god of new creation, is considered her creative principal. Saraswati is the energy that guides the engine of new creation in our lives. Let us meet the goddess of preparations for the new beginnings in our lives.

The Myth[21]

One of the three goddesses of the holy trinity, Saraswati was born out of the body of Brahma as the feminine principle of creation. She was both Brahma's daughter and his wife. Like many Gods in the Olympian tradition, they had an incestuous relationship. *Om* – the sound of the creation of the cosmos – emanates from the strings of Veena (a musical string instrument) held by the goddess Saraswati. She is born out of Brahma's head as the female principal of creation. Symbolically, this may be construed as Saraswati being Brahma's thinking, logical and cognitive principal. This is akin to Athena who springs forth form the head of Zeus.

In the Vedas, Saraswati is a river goddess. She has been identified with the rituals and hymns performed on the banks of the river, so she was called *Vach* (sacred speech). New consciousness is embodied in the spoken and written word. In the myth of the origin of the world, she was considered the instrument of creation. She is the flowing one who represents the union of power and intelligence. Her river nature symbolizes the flowing union of speech with thought. When words are tempered with thoughtfulness, they serve us to live a spiritual life. When words are guided by emotion alone, without thought, these words may hurt others and sabotage us. She is the patron of speech, knowledge, the creative and performing arts, and is depicted as carrying a veena, one of the oldest string instruments.

Attributes of the Goddess Saraswati

In the Vedic period, Saraswati is a river goddess, but in later Hindu culture, she is associated with clouds, thunder, rain, river and ponds. She symbolizes the life giving, purifying, and baptizing nature of all waters.

Later depictions of Saraswati are as the goddess of speech and the spoken word. She dwells in sound. The importance of the spoken word is greatly emphasized in Hindu culture, where **AUM** symbolizes the entire creative process, the idea of creation proceeding from *spoken word*, the ultimate reality in the form of a sound.

A stands for Creation
U stands for Preservation
M stands for Destruction or Dissolution
This is followed by silence or void, the realm of goddess Aditi,
who ushers in new creation.
This is representative of the Trinity of Gods and Goddesses in
Hindu tradition.

The importance of sacred speech is emphasized in the prominence of *Mantras*, sacred words as an essential ingredient of the yoga and other spiritual practices. Mantra is a subject unto itself, but it essentially relates to an individualized spoken word that forms a bridge between the individual and cosmic consciousness. It is a symbol that has the numinosity and energy to establish transcendence between individual ego to the soul and the soul to the Spirit.

Saraswati's association with science, learning, and knowledge reinforces her nature as goddess of speech and rational thought. Science, learning, and knowledge are the foundations of culture, and culture is defined by language. It is a paradox that culture is both defined and limited by language. Language can only define what is known consciously. Much of the culture is emergent and beyond conscious embodiment. It is in a state of continuing emergence. This explains why artists often leap frog into the future; they are not limited by the confines of language to express the creative spirit of human nature and its limitless possibilities. Thus culture is created and limited by its language. We can extrapolate that Saraswati is a goddess who inherently controls the very definition of culture. She is considered to be the womb of the Vedas (ancient Hindu scriptures) and dwells in all books. She is the creator of books, inspires the arts, and is the patron goddess of Brahmins (the priest class in the Hindu caste system), whose sacred duty is to preserve ancient knowledge.

Saraswati is depicted as graceful and riding on a peacock or swan. The peacock may be symbolic of our complexes (personality quirks and hang-ups). On our path to our soul, it is essential that we ride and tame our complexes and gradually assimilate them into the ego consciousness. If we don't ride our complexes, they ride us and run over the integrity of our personality and compromise our soul work. We become proud as peacocks, lose humility, and stray away from the path to the soul.

The swan is the symbol of spiritual transcendence, the one who rises above. Saraswati, as the one who rides the swan, represents the spiritual dimension of human existence that rises above the physical world into the realm of higher consciousness. When seated, Saraswati is depicted as sitting on a lotus. A lotus maintains its beauty, integrity and purity in the muddy waters from which it germinates. Like the lotus, she floats above the muddy waters of human imperfections to strive for the spiritual aspects of our existence. She inspires us to strive for our lotus nature. In this lotus mode we synthesize the opposites in our personality: the muddy and shadow aspects of our personality with the pristine aspects of our spiritual potential. When we unite these opposites in our psyche, we have a "burning bush" experience. A bush which burns and yet can maintain its integrity and form is the burning bush. A personality that burns in the rigors and trials of life but maintains its form and purpose is a truly spiritual life. Saraswati blesses a life that resides in the muddy waters of our outer existence. She invokes our lotus nature.

Her presence is not usually sought in homes but in libraries, schools, universities, and other institutes of higher learning. She is depicted as having four hands. In one hand she holds a rosary, symbolizing the importance of prayer, and in the other hand a palm leaf scroll, implying the value of knowledge. Sometimes she holds a book. In another hand she carries a lute or veena, symbolizing her patronage of music and arts. Her fourth hand holds a water pot, symbolizing her association with spiritual sciences and religious rites. Dressed in white, she depicts purity of true knowledge. On her brow is a crescent moon, identified with lunar consciousness and anima or *feeling for what is of real value* in our life.

The Workings of the Latent Code of Saraswati

Saraswati is the patron goddess of young adulthood, the life-stage of matriculation, where one undertakes an intensive course of education or craft to establish one's professional identity. Saraswati guides men and women to undertake the pursuit of a professional identity. When acting under the auspices of Saraswati, the individual has little time for play or the frivolities of life. Such an individual is a father's child, sitting at the feet of the guru or teacher in pursuit of knowledge. A Saraswati woman, like Athena in Greek mythology, is often out of touch with her body and stays in the realm of the logos.

With rapid advances in technology, globalization of the job market, outsourcing of jobs between nations, retraining for new jobs and new skills would be a rule rather than an exception. It will need emphasis on retraining and lifelong learning. Our citizens, our schools, our centers for higher learning will have to get in step with these massive global shifts to assist us in this lifelong learning enterprise to keep up and perform at our personal best in frontiers of science, industry, commerce, healing and personal growth. This should be seen as a spiritual not academic or professional enterprise alone, since lifelong learning not only makes us competitive in job market but soulful in performing our Dharma or Spiritual calling. Saraswati is the patron goddess of this process of learning. Institutions of continuing education need to prepare our citizens not only for survival but also for their Spiritual calling.

The Sacred Union of our Masculine and Feminine Potentials under the Auspices of Saraswati

Saraswati is the positive dynamic feminine or creative enterprise that initiates the process of initiation needed to constellate new life structures based on devotion to knowledge and new learning. She inspires the individual to mature transformation into adulthood, equipped with knowledge and trade. She fosters flexibility and openness to new ideas and possibilities of imagination and learning.

While initiation into the feminine realm usually is a watery initiation into the realm of the chaos and creative potential of the unconscious, the Saraswati initiation is both watery -- delving into the depths of one's inner creative potential -- and fiery, submitting to the rigors of the established academic order. Compared to Sati/Parvati, however, Saraswati's relationship with the masculine order is much more collaborative and complementary. Saraswati is both Brahma's wife and daughter, and she can readily move into dependent or mutual mode with the Masculine.

World-view from the Lens of the Latent Code of Saraswati

The Saraswati code fosters primarily the thinking and secondarily the sensate typology, creating a structural World-view. The Saraswati World-view fosters attention to facts and deals with the issues and challenges of life by application of facts to experience. Under the auspices of the Saraswati archetype, individuals find scope for their abilities in technical skills with facts and objects and excel in applied science and math, business, administration, banking, production and construction.

Comparative Mythology

Like Athena who sprang from the head of her father Zeus, Saraswati is born from the head of the father/ husband Brahma. Saraswati, like Athena, is the goddess of wisdom and crafts. While Athena presides over battle strategy in wartime and domestic arts in peacetime, Saraswati presides over the pursuit of excellence in the arts and academic pursuits. Athena is depicted with an owl, a bird with prominent eyes associated with wisdom, one of her traits. Saraswati is depicted as riding a peacock or a swan, symbolizing the importance of taming the ego and vanity if true knowledge and wisdom is to be achieved. Athena also values the ascendancy of rational thinking, will, and wisdom over instinct and nature. While Parvati like Artemis reside in the wilderness, Saraswati like Athena resides in the city and centers of higher learning.

Perils and the Promise of the
Latent Code of Saraswati

Individuals guided by Saraswati rarely lose their heads or hearts. While this fosters goal-directed academic and personal enterprise, it keeps them out of the emotional and relational matrix. Such an individual is rational, measured, and deliberate, which inhibits their spontaneity and playful encounters. Those caught in the realm of Saraswati, and overstay their welcome, become perpetual students. They use academic quest to avoid life, not prepare for it. They are caught in the archetype of Peur or Puella Aeternus or the Peter Pan syndrome, of perpetual childish youthfulness, at the expense of adult engagement of life, work, relationships and spiritual calling.

Joann was one such individual. She consulted me for academic underperformance in her graduate school. She had an impressive academic record so far, thus this problem intrigued me. On closer assessment, it became clear that this was her second graduate school tenure. She had already successfully completed her graduate work in a related field. The real problem was not academic but relational. She had been using graduate school as a defense against relationships, and the academic problem was her last stand against the challenge of entering the relationship sector of her life. She is a pretty, engaging and interesting person, and her problem was that she would ward off eligible men. Her history revealed that her parents were divorced when she was nine years old; her father was emotionally disengaged and her stepfather sexually abused her through adolescence. Relationships were frightening to her. In her therapy, she worked through the trauma of sexual abuse, reclaimed trust and self assertion and eventually established a successful relationship.

Another peril of the Saraswati archetype is that she was both Brahma's daughter and lover. Unfortunately, this dynamic plays out in the life of many young women caught in the dark side of the Saraswati archetype. These women get caught in the professional student syndrome and get emotionally and erotically involved with their mentors and teachers. While academic institutions need to maintain vigilance about this ethical violation, analytically this also needs to be understood from a dynamic perspective. These women often have distant mothers, and they have a childhood history of emotional tangles with their needy fathers. They get caught in the surrogate spouse syndrome to provide love and emotional nurturance to their fathers. In these situations, mothers are often depressed, alcoholic or chronically ill.

This childhood drama is replayed in their adult encounters. These women have a strong father complex, and they become emotionally and erotically involved with older men. In academic settings, this replays itself in the form of younger students getting involved with their older teachers who may be struggling with their own midlife transitions. Sara was one such individual. Her mother was depressed, and as the oldest daughter, she was her father's confidant. They slept in the same bed till her mid-teens. While there was no clear history of sexual abuse, the relationship was highly charged with erotic tension. Sara went to a prestigious college and fell in love with her professor. After she completed her school, they got married. In a few years, her husband fell in love with another younger student and abandoned her. In her therapy, Sara reconstructed her life narrative, recognized her tendency to be the daughter-lover of creative but needy men— the reenactment of Saraswati archetype. Eventually she established a relationship with a peer, and they are working on deepening their budding relationship.

Latent Code in Action

Anna's new beginnings

Anna's story illustrates the Saraswati's guidance in the life of one of my patients. Anna consulted me for therapy after her father's death. At first sight, it looked like a case of grief reaction. Then early in analysis, Anna presented the following dream.

I am at Marquette University's law school lecture hall.
It's the first day of my attendance at the law school. I feel
anxious. My professor is an impressive woman. She smiles at me
reassuringly.

I was somewhat puzzled about the dream of returning
to school in the context of grief over her father's death.
As we worked through this dream further, it emerged
that Anna's father was very keen that she go to law school
to study law. Their relationship had been contentious.
While interested in law, Anna felt as though her father had
usurped her ambition, and she decided to drop out of a
promising academic track.

Anna's parents had a very dry and soul-less marriage.
Her father was a successful businessman, who had numerous
affairs with his younger associates and secretaries over the
years. As Anna grew to be an adolescent and a young woman,
she felt envious of her father's successive mistresses, who
got much more attention than either her or her mother
from her father. He had the Midas touch in his professional
life, but his blossoming success only alienated him more
from his wife and children. This dynamic was recreated in
Anna's marriage. When Anna belatedly started law school
after her father's death, her husband was not supportive of
this initiative. However, she financed her own schooling
with her inheritance from her father. Midway through law
school, Anna fell in love with one of her older professors,
a charismatic father figure. This is the danger of the dark
side of the Saraswati archetype. Under the auspices of the
archetype, people can fall in love with their mentors and
teachers. This relationship with her professor was very
nurturing both personally and professionally.

Retrospectively, it seemed to her that when she dropped
out of college, it was a form of rebellion against her
father's authority. Later in her analysis, she differentiated
her authentic academic strivings from her father's wish
to vicariously live out his ambitions through her success.
When she resumed and successfully completed law school,

the Saraswati archetype had constellated to guide her path. The professor in her initial dream was a symbol of Saraswati, who came to guide her back to complete her academic goals and further her individuation.

With the help of therapy, Anna realized that she was caught in the shadow side of the Saraswati archetype, and through this realization, she was able to re-prioritize her life and rectify the situation. After completing law school, Anna was taken under the wing of an older mentor and joined him as a junior partner in a prestigious law firm. To her chagrin, she found out that her husband had been having an affair during her schooling, and her marriage fell apart. Eventually, she married her senior partner and blossomed personally and professionally. This is a classic Brahma – Saraswati alliance, but her continuing therapy needed to focus on her tendency to get caught in the role of the daughter/spouse of a powerful father/husband/ mentor.

Saraswati calls for the need for systemic study and devotion to the subject matter for the student to become a professional. We are all familiar with the realm of Saraswati whenever we undertake a new field of study or interest. We must then find a place for instruction and devote substantial inner and outer resources to the subject of our interest. As in the alchemic tradition, patience, practice and integrity initiate mastery of the art. Each time we learn a new skill, go back to school, take on a self-study course, learn about computers, learn a new game or hobby, get interested in spirituality or undertake a serious study of our chosen subject matter, Saraswati is invoked. If we honor her, she guides us towards expertise in our new enterprise.

Following my Trimurti dream, for example, several synchronistic events led me into the study of analytic psychology. I decided to undertake six years of advanced training in depth psychology to honor my artistic, spiritual and creative potential. Interestingly, it gave me a new language; I found my *vach*, my voice, to express my

authentic ideas. In the process I had to honor the watery
initiation by delving into the depths of my unconscious
and the fiery initiation of negotiating the academic hoops
of Jungian analytic training.

While young adults in the academic life stage are
familiar with the realm of Saraswati in terms of formal
studies and instruction, many adults in mid-life and older
age are having to retrain to adjust to a fast changing job
market and need to learn new skills. Virtually every adult
in the world will have to learn something about computers
and cyberspace at some point. Others elect to undertake
adult education to make an informed and soulful vocational
choice in mid-life. Each time we participate in continuing
education we are in the realm of Saraswati. If we recognize
this and honor the goddess, their academic enterprise may
become more rewarding and seamless.

Toni Morrison and the Latent Code of Saraswati

Saraswati is the patron of arts and academics. Individuals
inspired by the Saraswati archetype blaze out new trails in
the field of arts and academics to further justice and cosmic
welfare. One such individual is Toni Morrison, nee Chloe
Wofford, the first African-American woman to receive the
Nobel Prize in Literature; she also has won the Pulitzer
Prize for fiction.

Her parents had moved to Lorain, Ohio from the
South to escape racism and to find better opportunities in
the North. At home, Chloe heard many songs and tales
of Southern black folklore. The Woffords were proud of
their heritage.

Lorain was a small industrial town populated with
immigrant Europeans, Mexicans and Southern blacks who
lived next to each other. Chloe attended an integrated
school. In her first grade, she was the only African-American
student in her class and the only one who could read. She
was friends with many of her white schoolmates and did
not encounter discrimination until she started dating.

She hoped one day to become a dancer like her

favorite ballerina, Maria Tallchief, and she also loved to read. Her early favorites were the Russian writers Tolstoy and Dostoyevsky, French author Gustave Flaubert and English novelist Jane Austen. She was an excellent student, and she graduated with honors from Lorain High School in 1949. Chloe Wofford then attended, with the financial aid of her parents, the prestigious Howard University in Washington, D.C., where she majored in English with a minor in classics. Since many people couldn't pronounce her first name correctly, she changed it to Toni, a shortened version of her middle name. She joined a repertory company, the Howard University Players, with whom she made several tours of the South. She saw firsthand the life of the African-Americans there, the life her parents had escaped by moving north. Toni Wofford graduated from Howard University in 1953 with a B.A. in English. She then attended Cornell University in Ithaca, New York, and received a master's degree in 1955.

After graduating, Toni Wofford was offered a job at Texas Southern University in Houston, where she taught introductory English. Unlike Howard University, where African-American culture was neglected or minimized, at Texas Southern they "always had Negro history week" and introduced to her the idea of African-American culture as a discipline rather than just personal family reminiscences. In 1957, she returned to Howard University as a member of faculty, and there she met Harold Morrison, a Jamaican architect she married in 1958. This was a time of civil rights movement, and she met several people who were later active in the struggle. She met the poet Amiri Baraka (at that time called LeRoi Jones) and Andrew Young (who later worked with Dr. Martin Luther King, and later still, became a mayor of Atlanta, Georgia).

The Morrisons' first son, Harold Ford, was born in 1961. Toni continued teaching while helping take care of her family. She also joined a small writer's group as a temporary escape from an unhappy married life. Difficult marriages are a hallmark of individuals who operate out of the archetype of Saraswati – the patron goddess of art and academics. She needed the company of other people who appreciated literature as much as she did. Each member was required to bring a story or poem for discussion. One week, having nothing to bring, she quickly wrote a story loosely based on a girl she knew in childhood, Loraine, who had prayed to God for blue eyes. The story was well-received by the group, and then Toni put it away thinking she was done with it. Her marriage deteriorated, and while pregnant with their second child she left her husband, left her job at the university, and took her son on a trip to Europe. Later, she divorced her husband and returned to her parents' house in Lorain with her two sons.

Saraswati-inspired individuals continue to be much closer to their parents, and their relationships with their fathers become a yardstick with which they may measure their husbands. This usually sets up a very high bar for their marital expectations.

In 1967, she was transferred to New York and became a senior editor at Random House. While editing books by prominent African- Americans like Muhammad Ali, Andrew Young and Angela Davis, she was busy sending her own novel to various publishers. The Bluest Eye (1970) is a novel of initiation concerning a victimized adolescent black girl who is obsessed by white standards of beauty and longs to have blue eyes. The book received enormous critical acclaim for a first book even though it was not commercially successful. From 1971-1972 Morrison was the associate professor of English at the State University of New York at Purchase while she continued working at Random House. In addition, she soon started writing her second novel where she focused on a friendship between two adult African-American women. Sula (1973), which examines (among other issues) the dynamics of friendship and the expectations for conformity within the community, became an alternate selection by the Book-of-the-Month Club. Excerpts were published in Redbook magazine, and it was nominated for the 1975 National Book Award in fiction.

From 1976-1977, she was a visiting lecturer at Yale University in New Haven, Connecticut. She was also writing her third novel. This time she focused on strong African-American male characters. Her insight into the male world came from watching her sons. Morrison' third novel, <u>Song of Solomon</u> (1977), is narrated by a man in search of his identity. It won the National Book Critic's Circle Award and the American Academy and Institute of Arts and Letters Award. Morrison was also appointed by President Jimmy Carter to the National Council on the Arts. In 1981, she published her fourth novel, <u>Tar Baby</u>. Set on a Caribbean island, it explores conflicts of race, class, and sex, and it is the first time she describes interaction between African-American and white characters. Her picture appeared on the cover of the March 30, 1981 issue of Newsweek magazine.

In 1983, Morrison left her position at Random House, having worked there for almost twenty years. In 1984, she was named the Albert Schweitzer Professor of the Humanities at the State University of New York in Albany. While living in Albany, she started writing her first play, <u>Dreaming Emmett</u>. It was based on the true story of Emmett Till, an African-American teenager killed by racist whites in 1955 after being accused of whistling at a white woman. The play premiered January 4, 1986 at the Marketplace Theater in Albany. Morrison's next novel, <u>Beloved</u>, was influenced by a published story about a slave, Margaret Garner, who in 1851 escaped with her children to Ohio from her master in Kentucky. When she was about to be re-captured, she tried to kill her children rather than return them to life of slavery. Only one of her children died, and Margaret was imprisoned for her deed. She refused to show remorse, saying she was "unwilling to have her children suffer as she had done." <u>Beloved</u> was published in 1987 and was a bestseller. In 1988, it won the Pulitzer Prize for fiction.

In 1987, Toni Morrison was named the Robert F. Goheen Professor in the Council of Humanities

at Princeton University. She became the first African-
American woman writer to hold a named chair at an Ivy
League University. While accepting, Morrison said, "I
take teaching as seriously as I do my writing." She taught
creative writing and also took part in the African-American
studies, American studies and women's studies programs.
She also started her sixth novel, Jazz, about life in the 1920's.
Morrison has suggested that Beloved and Jazz (1992) are
the first and second books, respectively, in a planned trilogy.
A work of criticism, "Playing in the Dark: Whiteness and
the Literary Imagination," also was published in 1992.

In 1993, Toni Morrison received the Nobel Prize in
Literature. She was the eighth woman and the first black
woman to do so. Her seventh novel, Paradise, was published
early in 1998 and her most recent, Love, was published in
2003. Tony Morrison embodies the Saraswati archetype.
She embodies the best in the tradition of academic and
creative excellence in service of bettering the collective
consciousness.

Saraswati Yantra[22]

The Saraswati Yantra is helpful in focusing the energies of the latent code of the Saraswati archetype in our personal consciousness. It guides students, artists and those who undertake a new course of study, education or skill acquisition and higher studies. This yantra has two triangles at its core, symbolizing the union of masculine and feminine energies in optimal proportion. This signifies that the ideal attitude towards a new course of education must equally honor both the masculine and feminine perspectives to acquire a new attitude to subject matter of the study. We need the feminine guidance to discern what is of value to us and the masculine initiative to pursue a rigorous new enterprise. In chapter 2, I have clarified that these descriptors of feminine and masculine are not to be confused with gender attributes but rather unisex psychological potentials of both men and women. The terminology used in analytical psychology is Anima function or feminine values and Animus function or inner masculine drive in both sexes. The Yantra is surrounded by eight petals; the number eight is a symbol of infinity. The latent code of Saraswati opens up the realms of knowledge and infinite possibilities. To really experience our soul, we must prepare our consciousness with attention to academics and an artistic eye for life. Knowledge imparted by the code of Saraswati is the source of power, for knowledge is power. It is only with respect for the sacred words and speech that can we rekindle our relationship with the spirit and the universe and regenerate our personal consciousness in accord with our spiritual roots. The *mantra* for the Saraswati's latent code is *Om Sri Vidya Dayeni Saraswatiye Namaha"* (O great Universe, my salutations to goddess Saraswati. May she impart me the necessary knowledge and wisdom to fulfill my spiritual responsibilities in this lifetime).

Cultivating and Honoring Saraswati Code

Throughout North India today, Saraswati is honored in a special prayer ceremony, or Puja, in early spring.

On this day the images of Saraswati are established in schools and universities and special musical and cultural programs celebrate the goddess. It is a day when pens, books, musical instruments, and gurus and teachers are formally worshipped. Mantras such as "*OM Saraswatih Namaha,*" which honor the great goddess, resound. At a personal level, we honor Saraswati whenever we undertake any form of education, either formal or self-taught. When we undertake higher education as an intellectual exercise to enhance our personal and professional success only, it supports our ego consciousness and leads to the realm of material, outer success or *Maya*. When we devote such an effort to Saraswati, the higher education becomes a method to honor the goddess and her will for us. We then devote the enterprise to serve the higher and deeper calling of our soul— to fulfill our *Dharma* (sacred duty) to ourselves (*Sva Dharma*), our family (*Ashram Dharma)*, our community (*Varana Dharma*) and our higher consciousness (*Reta Dharma*). In *Maya* realm, higher education may lead to gold making but in *Dharmic* realm, Saraswati guides us to soul-making. One intervention we can make in our daily life to invoke the guidance of Saraswati is to maintain a daily written journal and chant a personal mantra or prayer to center ourselves during daily meditation. Another intervention is to maintain a course of personal study or education in a new subject that deepens our soul work.

In this chapter, we have met one of the three goddesses in the Shakti trinity. In the next section, we meet the second goddess in this sacred trinity, Laxmi, one of the most popular Hindu goddesses. She is the bearer of peace, prosperity and *Dharmic* or spiritual order in the lives of individuals and societies. Join me now in honoring the realm of Laxmi—the most revered of Shakti manifestations in India today.

laxmi

OUR SOUL POTENTIAL

CH 5
The Latent Code of Laxmi
The Code for Peace, Prosperity and Plenty

Laxmi is the most revered of Hindu goddesses and unlocks our potential for peace, prosperity and plenty in our inner and outer life. She is the consort of Vishnu, the preserver of moral order in our personality and in the world. Laxmi facilitates the maintenance of a soulful life. She is invoked by simplicity and purity of life and purpose. She provides our psyche with the necessary symbols and motivation to persevere in our goals to achieve our soul potential. She is the patron goddess of midlife transition. She ushers in our Vishnu nature – our psychic tendency to maintain order, focus, and soul purpose in our life in general and our mid-life in particular. Let us now meet the most revered of the three goddesses of the Trinity.

The Myth

When the kingdom of gods lost its prosperity and energy, they consulted Brahma for advice. Brahma counseled them to churn the cosmic ocean to extract the ambrosia, the elixir of eternal life. In this process a radiant beauty emerged from the ocean, seated on a lotus, holding a lily in her hand. Laxmi was ambrosia, the quintessence of the *magnum opus* of the gods, who grants peace, prosperity and life energy.

The power of all-pervading Vishnu is represented in the goddess of fortune and beauty. As the goddess of fortune, she is Sri, and as the goddess of beauty, she is Uma. Beauty (Uma) and Fortune (Sri) are the two wives of Vishnu. Both Laxmi and Sri are found in the Vedas associated with Fortune. Beauty is also the mother of Pleasure (Kama). She is known for her fidelity in her wife aspect, but as fortune she is known to be fickle.

Mythologically, Laxmi's association with Vishnu comes

about in the context of the churning of the ocean of milk jointly by the gods and the demons that seek the elixir of immortality. Ancient Hindu tradition asserts that creation proceeds from the womb of the primordial waters when it is agitated or churned. This is akin to individuation, when transformation and growth in an individual occurs, when the primordial waters of one's unconscious are churned either by life experiences. This transforms the junk of the human psyche into the gold of our potential. When the waters of the unconscious are churned like the cosmic ocean, Laxmi is distilled from the depths of the psyche, crystallizing our creative nature. She then marries Vishnu, who is the master of ceremonies of the churning of the ocean. The spoils of the enterprise fall to the victor. A pilgrimage on the path to the soul leads to the gift of Laxmi's code. The Laxmi archetype in turn provides a template for marital harmony, domestic order, and a model of mutuality between partners and between the Masculine and the Feminine aspects of our psyche.

Laxmi's appearance as a result of this cosmic oceanic disturbance symbolizes the alchemic process where purity, patience, practice and enterprise transform the base substance, the *prima materia*, of one's personality into a precious substance, the ambrosia of one's potential. The fruit of such an enterprise can be inner peace, creative prosperity, the experience of beauty and grace. This is the goal of every individual who undertakes the transformation of the personality into the higher soul potential and wholeness. A new order of the positive static feminine, the realm of Sri Laxmi, is thus established.

Attributes of Laxmi

Laxmi, when seen with Vishnu, has two arms, but when alone has four arms. The hands on the left hold the *amrit*, the ambrosia vessel, which she rescued from the ocean, and the conch shell, a trademark adornment of Vishnu's which identifies her with him. In the two right hands she holds a lotus and the bilwa fruit, called the Sri-phala, or the fruit of fortune. Sometimes one hand is in the *abhaya mudra*, the gesture of fearlessness, the palm held up with fingers pointing upwards, while the other hand is depicted as bestowing grace and prosperity. She sits on the red lotus, which signifies grace, love, and peace, and is symbolic of soulful living without which prosperity is dangerous, like a fast car without brakes.

Two objects are consistently associated with Sri Laxmi: the lotus and the elephant. She is seated on a lotus or wears a garland of lotuses. Throughout history, she is referred to as Padma or Kamala, meaning "lotus." The lotus is a symbol of fertility and life, which is rooted in and takes strength from the primordial waters of the unconscious, the wellspring of symbols and soul guidance. The lotus represents the fully developed blossoming of personality, the potential for wholeness. Jung considered this flower as a mandala symbol, a manifestation of the soul and the wholeness of personality.[23]

A popular rendering of the Laxmi image is one flanked by two elephants. Elephants have two symbolic meanings in the context of the Laxmi myth. The elephants shower her with water from their trunks, symbolizing our sense of feelings and values. What is of value comes from the heart not from the head. The elephants represent the imperial authority of our soul. Thus the elephants bring together two important themes in the Laxmi archetype: personal authority and authentic feeling. As a composite, this establishes the value of personal authority guided by feelings and value system in guiding the path to the soul and selfhood.

How the Latent Code of Laxmi Guides Our Path to the Soul

Laxmi is the patron goddess of adulthood and its corresponding developmental tasks. Her Aphrodite (lover) aspect brings an individual into a relational mode with a mate and psychologically into inner relationship with one's contra - sexual potential. A man meets the inner feminine and a woman meets the inner masculine under the auspices of Laxmi. Laxmi guides our efforts in the churning of the first half of life to achieve our personal and professional goals. If our efforts in the first half of life are soulful, we create good karma (actions and their consequences). If our choices in the first half of life are alienated from our soul's guidance, we create bad karma. When the chaos of the first half of life is churned, the cosmic ocean of our unconscious bears fruits and toxins. If our efforts in the first half of life are soul directed, our unconscious activates the Laxmi code. She then ushers in an era of inner and outer peace, prosperity and soulful life. The toxins are contained by the Shiva-Shakti vessel, which will be amplified in the last chapter. Developmentally, the householder stage of the life cycle is thus established, which provides the structure necessary for achieving personal goals and ambitions, raising a family and serving our community and the divine Spirit.

The Integration of Our Feminine and Masculine Potentials under the Auspices of Laxmi

The Laxmi myth embodies the archetype of the positive dynamic feminine that transforms, inspires and opens up the static masculine order to new creative possibilities in the mid-life transition. She then furthers our soul journey by ushering in the positive static feminine order of the great goddess, a new order of wholeness, self-acceptance and oneness with one's inner nature as well as peace with the laws of nature. While these are watery initiations in which one must experience the chaos of one's psychic depths, they have a fiery component as well in that one must agitate the unconscious depths and transform them in an alchemic enterprise of self discovery of one's personality potential. In this churning of the cosmic ocean of one's unconscious, engaging both one's gods and one's demons, the ego potentials and the shadow aspects must collaborate for optimal outcome.

A New World-view from the
Lens of the Latent Code of Laxmi

The Laxmi world-view is sensate (attention to details) with feeling as an auxiliary function thus imparting an experial worldview. To honor her typological World-view, the seeker of Laxmi's guidance needs to attend to facts, focus on details of daily life and attend to what holds a sense of value. One must maintain a friendly relational mode and find scope for his or her abilities in service to others. Later in this section, we will discuss the case of Larry – an introverted intuitive thinker – an ethereal World-view type. The Laxmi World-view put him in touch with the experial aspects of his typological mandala, honoring his feelings and attending to what he considered paltry details. This greatly enhanced his capacity to enjoy pursuits that he coveted but could not master, e.g., counseling, and to deal with his relationships with an authentic self-expression of his feelings. Typological wholeness was a necessary focus of his analysis and soul work as was evidenced in his dreams (see below).

Comparative Mythology

Laxmi is a complex goddess archetype and does not neatly fit any of the Olympian patterns. She is an organic composite of several Occidental goddess archetypes in a fluid continuum, unfolding to sustain or compensate for the demands of the conscious situation. Like Aphrodite, Laxmi is born from the sea, a fully-grown beautiful woman. As with Aphrodite, many of the gods are struck by her beauty and vie for her hand in marriage. Like Aphrodite and unlike other Greek Goddesses, (Persephone was abducted by Hades and Hera was seduced) Laxmi both chose Vishnu to be her consort and master of ceremonies of the churning event. Also, like Aphrodite, Laxmi had many liaisons. Her associations with many different male deities and demons gave her the reputation of fickleness and inconsistency. Even her associations with Vishnu came about because of her attractions to his many different forms and reincarnations. However, Vishnu had a steady, anchoring effect on her, and she became a devoted wife.

Once committed to Vishnu, Laxmi corresponds to the realm of Hera, the goddess of marriage and wife of the supreme god of the Olympians, Zeus. Once married to Vishnu, Laxmi develops the capacity to bond and make a lasting commitment through all of Vishnu's reincarnations. Symbolically, this marriage implies a sacred union with the deeper aspects of one's personality to establish wholeness. This inner marriage can be psychologically and spiritually nourishing but may also be contentious. Analytically this may be seen as the inner discord between the ego complex (our conscious personality) and the other complexes (our hang-ups or neurotic personality patterns) that threaten to usurp the central role in the personality.

Another archetypal characteristic of Laxmi is her Athena aspect. In Greek mythology, Athena is the protector, advisor, patron, and ally of heroic men. Athena sided with the patriarchy and always strategized to restore the patriarchal order in war or peace. In the great Greek epic *The Odyssey* by Homer, Athena is the patron goddess of the great hero and warrior Odysseus. She guides and protects him from many dangers in the war with his adversaries to reclaim Helen from her lover to her husband. After victory in battle, Odysseus provokes the wrath of the sea god Poseidon, who sabotages his return home to his kingdom Ithaca and to his lovely wife, Penelope. Athena protects and guides him during the ten years of his Odyssey and all his trials and tribulations till he finally reaches home only to find his wife held hostage by suitors who want to marry her. Athena once again guides Odysseus in battle and victory over the suitors to reestablish his authority over his kingdom and rekindle his relationship with his wife Penelope.

Similarly, Laxmi helps Vishnu, the lawgiver, to maintain cosmic order (*dharma*). When Vishnu is reincarnated in various avatars to restore *dharma*, Laxmi reincarnates

herself as a helpmate, assuming an appropriate form as
a spouse or consort. Laxmi is associated with upholding
social order, righteous behavior, orderly conduct, and
protocol. In many renderings of the Vishnu myth, he
is portrayed as outwardly passive, and it is Laxmi who
mediates and implements Vishnu's *dharmic* homeostasis on
his behalf.

Perils and Promise of the Latent Code of Laxmi

Women and men who are living out of the Laxmi
mode are extroverted individuals with a zest for life and
relationships. Her presence is seductive and invites
reciprocal response, often without consideration of
consequences. Until an optimal relationship is established
later in life, as with Vishnu, Laxmi may leave a trail of broken
hearts and shattered egos. Before optimal maturation, an
individual caught in the Laxmi archetype may be clinically
predisposed to borderline personality or hysterical states.
Her presence is transient, fickle, rewarding and energizing
in the present moment without any certainty about the
future or the consequences of actions or choices, which
leads to *karmic* debts (the consequences of our choices and
actions) to be repaid later in life.

Another peril of enmeshment in the Laxmi archetype
is an excessive preoccupation with material wealth and
peace at the expense of informed and necessary change
that one must make in the established order to make room
for new insights and new ways of relating. It can become a
"do not make waves" personality or culture. This can lead
to complacency and stasis in individuals or societies. Such
an adaptation ill prepares us to embrace the tides of time
and change inherent in life.

However, once the Laxmi energy moves from an
archaic to a mature dimension, she settles in for the
long haul, usually in a relationship with a mature, static
masculine animus, the Vishnu energy. But furthermore,
Laxmi energy settles in for the very long haul with Vishnu,
not only in this lifetime but also for all of his reincarnations,

his *avatars*. She collaborates with the masculine aspects of men's and women's psyche to establish a *dharmic* order that is living out one's essential nature. When an individual lives out of one's essential nature, one's *Dharma*, it ushers in an era of individuation, where wholeness of personality is established. Such individuals have tasted the gifts of their deepest psychic potential and live a full and creative life. Such an authentic and creative *dharmic* life (soulful life) blossoms into an era of inner peace, psychic prosperity and creative wealth. Such an optimal state is the heaven (Vaikuntha), where Laxmi and Vishnu reside.

The Latent Code in Action

Laxmi is the patron goddess of the establishment of the *Dharmic* order (living by our soul's code) in one's life. She is the most significant guide of individuals at the threshold of mid-life transition. In the first half of life, many of us get lost in establishing our outer life or *Maya* (pursuit of wealth, success and attachments). Our relational and inner life is often marginalized or ignored. Life becomes lopsided. For some individuals, this lopsidedness becomes conscious when they experience relational problems with an ignored spouse and children. For others, depression or substance abuse points to their lopsided lives and may even contribute to it. Such individuals have lost balance in their *Dharmic equation* (caught in Maya at the expense of the soul). Laxmi now beckons them to reestablish their *Dharmic* life. This involves reconfiguring their responsibilities to themselves (*Sva Dharma*), to their family (*Ashrama Dharma*), their community (*Varana Dharma*), and their spiritual life (*Reta Dharma*). In my own life, I had to honor Laxmi by simplifying the clutter in my outer life to make room for my inner life and thus foster my soul work. In psychotherapy with numerous individuals, Laxmi has been their guide and mine to restore balance.

Ian's Story

Ian's story illustrates the workings of Laxmi in the life of a businessman who was initially lost in the realm of Maya or outer success. Ian sought psychotherapy with me after a bout with depression. This was precipitated by a major showdown with his younger brother, who ousted him from a very successful family business and took over the reins of the enterprise. Ian felt humiliated and incompetent. While he got a golden parachute settlement, his pride was wounded. As a middle-aged man, his business empire was his universe. He had neglected his marriage, his two young daughters and his inner life. He felt like he had nowhere to go professionally or personally. His wife was skeptical of emotionally reconnecting with him lest he abandon her once again as soon as he warmed up to some new business adventure. Then he had a dream:

> *I am driving a red sports car. A police squad car pulls me over, and the policewoman gives me a ticket. My license plate registration has expired, and I need to renew it before I can drive.*

This dream had a significant impact on my patient. He explored in detail what aspects of his life had been neglected and what he needed to attend to. Over the next several years, we worked through the message of this dream. Ian took stock of the unfinished aspects of his *dharma*. The first half of his life was spent in the red sports car mode, the world of *Maya*, and the world of external success. This Maya enmeshment had accumulated considerable negative *Karma* in his professional and personal life. Ian started to acknowledge his personal strivings. He really wanted to be a counselor, not a businessman. His father had not been supportive of this choice but rather motivated him to take over the family business. Ian revived this ambition from his earlier life and took steps to complete his training to be a counselor. This was his *Sva Dharma* (Duty to Self). He started to take a deep interest in playing an active role in raising his two daughters. I remember one session in which he came in excited like a schoolboy because he had stood in line for six hours to get tickets for a rock concert to surprise his daughters. He had begun to attend to his *Ashram Dharma* (family and developmental responsibilities). Later, he volunteered as a counselor at a youth center thus honoring his *Varana Dharma* (responsibilities to his community). His sense of spirituality and inner life has deepened considerably. He is connecting with his *Reta Dharma* (spiritual awakening). Looking back to his initial dream, the goddess Laxmi as the patron goddess of the establishment of the *Dharmic* order in Ian's life had been constellated in the form of the policewoman who stopped him from driving on in his life under the auspices of an outdated license. The policewoman activated the latent code of Laxmi in his life.

SriLaxmi Yantra

The Laxmi Yantra is useful to invoke the latent code of the Laxmi archetype. It guides us to attain a psychological state of inner peace, material prosperity and success in Spiritual realignment of our life in accord with the program of the Universe for us. While the uninitiated may use it to seek financial success, the initiated invoke it to find inner peace. A Yantra is also symbolic of the human body, and when one mediates on a particular Yantra, it aligns the body to receive the energies and the blessings of the relevant sectors of the Latent Code.

Sri Yantra is a very ancient Yantra which aligns the masculine and the feminine, Solar and Lunar, fire and water, earth and sky aspects of our body and psyche to a central point or Bindu which represents the consciousness of our soul. The surrounding geometries represent the unfolding of the creative possibilities in the psyche when we are centered in the Bindu or the Soul. These infinite creative possibilities are inspired by the latent code of Laxmi. The Laxmi Mantra is "Om Shri Mahalaxmiye Namah" (Salutations to the Great Goddess Laxmi).

I will now discuss the symbolic aspects of Sri Yantra based on an excellent discussion by Arthur Avalon in his treatise on Shakti.[24] He discusses this great *Yantra* or diagram used in the worship of Laxmi.

It is composed of two sets of Triangles. One set is composed of four male triangles, denoting four aspects of evolved or limited Consciousness, and the five female triangles denote the five vital functions, the five senses of knowledge, the five senses of action, and the five subtle and the five gross forms of matter.

These two sets of triangles are superimposed to show the union of the masculine and feminine aspects of our nature. When united, they make the figure within the eight lotus petals in the full *Yantra*. These triangles are surrounded by four gates or doors, which are called *Bhupura*. It serves the purpose of what in Magic is called a Fence or the gate of our consciousness. Deeper mysteries of the universe can only be unlocked by the enterprise of our consciousness. This Yantra has nine *Cakras*, or compartments, formed by the intersection of the Triangles.

There is first a red central point or *Bindu*, the point of Bliss. The central point or *Bindu* is Supreme Divinity – the Mother as the Grand Potential whence all the rest which this diagram signifies proceed. It is red, for that is the active color of passion for what is valuable about life, and thus the color of the latent code of evolving Laxmi consciousness.

The object of the worship of the *Yantra* is to attain unity with the latent code. The *Yantra* is thus transformed in one's consciousness from a material object of lines and curves into a mental state of union with the Universe and its divine essence. This leads to the realization of soul consciousness. The *Shri Yantra* is thus the manifestation of the latent code of Laxmi. The worshipper becomes one with the *Shri Yantra* and realizes its healing potential.

Sri Yantra[25]

Celebrating and Honoring
the Latent Code of Laxmi

Sri Laxmi is one of the most popular deities of the Hindu pantheon. She is worshipped throughout the year in various festivals and holy fasts. The most important festival of Laxmi worship is *Diwali* or the festival of lights, which is held in late autumn. Several important themes are celebrated, including wealth and prosperity, fertility and abundant harvest, and good fortune for the coming year. She is the patron goddess of the merchants who seek her blessings.

Laxmi favors clean, simple environments. During Laxmi Puja, or prayers, the house is thoroughly cleaned to receive the goddess. The custom is to paint the house and light candles throughout. Psychologically, this may imply the need for the establishment of an adequate persona or stable outer life structures before the creative potentials is engaged under the watchful guidance of the latent code of Laxmi. In addition, the shadow or the problematic aspects of our personality have to be attended to before the light of Laxmi may prevail. This is symbolized by lighting the candles in the dark. The light of insight counters the darkness of ignorance of our dark side. A small candle in the new moon night is a symbol of the power of the individual human consciousness to counter the darkness in the universe. Prior to the final Diwali Puja prayer, Bali, a demon, is said to emerge from the underworld to rule for three days during which goblins and malicious spirits are about, with gambling and boisterous activities in command. The Laxmi prayers and invocations are supposed to ward off the harmful effects of the returned demons from the dead. *Alaxmi*, Laxmi's sinister twin, brings bad luck and misfortune but is banished by lighting the candles and lamps. Psychologically, this management of *Alaxmi* is meant to acknowledge and integrate the shadow aspects of the personality before the numinous aspects of our inner potential incarnate in our lived life.

In our personal lives, we best honor Laxmi when we simplify our lives and step back to examine the choices of our first half of life in order to attend our *Karma* and the *Dharmic* order in midlife or any major transition or new beginning in life. This may require us to reconfigure our responsibilities to ourselves (*Sva Dharma*), to our family (*Ashrama Dharma*), our community (*Varana Dharma*), and our spiritual life (*Reta Dharma*) in a manner that honors our full potential.

In this chapter, we have explored the realm of the goddess Laxmi. She helps us to usher in and maintain peace and prosperity in our life. This creates optimal conditions to pursue our path to the soul. However, there are times of transition and change when we need to adapt to new realities and circumstances. The latent code of Goddess Parvati presides over adaptation to change, and she is the subject matter of the next chapter.

THE SACRED FEMININE

parvati

FEELING • RELATIONAL • MUTUAL • MAT

CH 6
The Latent Code of Parvati
The Code to Integrate Our Masculine and Feminine Potentials

Shiva and Sati are as inseparable as cold from water
Heat from fire, smell from earth
Or radiance from the sun

– Vaivarta Purana

Parvati is the consort of Shiva and is the Goddess of cosmic welfare. Variously known as Sati and Shakti, she is the primal feminine force in the human psyche. The goal of the latent code of Parvati is to accomplish the sacred marriage between the masculine and the feminine energies in the psyche. This union of the Shiva and Shakti aspects of our personality leads to wholeness and the healing of our split psyche. In this lifetime, we gradually integrate the masculine and the feminine aspects of our soul at a gradually increasing level of sophistication. It is like a cascade to a higher level of consciousness. The ancient Hindu healing system of Kundalini yoga is a useful paradigm for the gradual integration of the masculine and feminine aspects of our psyche through the seven levels of development at a gradually higher level of spiritual development. The basics of Kundalini yoga are discussed in my earlier publications.[26] [27] As we undertake such a task of synthesis of our personality, the latent code of Parvati guides our soul work. Join me now in understanding and honoring the latent code of the great goddess.

The Myth

Parvati is also known as Sati and Shakti in her various incarnations and manifestations. She is always depicted with her consort, Lord Shiva. Parvati was first born as Sati or Uma, the daughter of Daksha and Prasuti. Even in her childhood she longed to be united with Shiva. She worshipped Shiva and thought only of him. Shiva, all knowing though he was, was not moved by her devotion. Her father, Daksha, hated Shiva and considered him impure and anti-establishment.

Daksha had 58 daughters, who abided by his dictums, but the 59th, Sati, was different. She felt more comfortable in nature rather than in her father's grand court. There she fell in love with Shiva, lord of animals and mountains. Eventually she married him against her father's wishes, and he disowned her. She shared Shiva's austere life and lived in the mountains.

Even in her sacred marriage with Lord Shiva, Sati valued her independence and, against Shiva's protest, decided to visit her father's house for the ritual sacrifice ceremony. Shiva acceded to her wishes, even though he was afraid that her father would not accept her as Shiva's wife. Shiva's fears were justified. Sati's father insulted Shiva in her presence. Sati immolated herself in the sacrificial fire in protest, and since then, a woman who burnt herself on her husband's funeral pyre came to be known as Sati. This is the origin of the Sati ritual in India, which since then has been grossly abused to suppress women's rights and serves as one of many tragic examples of symbolism in religious or mythological text being taken literally.

After Sati's death, Shiva was grief stricken. He threatened destruction of the universe. Gods and mortals made an emergency appeal to Vishnu for resolution of this crisis. Vishnu, the great protector of the cosmic order shot 52 arrows at Sati's burnt body, which fell in fragments all over the universe, and wherever it fell, gods and mortals built temples to pay homage to Sati. This act of homage to Sati appeased Shiva and he granted the world the relief from his fury and imminent destruction. However, Shiva himself gave up all pleasures and returned to his ascetic life in the mountains.

Sati was reincarnated as Uma or Parvati, the daughter of Himmavat, King of the Himalayas, and his wife, Manaka. Her parents were devotees of Shiva. Even in her reincarnation as Parvati she was in love with Shiva, who was still grieving her death as Sati. Parvati performed rituals of fasting and prayer and eventually won over Shiva's heart, and they were married.

Attributes of Parvati

In her aspects as Sati and Parvati, the goddess is a devoted wife. In her domesticated form, she is depicted as benign and carries no weapons. She sits next to Shiva while he looks at her with tenderness. Without Parvati, Shiva appears as the terrifying one, but Parvati brings him into a relationship with his feeling function and his domestic side. Thus the sacred feminine brings the raw and archaic masculine energy in the grove of its feeling, relational, mutual and mature potentials.

Though Shiva and Parvati depict the eternal Masculine and Feminine, they paradoxically did not have children of their own. However, this was meant to protect the pre-existent power balance. The gods were concerned that any offspring from such a powerful cosmic union would be stronger than any of the existing gods and could disturb the power dynamic. Shiva promised not to procreate, and frustrated by this dictum over her procreative potential, Parvati created her own son, Ganesha, from the rubbings of her skin. The myth of Ganesha is a major Hindu template of how masculine and feminine energies in our psyche and in relationships may organize their boundaries. Shortly, we will discuss the myth of Ganesha and how Shiva and Parvati negotiated their rapprochement. Interestingly, the myth of Ganesha has been a guiding myth in my relationship with my wife Usha as she asserted her own creative potential. After years of supporting my career and academic endeavors, she and my daughter Ami established a very soulful and successful Indian restaurant in Milwaukee, which they appropriately named "Dancing Ganesha."

THE REALM OF

ganesha

AUSPICIOUS NEW BEGINNINGS

ganesha

Myth of Ganesha and My Encounter with the
Latent Code of the Ganesha Archetype

My personal encounter with Ganesha started in mid nineties, when my daughter and I were visiting India. It was a very long and tiring journey. It takes twenty-six hours in the air, a stop over in London and Dubai. In Mumbai the first night we relaxed and then went for a stroll. Somehow in this huge frenetic and exotic metropolis unlike anywhere else on the planet, we ended up in a small curio shop. A small statue of Ganesha intrigued my daughter, Ami. It was made of solid cast silver and at first glance did not even look stable enough to stay upright. But it had an inexplicable charm, so we paid too much for it and took it home. Since that moment the symbol of Ganesha has come alive in my life. And I need, at the risk of being a little bit exhibitionistic, to share this story with you because there is no better way to communicate the power of the symbol without sharing with you how I lived it, or better still, how it lived me.

In order to illustrate how Ganesha altered my life, I must first relate the story of Ganesha. Parvati, a very powerful and beautiful woman, was married to Shiva. Shiva led a much fractured life. He would alternate between spending a thousand ascetic years alone in the mountains meditating and coming home to a domestic life with his wife. He would then return to the mountains, and the cycle would repeat ad infinitum. In a way I was caught up in the Shiva archetype, caught in my medical and psychiatric world, with precious little time for my family.

When Shiva would be lost in his introverted enterprise, Parvati would get rather bored after several thousand years of her husband's neglect. One day, as she was taking a bath in the holy Ganges, her frustration led to a fruitful idea. The Ganges is the river which flows from the hair of Shiva as he is sitting and meditating. So in a sense Shiva is the father, and Parvati is the adoptive mother of the river Ganges. Parvati was taking a bath in the river Ganges – her daughter, and suddenly she decided she must have a companion. So she took some of her skin rubbings and threw it in the Ganges. Out came a very handsome young man called Ganesha in his mammoth cosmic form, but to pacify those around him he assumed a human form.

Ganesha and his mother lived in a cave and had a very peaceful and playful time together. Parvati wasn't lonely anymore as she had Ganesha as a companion and son. One day she was taking a bath in her cave and instructed her son to guard the cave so no one should enter while she was undressed. Unfortunately that very day, of all the hundreds of years that Shiva was away, he showed up at the cave looking for his wife. Ganesha was guarding the cave, and he refused entry to Shiva. Shiva was very angry and took his sword and cut Ganesha's head off, oblivious that this was his son. Parvati came out and saw what happened, and she was extremely despondent and grief stricken to see her son murdered. Like Demeter, the Greek mother goddess whose daughter Persephone was kidnapped by Hades, she went into extended mourning and the entire universe came to a standstill. The gods pleaded with Shiva to reverse his sentence and to restore Ganesha's life. As they persisted, Shiva made a compromise. Ganesha could not have his old head back, but the next creature that walked past would be sacrificed and its head would replace Ganesha's head. Accordingly, the next creature that passed was an elephant, so Shiva kept his word, took the elephant's head and put it on the head of his son. That is how Ganesha manifests in the form that we now know him, the god with the head of an elephant. Thus Ganesha was reborn, an auspicious god of new beginnings. Later, Shiva adopted his son, and they lived happily ever after as a family: the father Shiva, mother Parvati, son Ganesha, and daughter Ganges. The four of them became a happy unit once again, and peace was restored.

Why did I find Ganesha? When my daughter and I came back from India, my wife vocalized her dream of the last eighteen years to open a restaurant. A few years later, with the collaborative efforts of my daughter, this wish became reality. The two of them played painstakingly with their list of names, much like when you name a child. And of all names that were on the list, they chose the name Dancing Ganesha. I was amused and found the name to be a fitting one. At that time I hadn't made the connection with the myth and the symbol of Ganesha.

So they planned very hard at this mother and daughter enterprise. Soon this idea and this whole project became a flourishing reality. Remember Ganesha was formed in collaboration between mother and daughter (Ganges and Parvati). So the symbol was living out in my life after I met Ganesha in Mumbai. Now it became real in Milwaukee, and it became a new child that was born in collaboration between the mother and daughter, but without father's input. Like Shiva I felt excluded from the cave. I felt incensed and wanted to cut the head of the project off. What about me? They told me I had my patients and clinic, and I could go back to my mountain. I wasn't deterred from my protest so readily and did my best to unconsciously sabotage the project. In the bloodshed that followed, my wife and I got to the negotiating table, and we arrived at a workable compromise – where my wife's mission and my passion for mutuality were honored. Now I gave full support to their business. We played out the myth of initially beheading the project by the male Shiva energy and eventual rapprochement between the masculine and the feminine to make room for the union and the emergence of the divine child, the Ganesha energy. When the masculine and the feminine energies in society, in relationships, and in psyche collaborate, the results are wondrous.

Something interesting happened a few months later which gave me some indication as to what motivated the beliefs which my wife and daughter infused into the Ganesha project. The restaurant had by now opened and received unilateral accolades from critics and diners alike. The resounding response was that the food was excellent and the atmosphere beautiful, but that there was something more, something different. It revealed to me the wonders and the working of goddess Parvati and her creative divine child-Ganesha.

It was a Monday evening, and my wife and I went to this rather highly acclaimed restaurant and had an enlightening experience, which gave me the insight as to why she and my daughter had to start their restaurant. The restaurant my wife and I were at was classy, expensive, clean and traditional. But the point of interest was that in this restaurant on a Monday evening all the patrons were men in suits. I wondered where the women were. There were two women who were quietly listening to the jokes of their loud and garrulous husbands, but other than these two women, there were no women in the room. I wondered where they all were. Surely, all these other men were not bachelors. Another interesting observation was that my wife and I were the only non-white people in the room. Where was the rest of America? Where had it gone from this room? We paid our bill and left with a strange feeling in our hearts.

I realized that it wasn't like this at my wife and daughter's restaurant. There, they had children and mothers, single and married individuals, men and women, couples and families, white, black and brown people, young and old, LGBT and straight. They were all together, forming a rich tapestry of culture and traditions. I had come to America in search of the great new frontier, with promises of racial equality, cultural diversity, respect for varying perspectives, a mosaic of the human race, a fractal of the promise of our civilization. It was a paradox that of all the places in America, I found it in my wife and daughter's restaurant! Such is the power of the feminine, of the blessing of Parvati and the wonders of the myth of Ganesha.

I researched: what is the definition of the word culture? The root is from the Latin word cultrae— to till, to break up the crust of the soil. Culture comes from breaking up the established order and tilling the ground to seed new order, new perspective, a new way of looking at and doing things. Perhaps this was the reason the Ganesha archetype had to reincarnate in this community to make way for creating ground for a new way of doing things. Where women are empowered and can take charge of their destiny. This is a whole new way of doing business for me and for my wife, and for our children, and for this community where new frontiers of cultural richness have integrated in the family matrix of this community. I think there is a very big difference between civilization and culture. Civilization has to do with established order. Culture has to do with new frontiers of civilization, the growth edges of civilization, which lay new foundation for new culture. And perhaps these were the sacrifices my family had to make to lay some ground for new culture in this community.

I was not only seeing the work of Ganesha, but I was living it as well. One important aspect of the Ganesha myth is the experience of your head being chopped off but then being replaced by an elephant's head. Losing one's head or the old attitudes is the sacrifice we must make to create room for the new beginnings and to find our higher, spiritual nature. Christ had to endure crucifixion to resurrect his divine essence. On our path to the soul, guided by Parvati and the archetype of the goddess Shakti, we must be prepared to make necessary sacrifices to find our higher nature. This involves letting go of old habits and business as usual.

So what does it mean to have the head of an elephant? What does that experience feel like? An elephant's head is close to the heavens, and its trunk is close to the earth. It symbolizes the union of these two extremes, the cosmic thinking and humble and human living close to the ground. When we bridge our shadow with light in our nature, our spiritual potential with our essential frail human existence, outer life with inner life, active life with reflective and spiritual life, where our darkest and highest potential unite we are living out our Ganesha potential.

The myth of Ganesha is one framework through which

we can negotiate the boundaries between the masculine and the feminine role relationships in our culture and potentials in our psyche. The myth of Ganesha is a gift of Parvati. Even though Shiva had promised the gods not to procreate in order to maintain political balance, Parvati managed to constellate Shiva's procreative potential via Ganesha. Similarly in contemporary culture, when a person sacrifices his or her creative potential for political and survival expediency, the power of the goddess Parvati helps the masculine realize its true potential.

This is a very limited rendering of one of the many versions of the Ganesha myth but is presented here since it forms a bridge between Shiva and Shakti and a myth that is a living myth in my life. The small statue of Ganesha that my daughter bought in Bombay still adorns a mantle place in the now well known restaurant.

The Latent Code of Parvati in Action

The archetype of Parvati is activated in women when they are developmentally in the phase of separation from their family of origin and their father's domain and are seeking their own relational matrix. In the developmental framework, this could be considered the individuation or separation phase. Psychologically, this can play out when women are seeking a connection with their inner Shiva or animus energy by emancipating from the father complex or dependency on the men in their lives.

This may often involve young women dating people that will invoke paternal disapproval. The task of development and individuation is to seek an authentic relationship with someone and with the inner masculine rather than merely a rebellious, oppositional object choice. The task of psychotherapy is often to help sort out the rebellious versus authentic choice in a relationship with the masculine. The same psychic dynamic may play out for men who may choose a certain directionless, Shiva lifestyle as a method to differentiate from their parental complexes rather than as an authentic lifestyle choice of Bohemian asceticism.

The Sacred Union of our Masculine and Feminine Potentials under the Auspices of Goddess Parvati

The Sati aspect of Shakti is the embodiment of the dynamic positive feminine energy. This ushers in creativity and transformation of the present order into new frontiers. She challenges the static masculine order of the father or the establishment and renders us flexible and open to new ideas and possibilities. She transforms both her father and her husband, Shiva, from the rigid to the dynamic and fluid masculine mode, from old order to new enterprise; Sati energy brings our rigid withdrawn Shiva nature into relationship with inner feminine and feeling function. This ushers in the creative flow of the individuals and the culture.

Through the watery initiation she represents, she dissolves both her husband's and her father's orderly, static world and sets up the framework for the creation of a new order. She herself is immolated in the process. In her reincarnation as Parvati, she comes into a new, peaceful balance with the masculine order of her father and her husband. She relates with love, not war, penance not protest, dialogue not dissent. This is akin to the contemporary feminist movement, which initially had been fiery in its confrontation of the static masculine order. Might it reincarnate as Parvati in a more collaborative balance with the masculine order? (This is not a recommendation, but rather a reflection based on the mythologies.)

A New Typological World-view from the Lens of Parvati

While the Shiva archetype may be considered an ethereal (thinking/intuitive) World-view, Sati and Parvati bring the personality into relationship with the oceanic world-view, the world of feelings and intuition. The Sati/Parvati world-view fosters the exploration of possibilities, an empathic relational attitude that includes the understanding of the aspirations of the other. Individuals under the auspices of the Sati/Parvati's oceanic world-view are enthusiastic and insightful, finding scope for their abilities in understanding and communicating with others. They tend to excel in psychology, research, literature, art and music, religious service, health care and teaching. Some of the characteristics of the Sati/Parvati World-view overlap with those of the goddess Saraswati.

Comparative Mythology[28]

In her Sati aspect, Shakti is a composite of Artemis, the virgin goddess of the hunt and the moon, who personifies the independent, achievement-oriented feminine spirit. In her Parvati mode, she is like Hera, the goddess of marriage, who considers her roles as student, professional, or mother secondary to her essential goal of finding a husband and being married.

Perils and the Promise of the Latent Code of Parvati

As Sati, the goddess imparts the necessary energy to women to find their own authentic ground as differentiated from parental complexes and separate out of their fathers' worlds. However, this may also take the form of extreme rebellion and feed oppositional behavior rather than authentic individuation. Sometimes this may have disastrous consequences in the masculine realm, where the woman squanders her energy battling the negative static masculine in its insistence on rigid order, complacency, organization for its own sake, unrealistic expectations and dehumanizing righteousness, inauthenticity and pettiness. Sati has to walk a narrow line between self-assertion and respect for the positive aspects of the masculine order while protesting its shadow aspects.

The Parvati Latent Code in Action

Tara's Story

Tara consulted me for psychotherapy in her late 40's for symptoms of depression and a gradual atrophy of her marital intimacy. Her husband, a successful professional in a large corporation, was getting increasingly caught in the corporate maze. For many years, Tara was a dutiful corporate wife, masterfully managing his professional matrix, organizing company parties and entertaining his clients and his associates. She was also responsible for raising their children, fulfilling the roles of a corporate wife caught up the role of homemaker and supporting her husband's success. She was his primary life line to the social and relational milieu.

Before getting married, Tara had aspiration to be an antique dealer, but this had fallen by the wayside as she got caught up in the archetype of her husband's Shiva dominated life. She increasingly got caught in the role of the devoted life. Even her role as a mother was motivated by a need to compensate for her husband's absence rather than a desire for an authentic connection with them. In her father's home, Tara was caught in a similar dynamic. Her father was a successful lawyer, and her mother had been caught up in the role of the devoted and supportive wife and mother, thus never pursuing her own dreams of being a jewelry maker.

Things came to a head when the older of Tara's two children left for college. The husband responded to this empty nest by getting more involved in his career and corporate life rather than working to rekindle the suspended intimacy in their marriage. Any attempts by Tara to engage her husband were ignored. Tara felt lost and abandoned by her husband and her children. Then she had the following dream.

I am visiting my best friend in New England in the fall while my husband is attending his company meeting in Boston.

My friend, Paru, and I are driving through the lovely New England countryside during full color. We stop in a small town for a cup of tea in a coffee shop. Afterwards we stroll about in the town to stretch our feet. I run into a lovely antique store, and I find a beautiful late 19th century chair. I knew that my husband would be irritated if I bought this period piece, but I decide to buy it anyways and risk the wrath of my husband.

This dream had a profound and empowering affect on Tara. Synchronistically, Tara attended one of my community lectures on dreams. She became curious about her own dream and consulted me for analysis. As the story unfolded, it became clear that Tara was caught in the Parvati archetype of the devoted wife with the primary task of keeping her husband connected to the emotional relational world, thus suspending her own personal and professional goals. Interestingly, she had no friend named Paru, but there was a student a few years her senior in college from India whose name was Paru. In India, Paru is often a shortened version of the name Parvati. I was amazed at the activation of the Parvati archetype in a woman with little to no connection with Indian culture, and even before she knew of my existence she had this dream. She then randomly decided to attend the lecture of an Indian Jungian psychoanalyst and ended up in analysis with me. I was amazed that her soul had set up this mysterious dream and then the meeting with an analyst equipped with the tools to decipher it. It was as if her soul could see into the future, even before our meeting.

Tara was deeply devoted to her therapy and its impact on her personal growth. The dream reminded her of her forgotten aspirations to work with antiques. She gradually rekindled this passion, and though her husband would not support her opening a full blown antique store, he begrudgingly tolerated her interest in attending antique auctions and shows. Tara was aware that a robust pursuit of this path could potentially threaten her marriage as her husband considered this interest as a trivial distraction from her role as a devoted corporate wife and mother.

A series of dreams and synchronistic events guided her on her path. Her challenge was to reconcile her dreams and her marriage. She stumbled upon a unique solution. Instead of an antique store, she became and antique dealer, buying antiques for large stores in her area. Interestingly, at one point, the financial success of her endeavor equaled that of her husband's. This was very threatening to him. At this point the tantric aspect of her sexuality came to her rescue. (Tantra is discussed in the chapter on Kali.) Tara had taken some belly dancing classes, and she started to implement some of her esoteric knowledge of belly dancing in the bedroom, which revived their sexual intimacy. This rekindling of their physical intimacy led to a deepening of emotional intimacy, which in turn led to her husband developing a respect for his wife's passions and goals. It is often in the watery realm of eros and feelings that Parvati transforms the static world of the Shiva ridden masculine into its relational potential and fosters the emergence of mutuality. As an added bonus of this activation of the Parvati archetype, Tara's mother decided to follow her suit and pursue her interest in jewelry making.

The Parvati archetype remains a precious guide for contemporary couples to renegotiate the boundaries of relationships. For supportive anima holding partners, it's a crucial template to make a transition from the roles of devoted partners to honoring their own personal and professional goals in ways that maintain the integrity of the tender threads of relationships. As women have claimed their rightful and equal place in the professional and corporate career arenas, it is their male counterparts who must seek the guidance of the inner Parvati archetype to engage a meaningful balance.

Robert's Story- the Kiss of Life from the Goddess

Let me share Robert's story to illustrate the impact of the Parvati myth in the life of one of my patients. Robert was caught in the high-powered world of medicine and academia. He was a successful surgeon, researcher and teacher, but he was alienated from his wife, children, and his inner life. His life mantra was "work, work and work." As a pillar of the medical establishment, he was the bastion of the static masculine order and deeply embedded in what may be termed Shiva consciousness. He sought analysis after his marriage broke up, and he sank into depression. Here is a fragment of his initial dream,

A very sick man is being rushed to the hospital in an ambulance. In the ambulance, a young woman paramedic gives him mouth-to-mouth resuscitation. The paramedic revives the man and takes him to the hospital for further treatment.

This initial dream became the guiding lamp of his analytic work. While his marriage was beyond repair, he began to reclaim connection with the unlived aspects and ambitions of his earlier life: flying small planes, skiing, blues music and poetry. He trimmed his work in half and established a playful alliance with his two sons. Subsequently he was able to establish a relationship with a soulful woman. More significantly, he made a connection with his inner life and inner feminine, his anima.

Archetypally, the Parvati myth was constellated in his initial dream. Just as Parvati infused new breath in Shiva's life, by connecting him to the world of relationships and feelings, the dream paramedic woman was a symbol of Parvati that introduced Robert to the world of feelings and relationships. This was the kiss of life imparted by the paramedic, the Shakti incarnate. Within the analytic matrix similar feminine images and energies emerged in form of further dreams, synchronistic events and feelings that gradually reconnected him with his life, love and wholeness. Robert was able to balance his masculine world view – work, work, work – with a new balance. In this new life, there was an optimal balance of love, work, play and creativity. When these four quadrants of our lives are balanced, the quintessence, the fifth emerges. This fifth is the spiritual dimension of life that imparts deeper meaning and purpose to our lives.

Professional Marriages and the Latent Code of Parvati

For many years, I have been a psychiatric consultant to the impaired professionals program at the local psychiatric hospital in my community. This involves working with physicians and other professionals who are impaired by substance abuse, depression or other psychiatric illnesses. Usually, they are individuals lost in throws of their mid-life transition. Their lives are out of balance. They get over-involved in their professional lives and alienated from their children, spouses, communities and their inner lives. In my work with these individuals, I have found that they are often lost in the dark side of Shiva consciousness on their mountaintops, disengaged from their inner and outer worlds.

For some male professionals in the first half of life, their partners carry the burden of attempting to keep them in relationship to themselves and others, like Parvati who keeps Shiva in life and in relationships. However, over time, such medical and professional marriages burn out as the wife gets tired of carrying her husband emotionally and her own life calls her. These men now feel alone and abandoned. They must now find the Parvati within rather than project this anima function onto their spouse. Within the analytic process, their impairment or illness can be the vehicle that brings them into connection with their inner feminine. It has been a very rewarding experience for me to be a companion to many such courageous individuals in their journey into the depths of their souls to seek the goddess within. They balance their lives with help of the goddess and reclaim their connection with their feeling function, with their aesthetic strivings for art, culture and spiritual life. Most importantly, they discover the possibility of authentic relationships with their spouses, children, peers and others. Parvati's code brings Shiva into relationship with the world.

My story-the rescue by the goddess

In my mid-life I too was lost in the realm of the static masculine: well-established professionally but disconnected from my inner life. Existential despair and disillusionment with outer success pulled me into introversion and immersed me in my inner life. Shakti presided over the new creation in which my inner spiritual life was acknowledged, my cultural roots and richness were integrated into my Western lifestyle. At this juncture in my life, I had a significant dream:

It is a hot sweltering summer day and I am swimming in an Olympic size swimming pool to cool off from the heat and the pressures of the day. Suddenly, I feel disoriented and start to drown. Thankfully the lifeguard, a beautiful woman, rescues me!

This dream had a profoundly soothing impact on me. I was feeling the heat of the fiery masculine order and needed to retreat to the swimming pool, to the healing, soothing waters of the unconscious for renewal. Initially, this felt very frightening, as if I was drowning in the depths of unconscious dangers. For my orderly medical orientation, these were murky unpredictable waters. However, the feminine came to my rescue. Interestingly, my personal training analyst was a woman. Erotic transference notwithstanding, I wondered if Parvati had constellated to rescue and guide me.

This dream and others like it reflected the disorientation that was resulting from my growing disidentification with the static masculine orientation of the medical establishment and the gradual relinquishing of external affirmation. My spiritual drive became domesticated through the lived experience of relationship with my wife. It was she who encouraged me to honor my longing for this inner connection. She was supportive of my spiritual researches, of my Jungian studies, of my tinkering with the integration of Eastern spiritual themes and Western medicine, of moving from a medical practice to a spiritually based psychoanalytic work with my patients. Gradually, I am internalizing this anima function that my wife has carried for me. As my wife was freed somewhat of the burden of carrying my creative, feminine, anima drive, she has been free to assimilate these energies in her own life. This has been to channel her energies to pursue some of her own cherished dreams and ambitions. In the process she has started a very successful restaurant in Milwaukee.

The Ganesha Yantra

To invoke the Yantra of Parvati, one may use the Sri Yantra. In this chapter, I will illustrate the workings of the Ganesha Yantra. The Ganesha Yantra illustrates the dance of the circle and the square. The Circle represents the unconscious aspects of the psyche that are Squared –or made conscious. This allows our consciousness to harvest the hidden treasures of the unconscious for purpose of fulfilling our spiritual tasks in this lifetime. A square has four doors that open to our four functions, four elements, four seasons and wholeness of consciousness. This permits the Lotus within (the Soul) to blossom into wholeness (individuation) with eight petals. At the core there is the union of the contra sexual complexes: masculine and feminine energies into an integrated, hermaphrodite soul.

While at the core the Ganesha Yantra is symbolized by the upright masculine triangle and the reverse feminine triangle in optimal balance, a necessary condition to make optimal new beginnings, both the triangles are enclosed in an upright masculine triangle. This signifies the need for a masculine initiative to make a new beginning. This calls for a dynamic masculine enterprise, which is ready to sacrifice the old attitude, as in the myth of Ganesha, who is prepared to behead the old thinking to make room for a new attitude and outlook to life. Once the dynamic masculine enterprise makes a new beginning, it must make room for an optimal representation of the masculine and feminine perspectives. This permits the new enterprise to have an enduring and beneficial impact on personal life and collective wellbeing.

The eight petals of the Ganesha Yantra symbolize infinity or wholeness of our psyche. The color rose symbolizes the soul, and the planet Mars, or power (Empowerment of the Soul). The color red also symbolizes the sacrifice of the Ganesha. This represents the process of atonement for the sins of our ancestors and the regeneration of our higher psychic potential. The concept of clan karma is discussed in my book *Retire Your Family Karma*.[29]

Ganesha-Yantra[30]

Honoring and Cultivating
the Latent Code of Parvati

For men who wish to establish a connection with their positive dynamic masculine potential, their inner Shiva, they must approach him through the invocation of Parvati. Shiva is an ascetic who does not directly respond to the pleas and prayers of his devotees. They must approach him by supplication of his consort Parvati. This may involve challenging their overly masculine, goal directed, thinking, orderly, narrow orientation to life and attending to the mandala or circle of their life, in which their thinking orientation is balanced by feeling, work is balanced by love, play, creativity and spirituality.

Likewise for women, Parvati is the archetype that could guide them to make a connection with Shiva potentials. While this may initially be projected onto an outer significant male relationship, in time they may reclaim this projection and live it out in their own lived life. This may involve several interventions that the archetype of Parvati prescribes for women. This may start out with holding one's ground and authority against the masculine order, no mean feat in a patriarchal world order. This could be a fiery initiation for women like Sati. This confrontation, however, is balanced by love and feelings, a uniquely feminine gift. Once they hold their ground, they must now risk establishing their own professional or creative enterprise, a new Ganesha energy – a divine child created by the feminine without masculine support. This is followed by sacrifice and compromise, so that the divine child of the feminine enterprise is informed and supported by the masculine order, a new synthesis, where both perspectives are honored and integrated to a higher synthesis. This stage of rapprochement is crucial for a higher synthesis where a woman can establish a new compromise with the outer masculine and a new internalization of the inner masculine potential. This could balance their feeling with thinking, relationship with enterprise, sacrifice with self assertion, and spiritually informed material enterprise. When women start an enterprise, it is usually more humane, balanced and spiritually grounded than male entrepreneurship. In India today, many young women invoke Parvati through their prayers and fasting on certain auspicious days so that they will achieve connection to their Shiva.

In the last three chapters, we have explored the latent code of the Shakti archetype as it manifests in the images of the goddess consorts of the Trimurti. I have portrayed some of the ways these goddesses have contributed to my soul work as well as guided my patients. These manifestations of Shakti are characterized by the relational aspects of goddess energy. In the next two chapters, we will explore the non-relational or autonomous aspects of the Shakti archetype. These aspects are imaged as the goddesses Kali and Aditi. Kali is constellated in order to destroy the dysfunctional order to make room for a new order in life of individuals and societies. As Kali destroys the existing order and cleanses the ego, she creates a void in our consciousness. The Goddess Aditi presides over this void. When we can sit with this void, Aditi guides us on the path of creation of new consciousness and a new life order. Join me now in honoring the latent code of Kali and Aditi.

INTEGRATE THE SHADOW

PAST   PRESENT   FUTURE

kali

CH 7
The Latent Code of Kali – the Dark Goddess

When we sacrifice the dark side of our personality, we make room for the light of the Spirit to guide our path to our soul. When we breakdown our hang-ups at the altar of the terrible, dark, mother goddess Kali, we permit the depths of our soul to break through into our life.

The latent code of Kali is the destroyer of the shadow in our personality and the community. Kali's code helps us transmute and assimilate this darkness and consciously harvest the potential for light embedded in the shadow. An angry, aggressive individual may learn to sublimate his self-serving aggression into altruistic advocacy of the rights of the disfranchised. She takes in the sins and the ills of her children and makes them into her own suffering. She is the protector of the meek and slayer of the despots, and she restores the just order in the world. She is misunderstood in the east and west alike as a dark goddess – the darkness she depicts is the embodiment of the dark side of the collective that she takes into her own being so that we may live in light, peace and plenty.

Kali is the fierce dark goddess who amputates the darkness of our soul and makes room for the light. Whenever a life is out of balance, the shadow aspects of the individual or culture get in the driver's seat. During such times of imbalance in the individual or the community the latent code of the dark goddess Kali incarnates in our life to destroy the darkness of the personality to make room for a new consciousness to emerge. While new consciousness emerges within the realm of Aditi (the grandmother goddess of void and new creation), this can only occur once Kali has cleansed the consciousness of its darkness to make room for the new. Both Kali and Aditi are non-relational goddesses and maintain the rhythm of destruction and creation respectively within an individual's personality and in collective human consciousness. The wisdom of latent code of the Kali archetype stops individuals in their tracks and forces them to take note of those aspects of their personality that remain in the shadow so that the *soul making* may proceed. Kali frightens and fascinates us. Kali renders our old attitudes and adaptations powerless, yet empowers us to undertake new ways of perceiving and managing life and its traumas. She is experienced as a paradox within our psyche. She is the bloodthirsty goddess, yet she infuses new passion and hope for change. She is dark yet she paves the way for the light in our personality to shine through the dark clouds of the situation. She embodies the *Complexio Oppositorium* – the union of the opposites in our personalities.

Kali's Myth

Kali's most common image is that of the angry goddess destroying evil and consuming it. Kali's warrior aspect is the goddess Durga, who is summoned by the gods to battle the demons. Durga is created by the gods when they have reached their threshold in maintaining cosmic order. When an adversary is beyond the scope of the male gods to cope with, they pool their energies to create the goddess Durga. Her face was formed by Shiva, her hair by the god of death, Yama, and her arms by Vishnu. Shiva gifted a trident, Vishnu bestowed his charka weapon, and the Himalaya Mountain gifted her a lion to ride. She embodies the power of the gods and is created to protect them. When a situation is beyond the power of the gods to manage, they summon Durga to restore cosmic order and welfare. Like Vishnu, she incarnates time and again to restore cosmic balance.

The buffalo demon Mahisa performed austerities and was granted a boon by the gods that he could not be destroyed by any man. He did not think he needed protection against women! He then terrorized the gods who felt overwhelmed and summoned Durga to rescue them. She defeated Mahisa and restored the order of the gods. In our present cultural context, it is interesting to note that when the male enterprise has reached its limits, it is the warrior goddess energy that may rescue us. Powerful women like Dr. Condelezza Rice, Senator Hilary Clinton, former British Prime Minister Margaret Thatcher, former Indian Prime Minister Indira Gandhi, Mother Teresa, Carleton S. Fiorina (Ex - Chairwoman Hewlett-Packard Company) and thousands of brave American women in our armed services are all trail blazing the latent code of the Durga archetype.

In battling the demons, Kali appeared twice to assist Durga. Early in the battle, the demons approached Durga with their threatening weapons. This provoked and angered Durga, and suddenly the goddess Kali sprang forth from her forehead, ready for battle. She tore and crushed the demons. Later in the battle, Durga summoned Kali to help defeat the demon Raktabija (one who arises from the seed of his own blood). He had the ability to clone himself instantly whenever a drop of his blood fell to the ground. Wounding him only multiplied him. Kali destroyed the demon by sucking his blood away.

In these two Durga episodes, Kali manifests Durga's embodied rage. Kali plays a similar role in her association with Parvati, Shiva's gentle spouse. When Shiva is threatened by the demon Daruka, who can only be destroyed by a woman, Shiva summons Parvati's assistance. Parvati then enters Shiva's body and transforms herself into Kali via the poison that is stored in Shiva's throat. (We will be discussing this story later: *Neel Kantha*, Shiva of the Blue Poison Throat.) Kali now destroys the demon Daruka, successfully playing the role of Parvati's dark, ferocious aspect.

Kali also appears in the myth of Sati, Shiva's first wife. (We discussed the Sati-Parvati mythology in the Parvati chapter.) When Sati's father Daksa infuriates his daughter by not inviting Shiva to the great sacrifice rite and later insults Shiva in absentia, Sati immolates herself in protest. Prior to self-immolation, Sati rubs her nose in anger – a signal to summon her dark inner twin Kali, who appears to save her honor. Sati, in a rage, transforms herself into ten goddesses, the Dasamahavidyas (Dasa=ten, maha=great, Vidyas=goddesses of wisdom). The first goddess in these ten goddesses is Kali.

Kali is of central importance in *Tantrism*, particularly the practices of left-handed Tantrism or Kundalini Yoga. In Tantric rituals, both physical and spiritual, the seeker or *sadhaka* seeks to gain *moksha*, i.e., freedom from opposites in human nature and the psyche. The crucial theme in this endeavor is uniting the opposites: masculine and feminine, spiritual and physical, microcosm and macrocosm, sacred and profane, life and death, order and chaos, Shiva and Shakti. The central theme in Tantric Yoga is attaining spirituality via sexuality. Sexuality here is not the practice of sexual intimacy but rather see the sexuality as a symbol of integrating the masculine and feminine potentials of an individual or a couple in a spiritual union.

The *seeker* practices prescribed rituals to achieve this goal and must undertake the ritual of living out the five forbidden things or truths. This supervised ritual includes partaking of wine, meat, fish, parched hallucinogenic grain, and illicit sexual intercourse. These ancient prescriptions should not be taken literally, but rather symbolically. They help the seeker experience, master, and then transcend the dark side of his or her own nature in order to establish wholeness of consciousness. In this context, Kali, the patron goddess of tantric rituals, not only symbolizes the dark side of the human psyche but also is herself a symbol of the experience and mastery of it. Taken on a more symbolic level, this paves the way for integration of the shadow into the totality of one's being.

Attributes of Kali

Kali crushes, tramples, breaks or burns the enemy. She is described as having a terrifying macabre appearance: she is black, naked, and has long, disheveled hair. She has four or more arms and wears a gruesome necklace of severed heads. Children's corpses serve as her earrings, and serpents as her bracelets. Her fangs are long and sharp. She has claw like hands with long nails and fresh blood drips from her lips. She sometimes is portrayed wearing a skirt of dismembered arms. When Kali is shown on the battlefield, she is often portrayed as a furious combatant who gets intoxicated on the hot blood of her victims. She resides in cremation grounds, where she sits on a corpse surrounded by jackals and goblins. Kali is usually depicted as an independent deity, but when she is depicted with a god, it is with Shiva, her consort and companion. Often, Kali dominates Shiva, who is portrayed as passive in her presence. She becomes his active principle. Eventually she activates Shiva, not into rage but ecstasy. While Parvati tames, socializes, and domesticates Shiva, Kali incites him to passion. Parvati is Shiva's numinous anima, while Kali symbolizes Shiva's dark and erotic anima. It is only in the presence of passive Shiva that Kali's erotic essence manifests itself. Powerful women manifest their erotic side only when men they trust yield to their moral authority.

Kali is the feminine aspect of *kala* (time). She is the origin and the end. She represents the energy of time and stands on the corpse of the cosmos, Shiva himself. Since she represents time, she wears a necklace of skulls signifying her sway over life and death. She is black, the ultimate color which assimilates all other colors. Like Shiva, she frequents lonely places at the outskirts of towns. Symbolically she gives voice to the marginalized aspects of society and personality, the shadow and the inferior functions of both individual and collective consciousness. She embodies the fury of the dishonored feminine.

Kali provides a world-view through the shadow lens. She gives context to why we have disease, disorder and anarchy, why the dark side prevails over the light forces of the numinous. She imparts a view that existence is not only about life but also about death, not only about order but also about chaos, not only about health but also about illness, not only about virtue but also about vice. These polar opposites create tension that we call life. When Kali connects us with the dark side, she opens up the possibility of wholeness.

In Tantric yoga she is described as garbed in space, clad but by sky. In her nakedness she is free from all coverings of Maya or illusions about attainment of power, success or attachments. Her garland of fifty human heads represents the fifty letters of the Sanskrit alphabet, symbolizes the repository of knowledge and wisdom, and also represents the fifty fundamental vibrations in the human consciousness. She wears a girdle of human hands, the principal instruments of work that signify the action of accumulated *karma*. This reminds us that we have the potential to accumulate tremendous amounts of positive and negative karma in this lifetime.[31] We also have considerable opportunity to retire this karma. However, if we don't retire our karma in this lifetime, we may leave it as an ancestral burden for our younger generations, grappling with their family karma.[32]

Kali's three eyes represent the past, present and future. Her white teeth symbolize the albetio (whiteness) or purity of soul, and her red tongue represents the rubedo (redness) or passion for life. Kali has four hands. One left hand holds a severed head, symbolizing the sacrifice of our shadow, and the other hand carries the sword that cuts the threads of pathological relationships or co-dependencies. One right hand gestures to dispel fear while the other exhorts to spiritual strength. In this form she is a constant, limitless primordial power acting in the great drama, awakening the Shiva (the unconscious masculine principal) beneath her feet.

How the Latent Code of Goddess Kali Rekindles our Life

The archetype of Kali is the guiding principal in our management of major life traumas. Whenever we face a crisis in our life that our ego or existing consciousness cannot cope with, we get overwhelmed and the crisis becomes trauma - that is, it leaves permanent scars on our psyche. At this point, we may regress to a survival mode of adaptation. Kali presides over this emergency survival operation. If we can honor Kali's code, our soul can move from merely surviving the trauma to mastering it, and this can result in a quantum growth in our personality.

In the ***survival-based psychology***, the soul activates survival focused psychic defenses. These include:[33]

Psychotic distortion: gross impairment of reality testing.

Psychotic denial: denial of a certain aspect of inner or outer reality based on gross impairment of reality testing.

Delusional projection: projecting our reality distortions and attributing these to the other.

Acting out: dealing with emotional conflict by actions rather than reflection or feelings.

Apathetic withdrawal: massive withdrawal of libido or life energy from a certain segment of life.

Help rejecting complaining: chronic complainers who solicit sympathy or support only to reject these once offered. They set us up by entangling us in a vicious cycle of complaint, elicitation of support and sympathy and rejection of these, thus frustrating the rescuer only to restart the cycle.

Passive aggression: passive behaviors as a way to sabotage the other.

Splitting: This involves seeing oneself, the other, the world, the present, past and the future in black or white, good or bad, all or none manner.

Denial: individual denies a painful conflict consciously,

Projection: attributing one's feelings and thoughts to the other.

Rationalization: avoidance of painful conflict by concealing true motivation disguised in some self-serving, inaccurate explanation.

Devaluation: of self or others to deal with conflict or stress.

Idealization: of the other to deal with conflict or

stress. Such an archaic idealization that is not based on reality testing may be an attempt to create an illusion of a powerful protector that would ostensibly make one feel safe and secure.

Omnipotence: feeling superior to others.

Displacement: transferring feelings to a less threatening substitute person.

Dissociation: the part of the consciousness that contains the conflict or painful memory is split off from customary ego consciousness.

Intellectualization: avoidance of feelings by focusing on logical explanations.

Isolation of affect: separating feelings associated with traumatic memories.

Reaction formation: feelings, thoughts and actions are consciously opposite of their unconscious counterparts.

Repression: of painful feelings from consciousness.

Undoing: symbolic actions to negate unacceptable thoughts, feelings and actions.

When our psyche heals the trauma and we switch from survival to mastery mode, the latent code of Kali activates the higher soul functions. These include:

Anticipation: capacity to build a dam before a flood.

Affiliation: capacity to establish a community and fellowship of peers.

Altruism: capacity to sacrifice individual gain for community welfare.

Humor: capacity to laugh at oneself and take a playful perspective on the ebb and tides of life.

Self assertion: capacity to present and be in our authentic personality

Sublimation: channeling potentially maladaptive feelings or impulses into socially adaptive and useful choices and behaviors.

Suppression: consciously suppressing painful thoughts and feelings. Repression on the other hand is unconscious

suppression of the painful thought. Denial is the conscious
avoidance of a conflict that is simmering in the present
reality.

Imaginal capacity: psychological capacity to create
mental images and ideas, to fantasize, to daydream, to
create mental, inner representations of outer events and
possibilities.

Spirituality: trust, faith and belief that a higher center
of consciousness guides our life. This will be discussed in
detail in the chapter on attending to your latent code.

Symbol making: When our consciousness has reached
the threshold of its capacity to manage a life crisis, trauma,
developmental challenge, initiation or transition, the latent
code gets activated to support and guide the consciousness.
It then gifts us a symbol via a dream, fantasy, synchronistic
event, illness or some emergent relationship to guide us.
The symbol is the best possible prescription that the latent
code of the universe has to offer us to deal with the dead
end life situation. The symbol invokes a sense of intrigue,
deep feeling and numinosity. If we acknowledge our
symbol, honor it, work with it, it will guide us by adding
the wisdom of the unconscious and the archetypes to
the conscious situation. This deepens our understanding,
management and mastery of the present life crisis.

Symbol making is the unique capacity of the
unconscious that unites our conscious with the unconscious
and the Universal consciousness. This symbol then
bridges our limited outer consciousness with collective,
cumulative human wisdom to impart timeless wisdom to
the temporary situation or crisis at hand. This symbol now
facilitates our path to the soul and a connection with the
Spirit. The symbol is created by transcending the bridge
between conscious and unconscious, between individual
consciousness and collective human consciousness, between
human and divine, between the soul and the primal Spirit.

Throughout this book, you will find examples of
symbols that are activated to guide us in time of crisis,

trauma and change. When I was struggling with my midlife crisis, the symbol of Ganesha appeared to guide me. When my patients get caught in dead end situations, they receive the gifts of their latent code's symbols in their dreams and synchronistic events.

Symbolic Attitude

One of the highest attributes of an evolved human psyche is the consciousness of a symbolic attitude to life. This symbolic attitude constellates in our psyche when we move from a victim to survival and mastery mode of adaptation. It is an attribute of a mature, psychologically evolved being, an old soul. The concept of the young and the old soul will be discussed in the chapters on attending to the latent code. So what is a symbolic attitude? We will now explore some of its characteristics.

Being in the Present

Our past is our history, our future is a mystery, but the present is the moment we must live in. This involves paying attention to the ego's chatter, fears, feelings, hopes and memories. This facilitates maintenance of an observing ego to monitor this chatter–what is the soul trying to tell us? There is a belief that a deeper center of consciousness, the Soul, guides our inner life and the overall trajectory of our life. While our ego manages our dealings with daily responsibilities and the outer conscious life, this deeper center of consciousness, or Soul, what the Hindus call Atman, guides our purposeful life. The soul is connected to the universal consciousness that we may call the Spirit, or Brahmana. There is a constant dance between the body, the soul and the Spirit. While the body embodies the soul's program, the soul gets its instructions from the Primal Spirit in guiding our life.

A psychological mindedness implies that we are open to the whispers of our soul in guiding our life path into its spiritual groove. It involves a reflective attitude towards life in which one is able to reflect on life and its problems as a password of our latent code that connects our outer life with our soul and connects our individual soul with the Primal Spirit. The symbolic attitude respects the unknown. Our Soul lives at the boundary between what we know consciously and what is not yet known. The unknown is the boundary where the precinct of the Soul and the Spirit begin. The symbolic attitude honors the void and sponsors the capacity to deal with the uncertain till one is able to reflect on and understand its symbolic meaning. It establishes the context of how this voids incubates our soul and intentions of the Primal Spirit.

The symbolic attitude respects the symbols of our Soul. These symbols inform our life and align it with the Spirit's intentions for us. To honor the symbolic attitude we need to establish a personal framework to maintain a dialogue with the soul and the Spirit. This includes a personal system to decode, honor and implement the intent of the symbols that emerge from the latent code of our soul to guide our life. Through mist of time, our collective wisdom has accumulated in our myths. These myths embody the archetypes that manifest as life patterns, dreams, medical and psychiatric symptoms, art and creative enterprises.

Archetypes are modulated by the wisdom of the universe and are activated to guide us through major life issues, initiations, developments, crises, transitions or catastrophes. A symbolic attitude is respectful of the guiding wisdom of these archetypes.

Impact of Trauma on our Psyche

Trauma that is experienced very early in life, before we develop our verbal function, tends to be stored in the body as a body memory. This leads to the host of somatic problems mediated via the psychoid space (the hypothetical space between the body, psyche, soul and the Spirit). This contributes to the evolution of psychosomatic problems. Such trauma occurs before the ego is firmly established. When trauma is severe, it overwhelms the existing ego.

126   Archetypal defenses of the Self are thus constellated activating an archetypal rescue. In Kalsched's view,[34] the goal of such a rescue is survival rather than growth. This subhuman or superhuman trauma calls for a corresponding divine or archetypal defense which is embedded in the latent code of Kali.

In the Hindu view, however, when an archetypal defense is activated, the goal is not just individual survival, but rather the potential growth of the entire human consciousness, or what the Hindus call the *Dharmic* consciousness. In this view, the individual life is sacrificed to enhance collective consciousness. The personal interests are sacrificed in the service of the collective growth. In this way, the individual who is called to this sacrifice lives out his or her highest potential for community good. It is as if the trauma recruits the individual to serve in the realm of the collective welfare. This raises the threshold of our culture onto a higher plateau. When Mahatma Gandhi was abused and traumatized by the racist regime in South Africa, he was deeply wounded and traumatized. This trauma led him to call upon his deepest potential to love his enemy's divine core in spite of their outer dark side. This was the beginning of the Ahimsa movement (nonviolent civil protest) and moved human civilization to its higher potential. His personal trauma was a gift to the rest of the human race. An angry response to abuse and trauma is understandable and human. However, if we can rise above the personal hurt and respond to trauma soulfully, we raise the rest of human civilization up to a higher threshold of culture and consciousness. The trauma isn't just a catastrophe for our ego but an opportunity for our soul to serve the Spirit.

I have had the opportunity to work with a very courageous woman named Helen. Her grandfather sexually abused her in her childhood and this led to deep trauma and subsequent emotional and relationship problems for her. She could easily have stayed wounded for the rest of her life. Instead, she saw her personal trauma as a calling to understand and assist abused men and women and is now an expert psychotherapist in trauma treatment and is a fierce advocate for the rights and treatment of abused women and children. Like Gandhi, she has turned personal adversity into a soulful opportunity to serve her fellow human beings. I deeply admire her, and she has profoundly impacted me.

In my clinical work with trauma victims and survivors, I have found the template of the Kali archetype to be a very useful framework for comprehending and working through the trauma experience. These groups of patients include the war veterans, sexual abuse survivors, survivors of catastrophic medical illnesses like cancer and life-threatening surgery among many others. When these traumatic experiences are seen as encounters with Kali that can overwhelm the ego and protect the archaic soul, then we get a framework within which we can begin to work on rekindling the journey on the path to our soul. Activation of the Kali archetype in trauma survivors leads to survival based adaptation at the expense of personal growth. Honoring and working through the Kali archetype experience ensures survival and then rekindles soul-making as discussed below.

These archetypal defenses have a profound impact on our ego consciousness. The ego may identify with the archetype and get inflated as in narcissism and mania. Alternatively the ego may be run over by the archetypes and succumb to depression or schizophrenia. When archetypal defenses are activated, they have archaic, primitive qualities; they are demonic or angelic; they have a black or white quality; they are disrespectful of the ego and may even be destructive of it with the sole aim of the survival of the archaic, rudimentary Self. The soul now seeks a relationship or experience that reflects its core need to feel loveable and competent. The down side of this dependency on such a relationship is that it makes one feel good about oneself only in the context of such an addictive relationship rather than just having a core sense of one's self worth. Other individuals seek an affiliation with a group to feel good or viable as individuals. This may make them susceptible to gang or cult memberships. Yet another group of such individuals may seek refuge in the strength of a powerful, parental individual like a teacher, guru or guide. They project their own power and authority on this charismatic figure but feel personally depleted.

These archaic relationships are likewise activated in the transference matrix in the analytic container between such traumatized patients and their therapist. Here patients may depend on their therapist to mirror their self worth, provide them with friendship, or become a source of strength and comfort for them. While such dependence may be acceptable in the initial stages of therapy, if this dynamic continues beyond this initial stage, it can lead to a permanent impoverishment of the patient's ego. A competent therapist needs to help patients reclaim their projections of power and inner authority. This is a difficulty task as the therapist must now help patients de-idealize the therapist. It is a daunting challenge to make oneself redundant in the life of one's patient! This is akin to a parent's task of making themselves redundant in the lives of their children as they grow and blossom to maturity.

Kali's Guidance in Survival of Trauma

When we are confronted with a life crisis that is beyond our ego's capacity to manage, our personality is overwhelmed and we go into an emergency survival mode. At such times, our ego steps aside and lets the latent code of Kali take over the management of our life and relationships. Our soul has a numinous side which guides our growth and a dark side which manages emergency survival. This is akin to the civilian administration during peacetime and the martial law during wartime. The martial law of the demonic aspect of our soul suspends growth and soulfulness and focuses on the mere survival of the personality. This is the realm of Kali, under whose auspices the archaic defenses discussed above are activated. Often, when the

trauma is resolved and the crisis is over, Kali refuses to 129
relinquish control, and it is the task of the individual to
gradually reclaim management of their personality from
the Kali archetype. Once the wartime is over, martial law
must end and management must be turned back to the
civilian authorities. The emergency survival mode must
be terminated in deference to peacetime ethos of growth
and culture. The following therapeutic approach outlined
by Kalsched amplifies this method as it relates to the
individual personality.

In analytic work with clients, the first order of business
may be to restore the integrity of the ego and consolidate
the adaptive ego defenses. Once the ego complex is
established or re-established, the restored personality sets
out on the difficult task of confronting the archaic demonic
aspect of the soul that has outlived its usefulness. At this
stage in treatment, Shiva or our ego consciousness can be
seen as calming Kali in order to restore the realm of ego
complex. This task of the Ego is no less daunting than
Job's confrontation with the dark side of Yahweh as Jung
discussed in *Answer to Job*[35] discussed below.

In the survival-based psychology of extreme trauma,
the dark repressive part of the soul (deeper, unconscious
layers of our personality responsible for survival) enslaves
the ego (the outer, conscious layer of our personality
managing our day to day life) and may suspend our true
growth potential in service of mere survival. The ego has
to be rescued from Kali possession or identification, in
other words from being dominated by primitive, archaic
aspects of the personality. The analytic treatment with
trauma victims where the latent code of the Kali archetype
is activated may be summarized as follows.

1. In the early stages of therapy, the emphasis is on
restoration of the ego complex (conscious personality)
and disengagement from possession by the survival
archetype (Kali energy). However, the personality may
resist relinquishing its romance with the dark side of the

soul (deeper, unconscious center of the personality), which depletes the total personality through identification with archaic archetypal defenses (such as splitting, projective identification, paranoia, etc.). When the ego complex gains the strength to stand up against the dark Kali, the split-off positive numinous aspect of the soul (the civilian authority of the soul rather than its martial law aspect) gradually starts to cooperate with the ego and the growth of personality resumes. Now Kali can still maintain its presence and bestow her gifts of passion for new life and discernment of reality on the individual as the resuscitated ego complex takes back the driver's seat from the dark demonic side of Kali. This involves honoring and making appropriate sacrifices to propitiate Kali. The ego must also relinquish its identification with the power of the Kali archetype in order to take on the responsibility of consciousness. The personality now moves from Kali's cruise control to the conscious personality taking control of the steering wheel of life and its challenges. It is only when the ego reclaims its authority in managing our daily lives that it can come to be in a mutual and true relationship with the soul. The Ego-Soul partnership can then replace the dark side of the Soul as director of the emerging personality.

2. **The dark demonic** aspect of the Soul as imaged in Kali archetype is always a tyrannical perfectionist. In analysis with trauma victims, it is essential to maintain the analytic stance so that the very frustrations that arise from maintaining analytic boundaries create a 'little bit of trauma.' This is a sort of psychological immunization from the bigger trauma. The Kohutian School of psychologists calls this optimal frustration. This forces the individual to modify the experience of the other or the therapist as limit setting yet loving. Such a new composite image of the other is mature and mutual. It transforms and transmutes the relationship and then makes it relevant to one's own life. This image is then internalized as a new role model. This is called transmuting internalization. This then helps

us lay new mature self-structures that gradually replace the
archaic self defenses and need for primitive, self-esteem
sustaining relationships. This little bit of trauma inherent
in the frustrations of the analytic situation acts as a vaccine
that helps the ego separate from its identification with
Kali in order to evolve adaptive ways of managing life,
relationships and growth potential. The dreams of the
trauma victims reveal this battle between the emerging ego
and the dark, demonic Kali. In this matrix, a third position,
a new synthesis constellates, in which our personality comes
up with a novel way of dealing with life. In the dream
discussed later in this chapter, the third position emerged
in a dream in which the female patient decapitated a rapist
and protected her child, a symbol of her emerging soul.

3. Transference issues in trauma patients who are
in the grip of the Kali archetype need particular attention.
Transference means the projection of feelings from an
important individual in your past onto a person in the
present life, usually a therapist. While Kali is in control of
the personality, the individual continues to re-experience
trauma. The neurosis is not only in the past, but it
continues in the present as a persecutory "Kali within," as
the patient responds to what it perceives as inner and outer
threats. Analysis itself may be perceived as a traumatic
threat with the analyst as a tyrannical traumatizer. In
the analytic working through, the ego must insist on the
Soul's numinous (light) potential, in spite of its apparent
darkness; in other words, the analyst has to keep in mind
the "Answer to Job" paradigm. In Jung's rendering of this
Biblical incident, Job is put through very traumatic trails by
Yahweh, the God of the Old Testament, to test his loyalty.
In spite of this trauma, Job continues to treat Yahweh with
love, respect, loyalty and expectation of fair treatment.
Eventually, this forces Yahweh to abandon his trial and
treat Job with kindness and fairness. Job's trust in God and
insistence on fair treatment eventually forced Yahweh to
rise to the occasion. According to Jung, this is akin to our

fragile ego's insistence on a fair and mutually respectful treatment by the soul, even when the dark aspects of the soul have temporarily taken control of the personality in a crisis situation. This is like martial law. In a civilized and advanced nation, the civilian law would always have domain over the military; however, the power dynamic may seem uneven in times of crisis. This differentiates a civilized nation from a primitive one and a soulful life from an archaic personality.

4. **Optimal violation of the therapeutic neutrality** is essential so that: a) the ego complex or conscious personality is reinforced in the form of support of higher adaptive defenses; b) the demonic dark pole of the Soul is confronted; c) the light numinous pole of the Soul is reinforced. In other words, in working with trauma victims, the therapist must be prepared to be flexible and sometimes violate therapeutic neutrality to support the conscious personality against its own dark side. For instance, on occasions, I have violated therapeutic neutrality and encouraged some patients to break their workaholic routine and make room to play and take vacations. While this violates my neutrality, it encourages the playful aspects of my patients to stand up to their repressive, dark, hard driving, perfectionist sides of their personalities.

5. **In working with trauma victims,** the analyst must consider several additional points: the appropriate management of affect (permitting neither too much nor too little expression by either party), the attunement to the meaning as well as the mystery of personal growth, working through loss and grief over the lost unlived childhood. One of the biggest challenges for individuals who have survived trauma in their lives is to make sense of this experience in their life narrative. They wonder why they were subjected to such trauma and what meaning it has in their spiritual life. They wonder if they are mere pawns in some impersonal cosmic joke or their suffering has some meaning. In my

clinical experience, if an individual survives a trauma, [133]
they go on to grow from it and make major contributions
because of the lessons learned from survival and mastery
over such an experience. The trauma then becomes the
sand grit around which the oyster of life weaves a pearl
of a soulful personality. A sexual abuse victim becomes
an advocate of the abused, the emotionally neglected one
becomes the champion of the underdogs, and the sick one
becomes the doctor.

It is important to prepare the patients in the grip of
the Kali archetype for breaks, vacations, absences, and
separations. This preparation permits the ego to maintain
an evocative memory of the numinous aspects of the Soul
as well as of the analyst in order not to succumb to the
demonic Kali experience during such vulnerable periods.
Perhaps one of the crucial healing interventions in the
treatment of trauma victims is for the analyst to admit to
"counter transference errors and feelings," what Racker
terms counter resistance.[36] The analyst's emotional honesty
with the patient constitutes a corrective experience that
helps the ego lay out new and optimal templates for normal
relationships.

Finally, the patient and analyst must honor the emerging
new myth of the patient and be prepared to dialogue with
it. Since the analytic task is to incubate the emergence
of a new creation myth for the patient -- to honor "not
knowing," "knowing" may impede the emergence of a
new creation myth from the patient's psyche. If we stay
respectful of the void that the Kali experience leaves in our
life, we make room for new beginnings in our personal
growth. The Goddess Aditi presides over this experience
of void and new beginning, which we will discuss in further
detail in the next chapter.

Trauma is divine suffering as it activates the deepest
layers of the soul under the auspices of the Kali archetype
and may lead to the growth and individuation not just
for the person but also the collective. This redeems one's

Dharmic potential: one's highest duty to the soul and the Universe.

The Integration of Our Masculine and Feminine Potentials through the Latent Code of Kali

Kali is the embodiment of the negative dynamic feminine par excellence as compensation to the negative static masculine order. When the patriarchal order becomes rigid, dehumanizing, inauthentic, and petty, with rigid expectations, organized for its own sake and complacent, the great Kali archetype is activated to behead it. In this bloody initiation, Kali decapitates and dissolves the existing dysfunction and the despotic static negative masculine order.[37] Kali accomplishes this transition by invoking the apparently negative, dynamic feminine.

Clinically, such a bloody initiation may be perceived as an altered state of consciousness, as emptiness, depression, alcoholism and/or drug intoxication, hysteria and borderline psychosis. These clinical experiences may lead to despair, even suicide and death. If the patient and analyst can hold on to residual ego and establish a connection with a deeper layer of psyche, the source, the soul, then transformation of the personality and the culture becomes possible.

However, the experience of the inner Madwoman is a disorienting experience, for both therapist and patient alike. Goal-directed exploration of the psyche modifies and transforms the personality into new awareness and a new state of being. In order to accomplish this goal, the individual must deal with the archaic, dark self-care system, transform it, and reassimilate the transformed substance into a higher *conuinctio or union* with the personality. An alchemic perspective facilitates this assimilation of the darkness, of the sacred essence of Kali in one's wholeness. Alchemy is an analogy for the transformation of personality as it encounters the dark and the light, the high and the low, the sacred and the profane.

World-view through the Latent Code of Kali

In the Hindu goddess pantheon, Kali is the singular archetype that imparts a structural world-view to individuals and cultures. Kali's realm is the one of clarity of facts and purpose. She is the "No Nonsense" goddess. Kali does not get caught in non goal-directed feelings or possibilities, but she is firmly grounded in relevant facts and how they impact life experience. She imparts an extroverted attitude to our personality and her presence is felt as that of a very solid handshake with an individual with an iron fist. Images of Kali depict the dark goddess holding the severed heads of her victims. This symbolizes the decapitation of the existing thinking function, making room for new logic to adapt to the crisis and the developmental challenges at hand.

Comparative Mythology:
The Innana Erezkegal Split

Innana-Ishtar, the Sumerian goddess of heaven and earth, journeys into the underworld to Erezkegal, and her dark sister returns. Innana[38] is the queen of heaven, goddess of the radiant morning and evening stars. She is the queen of land and its fertility. Like Durga, she is also the goddess of war. As the goddess of sexual love, she is passionate.

When Innana descends into the underworld to visit her dark sister, Erezkegal, she is gradually disrobed, humiliated, flagellated, killed and hung on a meat hook for several days before being resurrected and rescued by her loyal servant with help of the God Enki and his deputies. However, she is much the wiser for having encountered Erezkegal. Now she has a wholistic view of reality, being informed of the dark side through her encounter with her Erezkegal nature.

Erezkegal is the queen of the Netherworld and the dead. Her name means "Lady of the Great Place Below." She symbolizes the Great Round of nature, growth and grain above and below, the seed dying to sprout again. Repeatedly her husband Enil, in his various disguises, raped her, yet she followed him into the underworld when the gods punished him. This was a questionable decision. It is my speculation that this decision was based on her ambivalence. She loved him but also wanted to tame his dark side. Proximity with the abusive lover was essential to contain his darkness and transform it into light. This doomed her to the underworld. However, she was able to redeem this folly by empowering her sister Innana, whose husband also betrayed her while she was with her dark sister in the underworld. Like Kali, Erezkegal is the root of all potential energy -- inert but ready to sprout into action upon the battlefield of life. Erezkegal, like Kali, is enraged when Innana invades her realm. In anger her face turns yellow and her lips black. She is full of fury. She symbolizes raw instinctuality, split off from consciousness. She unleashes her rage like Kali unleashes Shiva's destructiveness. Like Kali, she symbolizes an energy we begin to recognize through the study of death, disease, and destruction.

Alchemic Perspective[39] of the Kali Archetype

Alchemy is the medieval art of transforming lead into gold. Carl Jung was fascinated by Alchemy as a metaphor for understanding the transformation of personality from its base to higher potential. There are essentially four stages of alchemy: black, white, gold and red. The Negrado (black) implies confronting the darkness of our personality. Once this has been accomplished, we encounter the Albetio (white) aspects of our personality. This is the experience of the purity of our soul after cleansing or baptizing of the psyche. After the albetio stage, we experience the yellow or golden stage of alchemy. This is the spiritual phase of our life. It is called the Citrinatio (citrus) stage when we are grooved in our spiritual moorings. However, the highest stage of alchemy is Rubedo (red): the color of blood and passion. All of our soul work and personal growth are academic unless we are willing to put our sweat and blood into what we believe in. This is the stage of sacrifice that Christ demonstrated in his crucifixion, to lay down one's life for what one believes in.

The nigredo (darkness), putreficatio (rotting) and mortificatio (death like) are the sub aspects of the Negrado stage of alchemy. These are necessary Kali experiences that form a bridge to our dark, neglected aspects of personality and thus establish wholeness of the soul.

The alchemists thought that in order for a given substance to be transformed, it must first be reduced or returned to its original, undifferentiated state, to its prima material stage. Kali mediates this experience of the primary substance of our personality. She strips our personality of all its rigid, dysfunctional, superfluous trappings and gives us a sense of who we really are and what we are about.

This procedure corresponds to what takes place in psychotherapy under the auspices of the Kali archetype. The fixed, habitual aspects of personality lead back to their original, undifferentiated condition as part of the process of psychic transformation by Kali. This formless state of pure potentiality is necessary in order for a new structure of personality to emerge. Fixed, developed aspects of the personality allow no change. They are solid, established, and sure of their rightness. Only the indefinite, fresh, and vital but vulnerable and insecure original condition symbolized by the child is open to development and hence is alive. We must experience the naïve, vulnerable child within from which we can start growing again. We must find our innocent, playful, creative, child nature to rekindle our soul.

In the chapter on Parvati, we explored the myth of Ganesha. Shiva promised the lesser gods that he and his consort Parvati would not procreate so that their off spring would not compete with the lesser gods and cause imbalance of power. Yet this was not acceptable to Parvati, so she created a divine child from her skin rubbings. When Shiva met this divine child Ganesha, he beheaded him.

Later, however, he adopted this child after transplanting an elephant's head onto the child. Similarly, when we deny our creative potential for political or relational expediency rather than confront the envy and competition of others, our anima, the inner feminine, the creative life force ushers us to find the divine child within in spite of our ego or outer consciousness. The child is the symbol of emerging consciousness.

We consider the image of a child in dreams as one of the symbols of the emerging soul, but it can also symbolize the *prima materia* of the personality, the building blocks of our potential. The dream of Rose presented in this chapter contains the child of the patient as a symbol of her emerging soul, rescued under the auspices of Kali.

The problem of finding the *prima materia* corresponds to the problem of finding what to work on in psychotherapy. Under the guidance of Kali, we may find it in a number of places. Although of great inner value, the *prima materia* is vile in outer appearance and therefore despised, rejected and thrown on the dung heap. Psychologically, this means that the *prima materia* is found in the shadow, the part of the personality that is considered most despicable. Those aspects of us most painful and most humiliating are the very ones to be brought forward and worked on.

The *prima materia* is infinite, without definite boundaries, limits, or form. This corresponds to those experiences of the unconscious that expose the ego to the spiritual dimension. It may evoke the terror of dissolution of our consciousness or the awe of the experience of unconscious eternity. In Kali we encounter both.

Motificatio and the Latent Code of Kali

The terms *"mortificatio"* and *"putrefactio"* are overlapping ones and refer to different aspects of the same operation. *Mortificatio* means "killing" and refers to the experience of death of a certain aspect of our consciousness. It is like pruning the psyche, which permits the rest of the personality to grow and blossom. *Putrefactio* means "rotting," the decomposition that breaks down dead organic bodies. Kali destroys the rotting personal complexes or hang-ups and the shadow or the dark aspects of our personality and culture.

Mortificatio has to do with darkness, defeat, torture, mutilation, and death. Patients struggling with depression and borderline disorders often struggle with these images and unfortunately sometimes act them out rather than reflect upon them as transitional alchemic images. However, these dark images often lead over to highly positive ones: growth, resurrection, and rebirth. The hallmark of *mortificatio* is the color black -- the symbol of Kali.

Putrefactio blots out our habitual, old nature and transforms our personality into its spiritual potential. This is akin to transforming the complexes that impede personality into bearing new potentialities to enrich the spectrum of personality.

In psychological terms blackness refers to the shadow. Awareness of our own shadow permits us greater consciousness of our dark side. This illuminates our self-knowledge, and thus we have a better map of our own personality. Then the darkness lights the way. On the archetypal level it is also desirable to be aware of evil because darkness is the beginning of the experience of the light. By the law of opposites, an intense awareness of one side constellates its contrary. Out of darkness is born the light. Out of night is born the day. The experience of the Kali archetype though dark leads to experience of the light of one's personality

The Latent Code of Kali Activating the Rubedo or Life Passion

While the primary experience of the Kali archetype is nigredo, if one successfully holds the tension of this experience, it leads to *rubedo*, or redness, the color of blood, passion and sacrifice. This also symbolizes our feeling or value function. This leads to re-animation of life informed by our feeling function where we factor in what is of value to our soul in re-setting the priorities of our life.

The four stages of alchemy – *nigredo, albedo, citrinitio and rubedo* – symbolize the parts, qualities, and aspects of the One,[40] the totality of our personality. When an individual has assimilated Kali's *nigredo* experience and experienced the guidance of Aditi (discussed in the next chapter), the Kali dimension now takes on a new significance. The Aditi invokes the experience of the void, the *albedo* that heralds the rising sun or emerging new consciousness. The growing *rubedo* that now follows denotes an increase of warmth and light coming from the sun. When we start feeling our feelings of warmth and passion again, we are in our soul's groove. Our conscious and unconscious now start doing a dance together. We establish a rhythm of personal growth to the music of our soul.

Red and rose-red are the color of blood, our passion for life. While Kali confronts us with what is dead or what must die in our personality, when we make these necessary sacrifices she reanimates life with feelings and passion for what really counts - our soul priority, or true calling. When we are willing to be crucified on the altar of life, when we are prepared to shed our sweat and blood for the calling of our soul, we resurrect our highest potential.

Kali Yantra[41]

Kali represents the disintegrative force in nature as displayed in the passage of time (Kala) or increase of entropy. Kali is symbolized in the Yantra as black, but the other colors used in the yantra (red, yellow, green and white) are also part of her traditional representation as discussed in the alchemic aspects of the Kali code above. The downward pointing triangle is a very ancient symbol of the primal female, the origin of all things—pubic triangle of the Great Goddess.

The eight petaled lotus is the eight-fold Prkriti or nature, consisting of earth, water, fire, air, ether, manas (mind), buddhi (intellect) and ahamkara (ego). Five triangles are the five jnanendriyas (jnana=knowledge; indriyas=senses), the five karmendriyas (motor organs) and the five pranas (breathing activities). Bindu or the center point is the symbol of the balanced Soul, which is pure consciousness. The five triangles also represent the sacred marriage: union of two (feminine) + three (masculine) aspects of our psychological potential. It may also be correlated to the Seal of King Solomon–a five pointed star; the letters of Jesus & his five wounds and the sacred Pentagram– the flaming star of the Gnostics. However, all five triangles are essentially feminine, pointing down. This symbolizes the essence of the Kali Yantra; it is compensation for the excessive masculine drive in the personality by the energies of the inner feminine potentials in the individual and the collective consciousness.

The Kali mantra to guide our consciousness through the Yantra meditation is *"Om Kareeng Kalekaye Namah"* (Salutations to Goddess Kali). Kali Yantra is invoked when one is dealing with a major life crisis or trauma, and it is an invitation to activate the latent code of Kali for purpose of survival and mastery of the overwhelming situation. Kali is invoked when our ego consciousness runs into a dead end street and we feel that there is no way out. When our ego surrenders to the universe, the latent code of Kali is activated to guide our path through the darkness into the light. It invokes the hidden potentials of our personality when ego and pride step out of the way. It overcomes our ego attitude to our adversities, and we may be able to see a reflection of our own shadow in the mirror of our adversaries.

The Perils and Promises of Kali's Latent Code

In analytic experience, the encounter with Kali consciousness is the confrontation with the shadow and the demonic aspects of the soul.[42] We must descend into our inner Kali realm, encounter and honor her to achieve wholeness. Kali consciousness puts us in touch with the death of our complexes or hang-ups so that the deeper potentialities of the soul can emerge. Anticipation of the possibility of fire leads us to build fire escapes. Acceptance of the possibility of disease leads to the discovery and the use of immunizations and vaccines. Factoring in the 143 possibility of war leads to peace via strength. An individual who has encountered Kali in life experiences can anticipate and build the necessary ego structures in order to confront the dark side of reality, which in turn can activate the experience of the numinous aspects of the soul.

Kali Code in Action: Rose's Story

Let me now share the story of one of my patients and how Kali empowered her to deal with traumatic experiences in her earlier life. Rose was in her third year of analysis when she had an important dream. She was then in her mid-forties. Since starting analysis, Rose had resumed her college education that had been interrupted in her early twenties. As the oldest of five, she lived in a family with an alcoholic father and untreated manic-depressive mother. Rose was the caretaker of her younger sibs and her father's confidante. Since Rose was five, her parents had slept in separate bedrooms. Until age nine or ten, she would go into father's bedroom and sleep with him for comfort. Whether there was any sexual abuse by her father has remained an unanswered question in the analysis. She had an idealized transference to me, but embedded in it were seeds of anger and rage that only gradually emerged within the safe container of the analytic vessel. In this context, Rose reported the following dream, which she titled *The Rage:*

> *I am back in college climbing a sheer rock wall with my friends. It is very dangerous, but we do it quite often. I don't like it. Now I am at a party in a house with all young men. They open the door to a larger room where many naked young men are lying in beds. I am told the only exit is through the window on the opposite side of the room. I have to make it past the men. I wonder briefly if it would be enjoyable to have sex with all these men but decide it would not. I run in the other direction and am chased and caught. I scream as I am carried down the hall.*
>
> *Next, it is night, and I'm walking back down the hall*

*carrying the head of a man. His hair is long, and I'm holding
the head by it. I enter the room of naked men. They are asleep
now. I jump onto the window ledge, facing the room. I throw
the head to the floor in the center of the room. I say in a loud
and chilling voice, "This is the head of the man that raped me.
For each woman raped, another head will fall." I see my son
on the ledge next to me. He is a baby sleeping in his Superman
outfit. I scoop him up and climb out. I climb the brick wall of the
building to a tall bell tower. I climb into the belfry and let out a
loud, shrill scream. I awake with the scream still in my head.*

Here are some of Rose's associations to some of the
dream images: Her son symbolized her vulnerable soul.
The superman outfit indicated a defense against her
feelings of vulnerability and trauma. She associated the
image of climbing the sheer rock wall with the danger she
felt as a teenager when dealing with boys, who she felt only
wanted sex. She went to a frat party with a young man in
her freshman year. It was horrible; the focus was to get
drunk. The scream in her dream indicated intense rage.
The tall bell tower reminded Rose of Holy Hill Church, a
church built on top of a very high point near Milwaukee,
WI, "a sacred place," and it also reminded her of "the
movie *Vertigo* where the hero is betrayed." "Betrayal by my
father," she said. "Something was breached, a line crossed,
he moves into my space and crosses my boundary."

Archetypically, I see in Rose's dream the incarnation
of the Kali archetype to empower and renew her. When
her vulnerable core self was feeling threatened and in
danger of fragmentation, the Kali archetype was activated
to empower her to confront the intrusion of the masculine
with a sense of her own voice and rage at the injustice of
the father's encroachment upon her space and her soul.
Like the great Kali, she decapitates the rapist and protects
her son, a symbol of her emerging soul. Then she lets out
the battle cry of Kali as she asserts her arrival and presence
from the top of her church, atop the Mother Church, the
great Kali reincarnate.

This dream had a tremendously empowering impact
on Rose as she worked on the dream in analysis. The
dream imaged her ego capacity to confront the shadow
of the masculine, the negative animus that dominated her
internal world. Kali helped her in this confrontation as
the dream ego embodied the goddess capacity to behead
this negative masculine force. Through this activation of
the Kali archetype, Rose began to cut through her identity
as a victim and began to reclaim her soul's authority. She
resumed her journey towards mastery over the academic,
creative, professional and relational sectors of her life.

Edward's Story- Reclaiming the Kali Within

Edward is in his early forties and consulted me to
explore his ambivalence about his marriage. He and his wife
were married over ten years, and Edward was a budding
professional, while Mandy did not work outside of the home.
The couple struggled with some intimacy issues. Edward
presented as a polished, mellow, sophisticated professional,
and Mandy came across as a cultured, extroverted woman.
Over the years, Edward assumed the role of a kindly, care-
taking, indulgent father and, in complementary fashion,
Mandy regressed to the role of a rebellious teenaged
daughter. While initially this was endearing, eventually
this became a major flash point for dispute in the marriage.
Mandy sought comfort in compulsive shopping, and this
led to substantial financial problems for the couple. Edward
managed to pull them out of crisis several times, but this
pattern continued. All attempts on the part of the couple
to deal with this problem were unsuccessful. Reluctantly,
Edward moved out of the home and filed for divorce. At
this point, he had the following dream, which invoked the
goddess Kali and turned his life around.

The Dream

*I am a passive observer. The famous singer Madonna (with
blonde hair) is in a new, luxurious private suite at the baseball*

stadium. The room looks like the living room of a modern expensive home...or perhaps a high-rise penthouse.

She is on the floor conducting business with her agent. He is standing. I see her but never get a clear image of the agent. She is making big demands and walking a fine line between arguing and throwing a tantrum. She is rude, vocal and watching the baseball game that is being played.

I observe a woman dressed just like Madonna distributing flower petals everywhere, pleasing the crowd. She is sweet and pretty...nothing like the woman negotiating upstairs in the suite...

This dream was a turning point in Edward's analysis and soul work. All his adult life, Edward had been a kind, sophisticated, soft-spoken man, raised in a pious, catholic family. However, he was in denial of his shadow, his own dark side, the tough and ruthless professional in him. This tough side manifested occasionally in his work and his leadership qualities, but mostly he suppressed this dark side. This was his dark anima, the Kali within. Over the years, this Kali aspect of his inner life was projected onto Mandy. Mandy's own inner dynamic was susceptible to getting hooked by this Kali projection as it was consistent with her rebellious daughter dynamic, unfinished business from her own family of origin issues. This collusion of mutual dynamic got their marriage in the strangle hold of the dark goddess Kali.

Clearly, Edward was living out the persona of the public Madonna. The dark Madonna was the Kali within and was projected onto Mandy. Over time, Edward reclaimed this dark, powerful anima energy in his professional and personal life. It revived his soul. He was vitalized, energized and assertive. He became more communicative of his needs and feelings in a timely manner. Professionally, he reclaimed his leadership and played out his fuller potential. While his marriage was now beyond repair, he established a new relationship on a firmer platform of mutuality. He now lived out both the Madonnas, the public polished one

and the private assertive one. The split in the Kali energy
was healed. Edward felt empowered. The darkness of Kali
lit his path to the soul. Mandy has continued her own
soul work with another therapist and is claiming her own
authority about her inner potential.

Helen's Encounter with Kali – Let the Darkness Light the Way

Helen is a survivor of sexual abuse by her grandfather
at age six. Later in life, her husband betrayed her and
abandoned her for a younger woman. In her mid fifties,
Helen found herself hitting the dating scene. Unprepared,
she felt out of her league in negotiating this relationship
challenge. She felt further compromised because of her
history of abuse by her grandfather and betrayal by her ex-
husband. Then she reported the following dream.

*I am in my condominium and see this black woman making
out with this white man.*

Helen was raised in a white upper class family. She
felt ashamed at her legacy as a great-grandchild of former
slave owners. In her conscious life, she had deep respect
for African Americans and harbored no feelings of
prejudice. However, her first response to the dream was
one of prejudice at what she considered the blatant and
promiscuous behavior of the black woman.

On deeper association to this dream, Helen
acknowledged a sense of envy and admiration for the
black woman in the dream and her freedom to joyfully and
spontaneously express her sexuality. She wished she could
be like her! In the past, she had considered erotic self-
expression disgusting and un-lady like. The black woman,
the shadow aspects of Helen's own personality, appeared
in her dream to guide her into the way of the Eros and
relationship. The darkness in her soul lit the way to the
possibility of relationship. It is as if Kali herself appeared
in her dream to guide her path. Subsequently, Helen felt

freer to express herself, and this opened up her capacity to experiment with the dating scene.

Honoring the Shadow

We must acknowledge and honor the descent into our dark side to honor the goddess Kali. This may involve dealing with the blackness of depression (*nigredo*); the deadness in one's personality and situation (*mortificatio*); and the rotting aspects of one's personality, relationships, and life situation (*putreficatio*). This may involve recognizing the complexes that darken the personality or are projected onto significant relationships. In the analytic matrix, this may constitute the early stages of analysis when shadow must be acknowledged, complexes confronted, and ego "beheaded" to make room for the soul and the deeper layers of the psyche to rekindle personal growth. The defeat of our ego is the victory of our soul.

Sacrifice

Once we have confronted our dark side, we must make the sacrifice. Sacrifice means to make sacred, implying the act of worshipping the goddess Kali. Sacrifice, in my conception, is a symbolic relinquishment of a certain aspect of one's psychic life. When one is skewed in either the instinctual or the spiritual role of life, Kali restores the balance. Where the optimal point of balance lay for each individual is the mystery that each one of us must encounter in our own life. When an old viewpoint is obsolete and not adaptive to deal with an inner or outer reality, an inner tension develops. At this point the individual is forced to challenge the perception and view of the self, others and the world.

Sometimes this tension or conflict is projected onto someone. We tend to project our dark side on an adversary. Once upon a time, I had a partner whom I really despised for his greed over patient care priority. On closer assessment and self-reflection, it became clear to me that this person

was carrying my dark side. I had to confront my own   *149*
shadow and unconscious greed. Paradoxically, this got me
more into my soul and my mission to serve my patients.
The greed was now conscious, subject to my conscious
monitoring and regulated somewhat. A known enemy is
easier to fight than an invisible one. For the soul journey to
continue and the personality to grow, we must recognize
this projection and dissolve it. This calls for a sacrifice of
our grandiosity to make room for a new personal myth.
My old myth was that I was somehow a superior soulful
psychiatrist. My new myth was realistic. I was a regular
human being, who had to constantly struggle to balance
my altruism and professional calling with my legitimate
self-care and self interests.

Such dissolution of projection is mediated by Kali
consciousness. Our path to the soul calls for breaking up
the unity of personality with the archaic, shadow aspects
of our unconsciousness and assimilating these shadow
and other unconscious potentials of the soul to relate to
the consciousness. Such dissolution is painful, although
freeing, and occurs under the auspices of Kali.

Sacrifice is accompanied with psychic and emotional
suffering, and both have to be experienced to move our
emotional, psychological, and spiritual development
forward. Kali demands sacrifice to usher in our soul making.
An inner pruning is necessary for our potential to blossom
and achieve its full flowering. These sacrifices lead to an
awareness of the successively higher dimensions of the
soul and eventually connection with our soul's latent code.
Kali at times overrides our individual well-being in the
service of collective well-being. This permits us to move
from serving our soul to service of the spirit. Jung calls
this a development of soul from "individuation" (personal
growth) to "divination" (spiritual alignment), from self-
focus to service of the collective goals and community
welfare. In the Hindu framework, this is akin to moving
from *sva dharma* (selfhood) to *reta dharma* (devotion to
higher consciousness), which is the zenith of an individual's

psychic and spiritual development on the Hindu roadmap of individuation. Analyst David Rosen calls this process egocide.[43]

Egocide

In egocide, the individual is trying to kill off a certain maladaptive aspect of one's personality. However, if this part of our personality is embedded in our life matrix, we may feel that to kill our self is the only way to kill this part. Instead of killing the cancer, the person kills themselves. Some individuals unfortunately even concretize this process and may attempt suicide, as did David Rosen's subjects who attempted suicide by jumping off the Golden Gate bridge in San Francisco.

When the existing consciousness is beheaded, it makes room for the new consciousness. Now a new dimension of our latent code can emerge on the stage of one's life and consciousness. New beginnings become possible. Kali paves the way for Aditi. A new creation myth then emerges for individuals and societies under the auspices of Aditi, the Great Grandmother Goddess of Void and New Beginnings, also the subject matter of our next chapter.

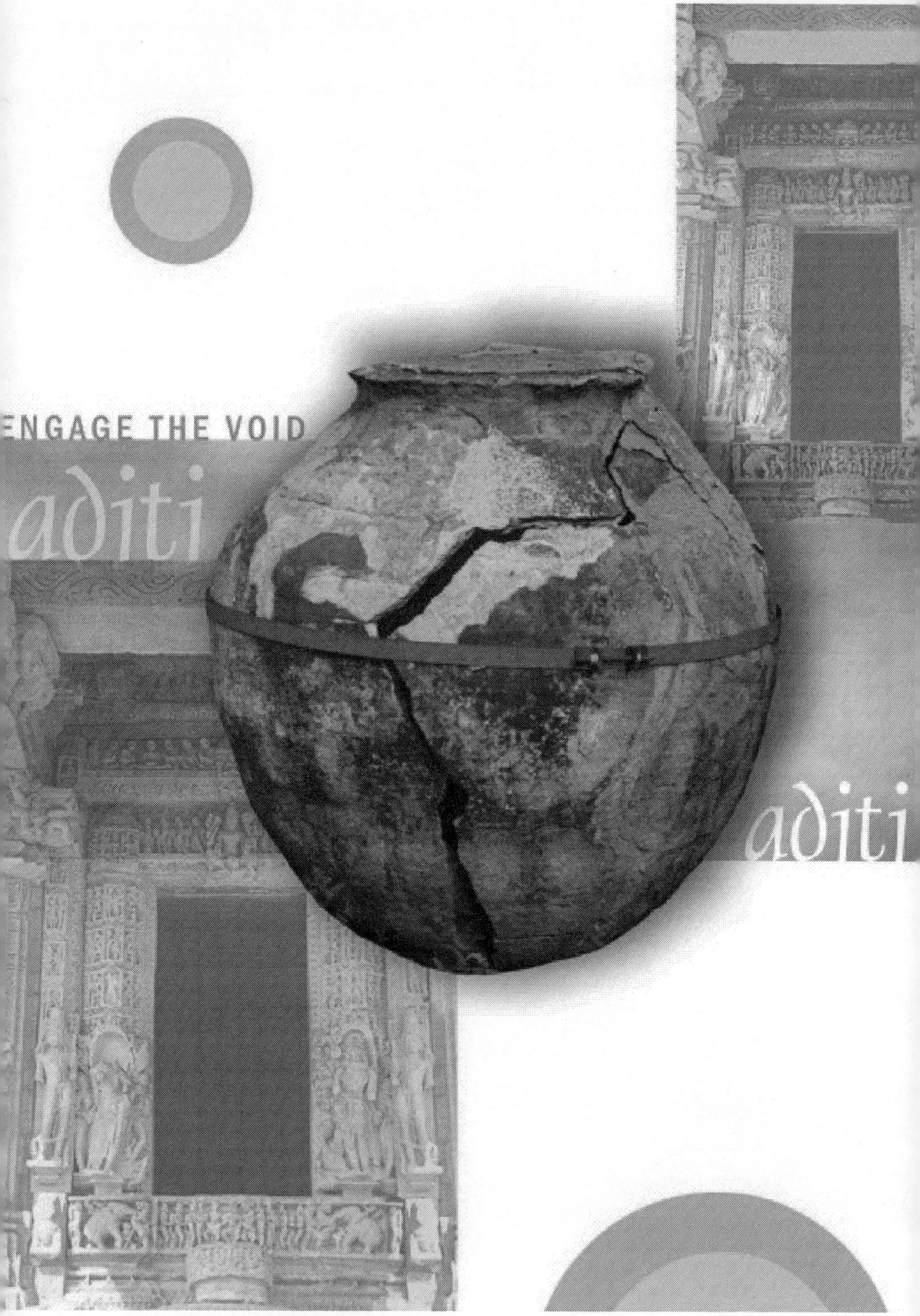

ENGAGE THE VOID
aditi
aditi

CH 8
The Latent Code of Aditi
The Code to Engage the Void and the New Creation

One of the most significant obstacles to engage our full potential is our discomfort with the dynamics of the Void. We are generally fearful of the void, but if we can hold the tension between the void and clutter, we can tune into the flow of the universe and tap into its infinite potential to help, heal and guide us. The great Rishis, the holy men and women of the East, have long postulated that we live in three states of consciousness: awake, asleep and dreaming. But the transition between these states involves engaging the "gap" in our states of consciousness. In this gap, we are tuned into the flow of the great energies of the universe, its timeless wisdom, its infinite void, its immense potential for new creation and countless possibilities. It is also a realm of great danger, where the uninitiated can get lost in the dark side of the cosmos and not find the way back into human consciousness. Different meditative traditions of all the great cultures have some guidelines to soulfully engage this sacred space. Transcendental meditation is one such tradition of the East. The latent code of Aditi guides us in this realm of the gap, the flow, the void, and paves the way to tap into the vast potential of the wisdom of the Universe.

Aditi, although the least understood, is also one of my favorite goddesses. She is the goddess that symbolizes the energy of the void—the sacred space that is essential to make room for new creation. In the extroverted Western culture and more and more in the rapidly materialistically driven Eastern world, there is disregard for the energy of the void. We as individuals and cultures have a tendency to want to fill in the void rather than honoring and nurturing it. If we are sitting quietly in the evening, we can't resist turning on the television rather than reflecting and meditating. When we are driving the car, we flip on the radio rather than permitting ourselves some musing time. When we are walking, we put on headphones rather than tuning in to the nature around us. We rarely permit opportunity for the void to whisper to us. If only we can resist trampling the void, Aditi may whisper to us from the depths of our soul and inspire us with a creative new fantasy, image, thought, impulse or possibility that can set in motion the incarnation of a new consciousness in our routine life. In my own life and the lives of my patients, whenever I have resisted the temptations of outer distractions and honored the sacred void, the inspiring and healing guidance of Aditi has blessed me. This has permitted my patients and me to make new beginnings on our path to the soul.

Mythology

The name Aditi is derived from the root word *da* (to bind or fetter) and suggests another profile of Shakti. As *a-diti*[44] she is the unbound, free one, and it is evident in the hymns that she is called upon to free the petitioner from the various hindrances of Maya and its karmic consequences. Aditi also plays the role of the guardian of *reta (The Spiritual Way)*, the spiritual connection between the individual soul and the primal Spirit. As such, she is called a supporter of creatures by providing or enforcing *reta*, those ordinances or rhythms that delineate order from chaos. In the *Atharva Veda* 7.6.4[45] she is described as the Great Mother in whose lap lays the atmosphere. Similarly, in *Vajaasaneyi Samhita* 9.5 she is represented as the support of the cosmos.

"In conception of strength, we call with speech, the great mother, Aditi, on whom this whole world has settled."[46]

The following passages, first from F.Max Muller and then from Pupul Jaykar, describe the many ways that Aditi is imbued with a cosmic significance.

The beyond, the unbounded realm beyond earth, sky and heaven, the visible Infinite, the endless expanse beyond the earth, clouds and sky. She is the unbounded one, free from bonds of any kind, whether of space or time, free from physical weakness, free from moral guilt. [47]

In a creation myth common to the countryside in India, the Aditi Shakti, the primordial ever-young goddess, spins the threads of creation. As she conceives and creates, she, in turn, is vanquished by the male gods, the static masculine order, who are born of her; she passes to them the power that ensures her own destruction, for she conveys the wisdom that in srishti, or creation, is the seed of bija of samhar, or destruction. In such a scenario of ending and beginning, death is an ending and yet passage to a new beginning." [48]

Aditi[49] is mentioned in the Rig Veda[50] as the mother of Gods. Although she is mentioned nearly eighty times in the Rig Veda, it is difficult to grasp her nature as she symbolizes the Void and New Creation. She is virtually featureless in her physical manifestations.

Attributes of Aditi - Motherhood

Perhaps the most outstanding attribute of Aditi is her motherhood. She is predominantly the mother of the Adityas, a group of eight gods. Aditi is also said to be the mother of Vishnu and Indra. Unlike Prithvi (Mother Earth), whose motherhood is central to her nature, Aditi does not have a male consort in the *Rig Veda* (similar to the Olympian goddess Hestia).

As a mothering presence, Aditi is often asked to guard the one who petitions her. Appropriate to her role as a mother, Aditi is sometimes associated with a cow. As an earthy cow, she provides nourishment, and as a cosmic cow, her milk is identified with the redemptive, renewing mythic drink Soma.

Archetype of Void and New Beginnings

Aditi is the archetype of void and new beginnings. Once Kali has cleared the psyche of the debris of dysfunctional complexes and assimilated the energy of the shadow and complexes into consciousness, the Aditi archetype is invoked. Initially it is experienced as void. If the individual can honor the void for long enough, then the possibilities of new beginnings emerge, e.g. in a big dream or a synchronistic event. This establishes the framework for the creation of new consciousness out of the personal myth of the individual.

Archetype of a Creative Impulse

Often Aditi is experienced as a new creative impulse just at the moment when the individual is exhausted and preoccupied with outer life. Jungian psychoanalyst Von Franz[51] describes this as a Spiritus Creator in the unconscious that manifests as a creative impulse and stirs up new possibilities. I once worked with a schizophrenic individual who would come to my office and keep fiddling with his fingers throughout the session. Later, he admitted to me his obsession with knives; he had a large collection at home. On his way to my office, he would pick up pieces of wood from tree branches near my office. He would fiddle with these twigs in his fingers.

Prior to one of our sessions, I had returned from a conference in Boston and bought a small Scrimshaw engraving on a nut palm (also called "vegetable ivory"). It occurred to me that perhaps my patient should try to do something creative with his fingers, knives and twigs, and I suggested he try whittling. Soon my patient started to make beautiful whittling images out of wooden branches, and his anxiety was much reduced. I was even able to cut down the dose of psychotropic medications he was on. I was still curious about his whittling, knives, and finger fidgeting rituals. I dug deeper into his family history and to my surprise learned that one of his great grandfathers was a member of the American Whaling Fleet. This American Whaling Fleet had ceased to exist, and this art form has being carried on by a few American artisans. Scrimshaw is the indigenous art form of the American Whale man. In his idle hours of cruising for whales, he devoted himself to fashioning articles and jewelry from whale ivory.

In an earlier publication, I have explored the concept of family or ancestral karma.[52] It was my patient's family karma to acknowledge and honor the art of Scrimshaw in some symbolic form. His compulsive finger rituals and knives obsessions were trying to reconnect him with his ancestral legacy. When he attended to this legacy, it opened up a creative sector of his life and helped him deal with this illness a little bit better.

Manifestations of Aditi in the Psychoid Space

At other times Aditi manifests in the psychoid space, a term Carl Jung used to describe the hypothetical synapse (junction) between our body, mind, soul and the spirit. Archetypes are the transmitters of energy in this synapse. It is the space where archetypes crystallize as attitudes, drives, complexes, apparently chance events, moods and body and psychological symptoms. These experiences are not only psychic but also physical and may evoke synchronistic phenomena.[53] When we experience a synchronistic event, Aditi may be whispering to us.

The manifestations of Aditi may take several psychological forms. When we are in the realm of Aditi, our psyche is in a state of void, or emptiness. If we don't confuse this as depression or pathology and hold the energy of the void for long enough, or unconscious steps in and activates the latent code of Aditi. The unconscious now manifests itself as creation of new consciousness. These manifest as mythological figures which are the signature of the unconscious. The language of the unconscious manifests through prehistoric and primitive images which we are familiar with from our fairy tales and myths. A big intuition manifests as an image of a giant, and a small inkling manifests as a dwarf. Sometimes these manifest as aliens, which signifies an intuition which is completely outside of the box of our consciousness. These images and impulses are flickerings of preconscious creative impulses, which, when honored, may lead to an expansion of ego consciousness.[54]

Aditi and the Feeling Function

Honoring Aditi can be experienced as swimming in the archetypal soup. Our thinking function can be said to have reached its limits in discerning the message of Aditi, and it is our feeling function[55] that zeros in on the most accurate promptings of the goddess. In any given enterprise, when we have followed our hunches, examined all the details, thought through all the logical options and are still uncertain about the path, it is our feeling, our assessment of what we value the most in any given situation, that guides our final decision. It is the heart, the feeling function, which is the final arbitrator of our most crucial choices. When I migrated from the UK to America, I did extensive research as to where I would settle within the USA. My gut feeling was to settle in California, where I had an intuition that my Eastern background may be better understood. My assessment of details suggested the Mayo Clinic, where I could flourish professionally. My logical assessment pointed to Chicago, where I could pursue my academic goals. But my heart called me to the solitude and peacefulness of Milwaukee where I could do my inner work in peace. That is what I chose, and it was a good choice. It has permitted me to do my work of integrating Eastern and Western wisdom in a relatively quiet space, uncluttered by other pressures and influences. This choice was the gift of Aditi.

My patient Virgo is another good example of the observation that it is the feeling that eventually redeems our soul under the auspices of Aditi. Virgo is a very logical man, attentive to details, traits that served him well as a physician. His Waterloo was in the realm of the feelings. After a turbulent divorce, he started dating his present wife. At this point of their courtship, he was uncertain of this emerging relationship and skeptical of his capacity to make a new relationship work. At this point he had the following dream, which helped him with his dilemma.

Jenny and I are married. We are living aboard an old rusty ship, possibly an old oil tanker which is no longer in use. We make love. An unknown person or persons disturb us, maybe attack us. I look out the old, rusty, loose-fitting door, but there is no one there. We have a daughter, a little girl who is about 6 or 7 years old. She has been taking violin lessons. I haven't heard her play for awhile, and I asked her to play. She plays a beautiful piece with lots of underlying fine rhythmic fabric as well as a melody overlaying it. I am very impressed with her ability and am proud of her. I am sort of shuffling around in bed and half awake. Jenny wakes me up, and I get up and ponder on the dream.

Virgo was ambivalent about his wish to marry Jenny as he felt burned out by his first marriage that felt like a rusty old oil tanker – an institutional medical marriage that had lost its soul. Maybe it needed restoration. The unknown intruder was equated to me as his therapist, who he felt was critical of his marriage plans. This was a projection of his ambivalence about the relationship. The little girl 6 to 7 years old was created by his dream maker, or the soul, as they were not yet married and had no possibility of children as Jenny had previously had a hysterectomy. In reality any future baby with her was not possible, thus this was a symbolic image. It symbolized his anima or feeling function. He took piano lesson at age 6 to7 himself, and his mother played piano.

The dream bodes well for positive prognosis in terms of new anima figure emerging in the dream matrix. The violin symbolized further amplification of his feeling function, the music of the soul. Jenny evokes feelings of love, desire, passion, and value, but most importantly, she touches the violin strings of his heart and soul. The dream was blessing his emerging relationship with Jenny. Aditi had blessed the emerging union.

Number Symbolism of Aditi

In the number symbolism, the *number three* indicates the presence of Aditi and signifies the creative flow. The *number four* indicates the number of differentiated consciousness (e.g. the four functions, the four directions, the four seasons, etc.) in which the creative thrust of the number three has been assimilated into emerging consciousness.[56] Four results from the flow of three and becomes still, visible, and ordered within ego consciousness. In summary, Aditi gets us into the void of consciousness, paving the way for the descent into the unconscious in search of new symbols for personal growth. When we have three fourths of the pie, we delve into our soul depths to look for the missing fourth quadrant of the circle. Usually, the answer to our riddle lies in the missing fourth piece. In my search for an optimal location to settle in America, I initially looked at three other alternatives, California for acceptance of my ideas, the Mayo Clinic for professional ground, and Chicago for academic possibilities. However, the choices still gave a sense of something lacking. Milwaukee provided me with that fourth dimension. It was the possibility of doing what I valued most— the soul work that clinched the final decision to settle in Milwaukee. It is the three that leaves a sense of unfinished assessment and provokes the search for the fourth dimension. The fourth dimension then incarnates the creation myth of the individual, most apparent in the initial or the big dreams of individuals.

How Aditi Manifests in the Initial and the Big Dreams

Jung attached special significance to the *initial dreams* in the therapeutic process. He postulated[57] that the dreams that appear at the initial stages of analysis often bring to light the essential root cause of our problems and also hold the key with which to unlock our path to the soul. Jung observed[58] that initial dreams are often amazingly

lucid and clear cut, but as the work of analysis progresses, 　*161*
dreams tend to lose their clarity. It seems that initial
dreams provide individuals with the best possible glimpse
of the unconscious and provide a map of our personal myth
that guides us to initiate new beginnings. As an analogy,
we can see that the best view of the sun is at sunrise as
it dramatically crests the eastern horizon at dawn out of
the darkness of the night (the unconscious). But as the
day progresses, the sun blends into the glare and glitter of
daylight, and the view that comes from the juxtaposition of
day and night, the past and the future, the conscious and
the unconscious is lost. The initial dream is the unique
window into the mystery of the Soul under the auspices of
the Aditi archetype. Whenever there is a feeling of void in
our personal life, and our ego consciousness has reached its
limit in the management of a problem in our outer or inner
life, Aditi presides over the psychic situation to guide us.
She gifts the consciousness with a dream, a synchronistic
event, an image, a fantasy or an inspiration that ushers in
the creation of new consciousness that helps us overcome
the life crisis at hand and gives us inspiration for a new
beginning. In the mid-eighties, when I was feeling lost,
exiled and burned out in Milwaukee, Aditi gifted me with
a dream that pointed me to my path. In this dream which I
have outlined before in a different context, I dreamt that I
had a meal with my mentor from India, Father Valles and
two other Jesuit fathers. Later, we prayed together at the
college chapel. The three fathers held the association of
Christian trinity (Father, Son and the Holy Spirit). Later,
I related them to the Hindu trinity (Brahma the creator,
Vishnu the preserver, Shiva the destroyer). Still later, I
learned of the dynamic energy system that drives these
three gods, which are the goddess consorts that engine
these three gods: Saraswati, Laxmi and Parvati. This dream
reset me on my path to my soul, to integrate Eastern and
Western wisdom. Later, it became the inspiration to write
this book on the healing and guiding wisdom of the latent
code of the goddess. This one dream still inspires me and

keeps instructing me on my path to my soul in new and novel ways.

John's Aditi Encounter

John's story is another example of the guiding light of Aditi that guides our way in the darkness of life via the gift of an initial dream. John is a gay professional who sought analysis to deal with his grief about the loss of a relationship with his previous partner and generalized lack of passion in life in spite of considerable professional success. He was in his late thirties with boyish charm. He seemed overburdened by life and outer success while at the same time disconnected from the care of his body and from attending to his inner life. He presented with a sense of grief about the loss of his relationship with his partner who was tall, handsome, blonde, blue-eyed and did occasional modeling jobs. His ex-partner's new partner was a Latin American man the same age as John. He presented the following initial dream:

I am at a party and sitting across the room from my ex-boyfriend's table. My ex-boyfriend has not shown up, but his present lover is at the table.

In this brief vignette, John's initial dream held the mystery of his individuation and new beginnings. As we worked with his dream in the following weeks, we came to understand that both his ex-boyfriend and his present lover were reflections and fractals of John's soul. These dream figures could be understood as unconscious manifestations of his soul needing to be assimilated into the wholeness of his personality. The necessary prerequisites for his new beginnings were to honor the void of his present life, the chaos in his relational matrix, the grief over lost love, and the hope for new beginnings. The archetype that ushered in this new beginning for him was the archetype of Aditi as she constellated in the session following this dream. John reported that he was feeling somewhat sad,

blue and tired. It had been a professionally burdened and   *163*
tiring week with a tremendous output in the work sector
of his life. I proposed a guided imaginal dialogue with this
mood to give it form and personhood. His image was of
his maternal great aunt, Mita, who was a simple soulful
woman, never married, who had raised John's mother and
uncles after his grandmother's death. She lived an austere
life with few trappings. Upon further analysis, it became
apparent that his aunt Mita was an anima soul figure,
who had come to guide John in his hour of distress and
loss. While his outer life was overburdened and riddled
with striving for outer success, his anima, his soul guide
crystallized as his sad, blue mood and led him to a precious
image of Great Aunt Mita. This image of his Great Aunt
Mita came to be understood as his doorway to the void, to
the solitude, simplicity and austerity of his soulful life, as a
compensation for his success-driven outer life. At the core
of the image of Mita was the archetype of Aditi. In this
initial dream, Aditi appeared in an image of void, the empty
chair reserved for the missing ex-boyfriend. Incarnated
within his blue mood, Aditi appeared as a soul figure to gift
him a glimpse into a compensatory attitude of a spiritually
informed life. The new John had the potential to be more
balanced, valuing not only his outer success but honoring
Aditi's call for a reflective life.

My Encounter with Aditi

Sometimes the meeting with Aditi comes about in a
synchronistic event. In the early nineties, I had become
professionally burnt out by the pressures of managed care
and administrative responsibilities at a local psychiatric
hospital. A brief stint at the Freudian training did not feed
my soul, and I was resigned to life in the clinical trenches
in the sober Midwest. Then one of my associates, whom
I had mistakenly perceived as a professional adversary,
to my utter delight decided to relocate to another part
of the country. I perceived him as self-aggrandizing and
narcissistic. Of course, in retrospect I see that he carried

the projection of my dark side. I disliked in him what I now understand as my own unconscious narcissism. However, at his farewell party, my wife and I were seated next to him and his wife. I tried to make small talk with his wife, and the conversation moved to dreams. I had just re-read Freud's classic Interpretation of Dreams, and I talked excitedly about my views on it. She listened attentively and gently said that Carl Jung also had some interesting things to say about dreams. I had minimal familiarity with Jung. In mainstream psychiatric training, we were taught about Jung for less than one hour! The next day, she left Jung's anthology on dreams as a parting gift in my mailbox. It sat on my bookshelf for over a year before I stumbled upon it again trying to analyze a difficult dream. Suddenly, I was hooked on Jung, and this chance event gradually culminated into a deepening interest in Jung and formal training. It was my apparent adversary's wife who introduced me to my life's calling. The soul whispers in mysterious ways. It was a brief but life changing encounter with the goddess Aditi incarnated in my colleague's soulful spouse at a chance dinner table encounter.

Aditi's Guidance on Our Path to the Soul

Aditi is the presiding goddess over the path to our soul. She ushers in the new creation of necessary consciousness at every bend and crossroad of our soul making. She guides us via her manifestations in our dreams, synchronistic events, creative impulses, and nagging and nudging medical and psychiatric symptoms until the necessary void is created to make room for new attitudes and corresponding life structures. How our dreams, synchronistic events, bothersome complexes, medical and psychiatric symptoms usher us onto the path to our soul is discussed at some length in one of my earlier publications[59].

The Fourth Quadrant

If we imagine our life as a circle, we can divide it into

four quadrants. Three of these are well-recognized and the focus of much of human enterprise: the quadrants of love, of work, and of play. The fourth less visible one is the quadrant of creativity. We often meet Aditi in this neglected quadrant of our life.

In my psychotherapeutic work with men and women over the years, I have found that when this fourth invisible quadrant of creativity is addressed and honored in some way, it has tremendous potential for healing human suffering. This emphasis, this acknowledgment, this honoring of the creative quadrant of life leads to a sense of completion and satisfaction in human existence that restores mental health and fulfillment to one's life. Highlighting this fourth quadrant of creativity brings the other three into a relative balance with the rest of the personality and leads to a sense of emotional, psychological, and spiritual fulfillment.

I have learned from my clinical experience over the years that while the other three quadrants of love, work, and play are crucial in managing our connection with day-to-day life in our routine world, the quadrant of creativity puts us in contact with our soul and the Spirit. In the fourth quadrant, that of inner experience and creativity, we recognize important aspects of our spiritual potential. Aditi guides us in the realm of creative enterprise. An example will illustrate the healing, whole-making power of creativity coupled with knowledge.

David' Story

David was a medical professional who came for psychotherapy with complaints of depression, drug addiction, and lack of intimacy with his wife. He responded very well to psychotherapeutic treatment plus a program of conjoint marital sessions. After two years of therapy, he was able to maintain abstinence from his substance of addiction; he had regained his professional ground and was highly respected in his field of work, and his marital situation had stabilized substantially. However, he continued to feel there was something missing in his life, some crucial secret ingredient.

In one of his sessions I asked him, "What is the very last thing in the world you would consider doing?" Initially he gave a somewhat flippant response that he would start making metal jewelry set with stones. I recommended he do precisely that: take a noncredit course in jewelry making at one of the local university centers and start making jewelry. At first, he was amused and somewhat irritated at my offbeat recommendation, but out of some sense of reverence and trust in me he half-heartedly went along with my recommendation. But then something unexpected emerged: when he started making jewelry under the guidance of his teacher, he found it was his true calling. He created exquisitely artful pieces set with stones, and several retail boutique owners vied to sell his work, albeit on a small scale.

Although the financial aspect of this enterprise was not his primary concern, he was amazed to see how successful he had become and how much more alive he felt. Living creatively had a beneficial impact on all the facets of his life, including love (his marriage), work (his profession), and play (his relationship with his children as well as in his own life). The fourth quadrant, creativity, had a binding, cementing, healing effect on all the other aspects of David's life, and it imparted a sense of completion and wholeness to his existence.

Most of us would benefit by honoring and nurturing the fourth quadrant of creativity in some tangible but individual way. Perhaps there is a special talent we have, or a dream or a waking fantasy leads us to cultivate a heretofore neglected aspect of our being and our potential. An acquaintance, friend, or stranger might make a suggestion that resonates in us, or an idea comes about through a random or chance event. Once a certain interest chooses us and we decide to honor and follow the path opening out before us, which is our fourth quadrant, creativity, we must nurture it by acquiring the necessary knowledge and skill. We must also make sure our creative endeavor does not get co-opted

by the three other frontiers of life: love, work, and play.
In other words, our creativity should not be placed in the
service of establishing a relationship, furthering our job, or
making us better at a recreational activity that we already
have undertaken. When we give space to the creative
principle in our lives, our creativity grounds and solidifies
our sense of a whole and integral existence.

The Trap of Usefulness

One clarification is necessary. Although the creative
enhancement of the realms of love, work, and play is most
desirable, and our creativity significantly enriches these
three dimensions, I am not talking about opening to the
creative force for practical or utilitarian purposes. Rather,
I advocate letting whatever is moving just beyond the
threshold of directed consciousness emerge into view. The
first step toward letting creativity flow through us is getting
our directed consciousness out of the way and placing our
skills of expression in the service of the nature in us that
wants to take visible, audible, tactile, or kinesthetic shape.

In its first emergence, the expression of the creative
force is for our eyes only. The creative force connects us
with the movement of the spirit in us, with our spiritual
potential. It can become a road to our deepest inner core;
it can connect us with the universe in unique ways. But if
creativity is to lead us further along the path to the soul, it
must start as private creativity— that is, creativity that is
not a means to any ends. Of course, later we may shape
for "public" display what has initially appeared to us in
private. But at first, we have to let Aditi express through us
whatever is there and ready to be born in the spontaneous
exercise of our skills and knowledge. Inasmuch as we can
give expression to our private, "personal" creativity, it will
connect us with the Spirit moving within us.

It is important to distinguish between "purposeless"
and "purposeful" creativity and to honor both of them
intelligently. Purposeless creativity is pure "being."
Purposeful creativity that may enhance our love, work,

and play falls within the realm of conscious and intentional "doing." Purposeful creativity seduces us by the prospect of enhancing some known aspect of life; purposeless creativity is closer to spontaneous play. When we honor it through spontaneous expression, Aditi's awesome healing power flows unhindered into our lives. We need not become accomplished artists in this endeavor, but only channels that permit the movements of Aditi to inform and enliven us.

In my personal and professional experience, I have found that the biggest problem in tapping the creative process is not that we lack creativity. Often we have so much of it that we get overwhelmed by the power of the creative force. Rather, the obstacles to our creativity are often twofold. First, we may have structured our lives in such a way that we have not set aside regular time to open to creative impulses. Second, we may need to focus on the dimension of creativity that we are going to explore and to improve or augment our skills of expression.

Fig. 4 The Four Quadrants of Our Soul

The Integration of Our Masculine and Feminine Potentials under the Auspices of Aditi

The initial experience of Aditi is that of the positive static feminine, organic undifferentiated wholeness, the uterus, nature in the round, being and self-acceptance, the Grandmother Goddess – the mother earth. Once this static ground is experienced, Aditi leads to the creative experience of earth melting into the water. When we enter from our outer consciousness into our soul or inner consciousness, it feels like baptism – a new birth of our personality. This watery initiation into the mystery of our unconscious initially may feel like we are drowning in our own frightening depths as we experiment with new attitudes and behaviors. At this point of watery initiation into new consciousness, the individual is in the realm of the dynamic positive feminine aspect of one's soul potential. The creative impulse inspires flexibility and openness and leads to new possibilities and eventually to transformation and renewal of the personality.

The New World-view from the Lens of the Latent Code of Aditi

Aditi is the balance of one's typological mandala. She speaks through all four World-views as necessary to relay its promptings of new creation and new beginnings. The creative impulse may manifest as an intuition, a hunch, an idea, or a feeling about a certain possibility. It can also manifest as a certain sensate detail that catches one's fascination. However, to implement Aditi's creative promptings, one must exercise the experial world-view, a sense of feeling or value for the new enterprise, and the necessary attention to details to translate the impulse into reality. In my own soul work I have had to cross such a threshold. I am an ethereal type-thinking/intuitive, judging my world by logic and intuition. When I made a transition from being a medical doctor and a psychiatrist to a psychoanalyst, I had to cross several barriers. Firstly,

I had to evaluate how important it was for me to move from a medical to a spiritual model of healing my patients. In soul searching, I found that the spiritual tradition held tremendous value for me and the rigors of Jungian analytic training were worth my while. This was attending to my feeling or value function. Secondly, I had to manage countless details in my personal and professional life to make time, room and money to undertake such a rigorous training, which was undervalued by my peers and often by patients who sometimes want a quick fix. This was attending to the piddly details, the sensate function. When I balanced my thinking and intuition with attention to my feelings and confronted my dislike for small details, I was able to make room for guidance from Aditi and make a new beginning as a soul maker rather than a medical worker.

Comparative Mythology

The oldest of Greek gods is the goddess *Gaia*, or Earth. It is she, the mother of all things, who produces her own mate, Uranos, the sky. This primal couple, like Nut and Geb in Egypt, spawn the first beings. In ancient times, the archetype of the Great Mother might have been derived from Gaia. She created her own mate out of the void, and the primal couple became partners in creation. This primal couple is the prototypical motif in masculine/ feminine alliance myths: Papa and Rangi among the Maori; Sky Man and Earth Woman among the Navajo; the Sun God and Spider Woman among the Hopi; Izanagi and Izanami among the Japanese; and Geb and Nut among the ancient Egyptians. Earth was worshipped as the source of birth, life and death.[60]

Gaia, the Earth Mother, the Great Goddess, and Aditi represent the nature and the mystery of creation and the unconscious, the source of creation of all consciousness. They can create but also destroy. All that is conscious eventually returns to the unconscious, an Uroborus phenomenon (a serpent biting its tail and creating a closed circle) that sustains and gradually matures collective consciousness. Her representations in myths and fairy tales are the wise old woman, the fairy godmother, and the witch. In the Christian tradition she is the Madonna, who has lost her dark side. But in the Hindu Shakti tradition, Aditi is worshipped both in her benevolent form as Saraswati, SriLaxmi and Parvati, and in her dark aspect as Durga and Kali. The cow, the holy symbol of the Great Mother in India, symbolizes Aditi. Interestingly, the Sanskrit term for the cow is *Gaia*.

Promise and Perils of the Latent Code of Aditi

Aditi lays down the foundation for the creation of new consciousness for individuals and cultures. She restores our connection with our soul. However, the experience of Aditi is not without perils. One significant danger of experiencing new creativity or consciousness is the *feeling of reality being evil,* based on a Gnostic idea.[61] This may come from the Buddhist notion that reality is *Maya* and the aim of life is to escape from it and achieve *Nirvana* (freedom from this miserable reality). Nirvana must be differentiated from the Hindu concept of *Moksha* or freedom from the opposites. Some of these philosophies consider creation a bad mistake, an enterprise of God's shadow, which got it into creation. Simply put, had God been conscious of what he was doing, he would not have created this miserable reality.

Another peril of the creative Aditi impulse is ambivalence. This is based on the dual tendency of the unconscious to bring something into consciousness and then to not want to hand it over.[62] The creative impulse is always ambivalent. Ambition alone does not provide enough drive to implement the creative impulse. It needs the support of the feeling function to achieve it. It needs the love of the creative enterprise to actualize the creative impulse. Creativity is a labor of love.

An additional danger of Aditi's creative impulse is archetypal possession. Whenever there is a creative impulse in the unconscious, the conscious gets possessed by it until the creative impulse is played out in some form. If the creative impulse is not expressed, it remains preconscious and gets secretly inflated by contamination with unconscious archaic processes. Individuals sometimes resist becoming creative because the fantasy of creativity is much more magnificent than the drudgery of creative work.[63] Often the creative output is a mere remnant of the perceived magnificence of the original creative impulse. This birth of creative output is experienced as deflation and often depression. Every creative person has to experience the high of the creative impulse and the low of the creative output. Perhaps post partum blues/depression in pregnant women is such a phenomenon. Nevertheless, unless the creative impulse is played out, it keeps nudging the individual as constant irritation, nausea, bad moods, and restlessness.[64]

Individuals who do not recognize and honor their creative impulses may get obsessed by and addicted to various substances or activities in order to divert and drain off the creative drive. Sexual addictions and other addictive behaviors may be a particular danger in predisposed individuals. The psychodynamic context of addictive behaviors is the difficulty in holding and honoring the void. In over thirty years of treatment experience with recovering addicts, I have found that if the craving is traced back to its psychogenesis, it is rooted in the dread of the psychic void and the tendency to abate this feeling quickly with addictive behaviors. The twelve-step recovery program provides an invaluable service by providing a framework to deal with this void through fellowship, twinship, and spiritual contact with the Higher Power -- the great Aditi.

While frantic attempts to flee the void may lead to susceptibilities to sundry modes of addictions, succumbing to the void and inner chaos may lead to a host of other psychiatric conditions. These include avoidant, schizoid, and schizotypal personality disorders,[65] and, in extreme cases, schizophrenic spectrum disorders. In these mental disorders, the individual becomes preoccupied with inner world to relative exclusion of the demands of the outer world.

Von Franz postulates that frustration, fear, loneliness, and boredom are common accompaniments of the creative process. When an important content of unconscious crosses the threshold of consciousness, it is an energetic phenomenon. When the creative content approaches the ego complex or our outer daily consciousness, it attracts libido or psychological energy from it, away from other complexes or hang-ups and personality traits. Ego consequently feels low, tired, restless, and depressed until the thought or creative impulse breaks through into consciousness.[66]

Aditi Code in Action

Aditi will guide us, but we should be willing to be led. The goddess can bring the horse to the well, but only the horse may decide to drink from the sacred well. All our symbols are hollow unless we make sacrifices in our present life to welcome them and display courage to implement their direction in navigating our life. Hence soul making is an act of sacrifice of our comfortable present existence and courage to take a leap of faith into the future.

It is crucial to find a balance between the *intent* and the *content* of Aditi's path. If we cannot deal with the personal content of our life, we have nothing *real* to deal with. But unless we deal with that personal content in spiritual terms we do not touch its driving power and *meaning*, nor do we reach that which is to be transformed.[67]

My Aditi Encounters

In my own continuing individuation, the guidance of Aditi has been crucial. In the first half of my life experience, I was an overburdened medical professional, struggling to juggle the competing demands for professional success, parenting my children, maintaining intimacy with my spouse, and surviving as an immigrant in an extremely competitive American environment. In the second half of my life experience so far, the soul keeps tugging at me to connect with my inner life, my cultural roots, to make some meaning out of my exile away from my land of origin. The professional and spiritual, the Eastern and Western, the medical and holistic aspects of my psyche felt *split*. Even in India, my schooling was under the caring auspices of Jesuit fathers, while my parents were devout Hindus. Latent in between these splits in my psyche resided a sense of void. I was having an Aditi experience.

It is significant that the Aditi photograph in this chapter was symbolic of my inner state at the time. I found this rendering of Aditi on the grounds of a Jesuit University (Marquette University) in Milwaukee. Perhaps the splits in my psyche were ready to heal, and I was ready to be whole. Certainly, this image was that of the goddess holding the **broken vessel** of void in her tight embrace and healing the fissures, not to perfection but towards wholeness and unity.

Gradually Aditi guided me to make room for my soul. Initially this involved encountering the void by relinquishing the trappings of external success and professional security. As I started to let go, the void presented me with frightening thoughts and feelings. Would I lose all my patients if I set limits on my work? Would I be a bad father and husband if I did not make a lot of money? As I struggled with these fears, new creative impulses popped up in the form of interests in depth psychology, Jungian training and down the line photography and computers. I eventually understood these new interests as gifts of the goddess Aditi. As I continue to gratefully and gradually attempt to integrate these new creative structures into my life I continue to endure the splits within myself under the holding embrace of Aditi. Of course my own struggle informs my work with patients. Let me now share with you the stories of some of my patients who met and received the guidance of Aditi on the path of their individuation.

Edmund's Story

Often, our significant relationships carry the fractals of our soul. They become the passwords that open the door between our soul and the Spirit. Edmund is one such individual. He is a neurologist who at age 58 consulted me on the Friday before he was to start a new job as a junior partner in a new group practice with three other neurologists. He had practiced in Michigan for seventeen years and burned out. While in Michigan, he got lost in his pressure cooker job and subsequently lost his emotional connection with his wife, which led to a divorce. However, he stayed on in Michigan for five more years till both his sons left for college. Then he moved to Milwaukee and worked in a group practice for seven years till a large HMO acquired his group. His job was eliminated. He was now in a second marriage to a soulful and supportive wife. He had financial resources to retire but felt he had no consuming interest or skill outside of medicine to sustain his interest and was fearful of the void of retired life.

In our work together, I had to deal immediately with the deep sense of depression and void he felt in his life, and this void played out for him every evening as he sat alone, lost in Milwaukee, unable to decide what to do with himself. I, as his therapist, had an intuition that this sense of void he felt every day was a significant starting point for him. It was a sacred place where Aditi had appeared to cleanse him of the Maya of the past and guide him to his future. We started by stopping the drinking in the evening and replacing it with the simplest of starting points: daily walks, journaling for twenty minutes, meditation. As he honored his void and created sacred space, Aditi gifted him with guidance to create new life structures. He started to attend AA meetings, joined the local medical society and volunteered to be on a committee to connect with his peers. He started dating his wife, and they would go out on the town twice a week. Gradually he fine tuned his practice and started to focus on those aspects of his practice that he enjoyed the most. He even gave several public education presentations at his local hospital. Life was infused back into his practice and relationships. He resumed his interest in flying a small plane and plans to pursue this further. Out of the void of his depression, Aditi's guidance blessed him with new structures in his life matrix.

He reported that his elder son, Robert, was model son, a Michigan State graduate like himself and well-established as an investment consultant in New York City. His younger son, Stan, was the black sheep of the family. He almost got kicked out of high school, and after many years in college, he barely finished his undergraduate degree and settled as a realtor in Las Vegas. He lived the life of a virtual beach bum and enjoyed himself. On closer analytic reflection, it became clearer that Stan lived out the unlived life for Edmund. Edmund was over-responsible, while Stan was irresponsible (playful, carefree, social and spontaneous).

In analysis, Edmund gradually claimed his Stan side, his playful side, the "Stan within." He decided to work in a low stress environment as a part time urgent care physician in an under-served part of Milwaukee and started to nurture his interest in other sectors of his life. He now feels much more connected with his wife and sons and has earnestly started to attend to the love, play, creativity and spiritual dimensions of his life. In my clinical practice, I am amazed to learn how often children carry the unlived projections of their parents' lives, both light and dark. Sometimes they carry our unlived virtues, and at other times they carry our unconscious vices. The more conscious we become of our souls, the less we project onto our children and other significant relationships. We then can live a fuller life and unburden our relationships from having to carry our unlived life. While we give birth to our children, it is humbling to note that often they give birth to the potentialities of our soul.

Ways to Honor Aditi

Attending to the latent code of Aditi involves attending to the whispers of our soul. The latent code of the soul speaks via our dreams, fantasies and day dreams. It speaks via our creative process of the artists in poetry, prose, art, cinema and other media and the psychosis, hallucinations and delusions of the mentally ill. It manifests in our hang ups or complexes and our relationships. It manifests in the margins and the small rather than the center and the big aspects of our life and personality.

We can tune into the latent code of Aditi by creating the sacred space to tune into this void. This includes incubating solitude, silence, studio time, meditation, journaling, and attending to the present moment. It involves a more advanced technique called Active Imagination. One important method to invoke and honor the latent code of Aditi is to honor your creative process or the fourth quadrant of your life. This has been discussed earlier in this chapter. The central intervention to gestate the latent code is to evolve a reflective and a symbolic attitude to life. This involves an attitude that respects and explores the meaning behind the outer manifestation in life and relationships. It attunes us to the whispers of our soul's code in all aspects of our life and events, relationships and problems, creative process and problematic medical and psychiatric symptoms. This will be discussed in detail in the chapter on attending to the latent code.

Yantra and the corresponding Mantra are useful ways to tune into the latent code of the relevant archetype. However, since Aditi represents the void, there is no specific Yantra for it, but in my clinical experience, I have found that one may meditate using an empty vessel as an object of meditation to honor Aditi.

In the chapter on attending to the Latent Code, these methods of attending to the latent code in general and Aditi in particular will be addressed in great detail. In the preceding chapters, we have explored several profiles of the latent code of the goddess archetypes as they guide our soul on our life path. In the next chapter, we will explore of the famous MahaLaxmi temple in the Indian metropolis Mumbai, formerly called Bombay. The story

178   of the construction of this temple on the Indian Ocean is intricately linked in the original construction of the great city of Mumbai, which is one of the world's leading centers of population, culture and commerce. It illustrates how the wisdom of the goddesses played out on the larger stage of the collective consciousness in the construction of this great city. I will also portray my own personal experience of this goddess energy that occurred when my daughter and I visited the holy temple of the three goddesses, the Maha Laxmi temple on the beaches of Mumbai on the Indian Ocean.

HONOR
THE
DYNAMIC
FEMININE

mahalaxmi

CH 9
The Slumbering Goddesses of Mumbai

While the latent code of the soul guides individuals in their life towards their destiny, it is also instructs communities and other fundamental structures of our civilization. Each monument, each city, each new idea in our civilization is guided by a latent code. If we study these structures with a discerning eye, we may be able to decode their code and understand the soul of these great structures. The archetype of love and Eros was the latent code of the magnificent Taj Mahal, the quest for after-life was the latent code for the lofty Pyramids. The archetype of justice and freedom is the latent code for American constitution. If we tune into the latent code of these structures that define our culture, we may better understand the origins of our nature not only as individuals but as a human family with a rich and diverse latent code, all weaving the fabric of our unique culture on this fragile planet. This chapter is a study of one such structure. It examines how seven disconnected islands were woven together to become what is now one of the leading centers of culture and commerce, the heartbeat of India, the great city of Mumbai.

In the winter of 1999, my daughter Ami and I visited the famous MahaLaxmi temple on the shores of the Indian Ocean in Mumbai. We interviewed its trustee, who kindly gave us permission to record previously un-photographed pictures of the goddess and gave us the valuable history of the temple. The MahaLaxmi Temple in Mumbai (Bombay)[68] was established sometime between 1761 and 1771. At that time Bombay was composed of seven different islands, and the British government of India sought to join them by a road for the convenience of the people. The contract for road construction was given to Mr. Ramji, a well-known building contractor. He was carrying on the work of construction every day, but during the night when the tide was high the entire construction bed would be washed away. This went on for some time, and there was virtually no progress in the construction of the road.

In despair, Ramji prayed to the gods and the goddesses, and one night he had a very numinous dream in which the goddess Laxmi appeared in his dream. She instructed him that the three goddesses (Laxmi, Saraswati, and Parvati) were lying in the seabed. Unless he searched for them, retrieve and honor them, and install them in a temple, the construction work could not be completed. The latent code of the great city was thus revealed to Ramji, even though he did not know it. He was the channel for the transmission of the code for the construction of the future metropolis. Ramji in his own words narrated this dream to the British officer who was supervising his work. Since there was no way out of the dilemma, he agreed in desperation to go along with Ramji's proposal to search the seabed for the goddess statues.

According to the dream's instructions, Ramji cast a fisherman's net in the sea. To his utter surprise, he netted three stones resembling the likeness of the three goddesses. To dislodge the statues of the slumbering goddesses from the seabed, the workers had to dig out a large amount of sand. This created a mound that held the tides at bay in the cavity formed by the excavation, and the mound provided the high ground above the sea level to build the bridge between the two islands. Later, Ramji constructed a small temple on this mound from his own money. At that time, the governor general was Mr. Harmbe. To this day, the road is named Harmbe road to honor him.

After the construction of this temple, the management of the temple remained with the Ramji family for many years. Ramji had approached the government and obtained the lease for the temple site. Thereafter, there was little expansion of the temple precinct. The family managed the administration of the temple until differences arose among the family members about the way in which to manage the temple and how to share the income.

Finally in 1912, the attorney general of Bombay filed

a petition in the high court of Bombay on behalf of the   *183*
entire Hindu community to safeguard the interest of
the Hindu deities and the temple. That legal proceeding
continued up until 1928 when it was decreed to a
community board of trustees. It was not until 1935 that a
first board of trustees consisting of outsiders (that is, other
than members of the Ramji family) was appointed and
undertook the administration of this trust. In that decree,
all the rights of the Ramji family were terminated, and a
board of trustees consisting of five people was appointed.
A scheme was framed by the high court for the day-to-day
administration and management of this trust. Since then
this administration has been carried on by a board of five
trustees in accordance with these provisions. In 1935 when
the management was taken over by a board of trustees, the
temple was facing a lot of fiscal difficulties. The treasury
of the temple was practically empty. Thereafter, the board
of trustees undertook a successful fund raising campaign.
Over and above maintenance of the temple, it now supports
scholarships for students and medical care for the needy.

The three deities from the seabed are the original black
stones which now adorn the temple center and have been
preserved handsomely for over 200 years. MahaLaxmi is
considered the goddess of wealth and prosperity, but her
twin sister ALaxmi is the goddess of poverty. It seems that
the temple went through the successive cycles of Laxmi,
ALaxmi and MahaLaxmi.

Interpretation

The British and their Indian subcontractor were trying
to build this bridge connecting two of the seven islands of
the original city of Mumbai, but the high tides kept washing
away the construction. Then Ramji had a dream which
revealed the latent code to proceed with the work. The
three goddesses revealed themselves in the dream to the
Indian supervisor of the construction project, instructing
him to salvage the three goddess stones from the shallow
sea bed and construct a small hill and a temple. Once the

goddesses were honored, the construction project could proceed. Of course, the construction of the hill which houses the MahaLaxmi temple was a necessary architectural innovation to get the construction site above sea level for the construction project to be completed. The supervisor's dream was the embodiment of the latent code, which gave him the necessary instructions to finish the project.

From an analytical perspective, we could postulate that conventional wisdom had reached its limit in constructing the bridge. This impasse activated the latent code of the great city. This inspired the dream of the construction supervisor that would guide him to complete the project. In an archetypal sense we could say that when the city of Bombay was struggling to establish its wholeness connecting the seven islands, the seven complexes of the city's psyche were attempting to establish wholeness. At this juncture in the life of this city, the latent code was activated to guide the growth of the great city. The city's soul gifted a dream to its construction supervisor. The latent code of the city's soul created a symbol in form of the goddess, inspiring a template to connect the seven islands to the mainland.

In an archetypal context we could say that the latent code of the Great Mother was constellated to help the city of Bombay fulfill its potential for wholeness and connection with the mainland. This is not unlike what happens in the individual's soul journey when the archetype of the Great Healing Mother constellates to provide appropriate symbols to establish wholeness.

The Integration of the Masculine and Feminine in the Latent Code of Mumbai

In the road construction project, the seven islands had to be connected. The city architects and builders approached this task from the masculine perspective: planning the project with the help of the available technology of the time and implementing the plan in a linear, goal-directed, heroic manner, with sheer manpower. However, the planners had not factored in the intervening presence of

the ocean, its tides, and their impact on the road-building   *185*
project. Dynamically, we may postulate that the builders
had approached the task purely from the vantage point
of the static and dynamic masculine consciousness. The
power and the presence of the ocean, the unconscious,
were not honored. In this instance, the solution to the
riddle of the architectural impasse lay in the ocean, the
unconscious itself. The cause of the problem also held the
key to its solution. Such is the case with the matters of the
deeper consciousness.

The task at hand was to connect the seven islands
with a road over the ocean bed while combating the
tides which would wash away any structure. The task was
connection, establishing wholeness – a mandala of the
city structure. Such a soul task called for the dynamic
feminine consciousness to assist the limited masculine ego
consciousness with which the planners were approaching
the task. This was the watery initiation, the ocean ritual,
to further the building process. The masculine ego
consciousness had to be humbled and dissolved into the
watery depths of the Indian Ocean to further the task.

When this watery initiation ritual was honored, the
necessary feminine consciousness emerged to guide
the project. In this watery initiation of the project, the
masculine pride had to be tamed, the limits of existing
technology accepted and the guidance of the unconscious
feminine consciousness sought. The goddesses had to be
honored for the project to proceed. The ritual invoked
the dynamic positive feminine that led to flexibility and
openness to new ideas and possibilities, imagination and
inspiration, and eventually the transformation of the city
into its fuller potential towards wholeness.

The image of what transpired in the process of searching
the seabed for the goddess stones is very instructive. What
was formerly the flat seabed was transformed into a mound
and a mini valley; what was flat became three-dimensional.
This provided the containment of the energies of the
ebb and flow of time and the ocean. The valley absorbed

the impact of the tides, while the sand mounds provided the foundation for the connecting bridge/road over the sea bed. The flat, inert sea bed was transformed into an architectural innovation when it was dug in a specific manner and became a living, interacting entity which permitted the task of completing the mandala of the city building to proceed. Such is the power of the transforming dynamic feminine consciousness in the lives of individuals and cultures.

Comparative Mythology

King Vortigern's fortress on Snowdon kept tumbling each night after expert masons had worked on it. His wizards advised him to find a youth that never had a father and sprinkle his blood on the foundations. After looking throughout Britain, Vortigern found a youth in Wales named Merlin. In Vortigern's court, Merlin's mother testified that Merlin's father had been a spirit, an incubus. In the face of imminent death, Merlin appeared unafraid. He told the king that an underground lake prevented the fortress from standing. When he had given directions for draining the lake, Merlin prophesied that two dragons lay asleep on the bottom, a red one and a white one. The dragons were duly found, and they awoke and began fighting. The red dragon won. Vortigern asked what this meant, and Merlin told him he would soon be defeated and killed. Soon after this, Ambrosius landed and proceeded to conquer Britain.

This myth of Merlin has interesting correlations with the MahaLaxmi temple construction. The dragon is a mother symbol. In both stories the underlying mother goddess archetype had to be acknowledged and honored for the building process to continue. Dynamically, we may say that unless the feminine aspects of the latent code are acknowledged and honored by the masculine enterprise, construction of the individuals, communities, structures and civilizations cannot proceed.

The symbolism of the red and the white dragons is

instructive in understanding the latent code of the city. In the alchemic template of soul making, the personality has to go through four stages of alchemy. These are the dark, white, yellow and red in that order. First we have to deal with the dark or the shadow aspects of our personality. This leads to baptismal rebirth of the whiteness or clarity and insight into our own personality. This leads to spiritual connection symbolized by yellow, gold or saffron color. However, the highest alchemic stage of personality is red, the color of blood, passion, life and embodiment of our highest values. This is when we are ready to pay with our blood for what we believe in. This is what I call Christ consciousness. Jesus Christ was willing to, and did indeed, pay with his blood and highest personal sacrifice to show his love and devotion to his fellow human beings. When we are ready to make such a sacrifice to embody what we value the most, we are closest to our soul and the divine Sprit.

Archetypal Awareness versus Archetypal Possession by the Latent Code

In the eastern motif there is the reverence for the latent code, which is not without its dangers. At times, reverence leads to possession by the seductive energies of the latent code, which then precludes the reflective or the analytic capacity of individuals and cultures. This was exemplified in my own experience on the occasion of my visit to the MahaLaxmi temple.

The trustee, Mr. Breder, invited me to attend the aarti, the daily prayer ceremony, as well as to take pictures of this important ritual. It was a magical moment of ecstasy where thousands of people gathered to hear the sacred goddess chants and prayers at the aarti services. Thousands of candles were lit on the temple grounds, reflecting the bright glittering stars in a clear tropical sky above the Indian Ocean. A crowd of thousands was hushed. We could hear the waves breaking on the rocks behind the temple. Devotees stood with their hands folded and eyes downcast in reverence to the goddess. Strong incense was burning and permeated the atmosphere. Then the drums started echoing throughout the surrounding area as the temple priests started to beat the age-old drums to honor the goddess. The great throng of humanity started to sing the hymns of the goddess in harmony, synchronized with their heartbeats. Stars were twinkling in the dark tropical sky reflecting back thousands of candles on earth. I felt transported back in time to thousands of years ago in some timeless realm. I was ready with my camera and my tape recorder. However, I got so enchanted by the aarti and the mass ecstasy and was so mesmerized by the ritual that I completely missed the rare opportunity to take the photographs. I failed to maintain my photographer's stance, to stay detached as well as connected in order to accomplish the important task of photo recording the event.

In other words, you could say that I was possessed by the timeless energy of the latent code of the great city, or I was in the grip of the archetype of the Great Goddess and was unable to stay in my consciousness to attend to the task at hand. Similarly, some Hindus and other individuals deeply immersed in their religious traditions tend to be extremely reverential to the spiritual dimension of life almost to the extent of being possessed by it. This then precludes an analytic capacity to use the latent code to instruct the task at hand. This sense of awe and reverence for the spiritual leads to possession. In a more generalized perspective, such individuals may then have difficulty standing their ground, going eyeball to eyeball with the archetypal energy, and establishing a democratic partnership with it rather than becoming involuntarily possessed by the latent code. This, at times, leads to mass possession and a sort of participation mystique with the spiritual energy. It manifests as unquestioning devotion and reverence for the archetypal forces and resignation to fate and destiny. Individuals then loose the capacity to establish a sense of democracy between consciousness and the latent code, which is the goal of individuation.[69]

Perhaps these are gross generalizations and a simplistic view of the spiritual traditions; nevertheless, it is the dark side of an otherwise very soulful perspective on life and the universe.

How does Laxmi's specific incarnation as a form of Shakti, as the goddess of peace, prosperity and plenty, relate to the concept of the latent code? The latent code of Laxmi involves both prosperity and poverty. In other words, only when prosperity integrates poverty can one actualize their potential for wholeness and individuation.

India as a nation has historically been caught up in the latent code of the dark side of Laxmi, which is poverty and its compensatory spiritual wealth. The whole concept of prosperity was in the shadow mode. Prosperity in India was seen as materialism, as spiritual naiveté, and considered as a shadow attribute of the Laxmi archetype. Most recently, the trends in modern India have changed this outlook. India's growth edge has thrust it dramatically and suddenly into the global economy as a contender for second world status, and eventually it will likely and hopefully attain first world status as well.

It is interesting that the MahaLaxmi temple has mirrored India and has also gone through cycles of poverty and prosperity. Presently the temple is handsomely in the *black* in terms of its finances.

Reverence, Reflection, Respect - East and West

As I reflect on my visit to the MahaLaxmi temple in Mumbai, it seems apparent to me that while the East is lost in reverence for the latent code, it has compromised its capacity for discerning the totality of the code. This suspension of the reflective capacity then compromises the ego consciousness of the East, preventing it from reflecting on the archetypal intent of the latent code. This is apparent in glorifying suffering and poverty. This was made apparent to me when I was lost in reverence at the MahaLaxmi temple during the aarti prayer service that evening and suspended the task at hand.

The West, on the other hand, is so seduced by its ego consciousness, to the extent that it has relatively ignored the necessary reverence for the archetypal dimension of the latent code. While this ego identification appears to enhance the western sense of material mastery, it also may marginalize the spiritual dimension of their latent code. In the West, the balance is skewed in favor of reflection rather than reverence. While this certainly strengthens the ego consciousness, it may often compromise the connection with the sacred dimension of life and reduces it to a mere and relatively minor ego function. The whispers of the latent code are merely taken as one of many variables in the total economy of consciousness.

The danger in the West is that since archetypal intent of the latent code is marginalized in comparison to the ego consciousness, it must then speak through other mechanisms. In individuals, these manifest as medical or physical illness. In cultures, these mechanisms are seen in the reactivation of the demonic dimension of the archetype as was apparent in Nazi Germany and which Jung postulated as the activation of the dark side of the code of the pre-Christian warrior god Wotan archetype.[70]

I wonder: where does a happy and optimal balance in the total scheme of things lie as far as the relationship between the ego consciousness and the archetypal intent? I agree with Carl Jung that an optimal encounter between the two is one of a democracy between ego consciousness and the archetypal intent. Here both are equally represented in the final synthesis of consciousness. When either is marginalized, it may manifest in ways that are not always conducive to the optimal health of individuals, nations, or cultures. When the West is lost in its material ascendancy and its ego consciousness, the archetypal intent speaks either through medical or psychiatric symptoms, or through regression to primitive, cultist, spiritual regression, what one Indian author Gita Mehta calls "Karma Cola."[71] The East, on the other hand, struggles to establish the ascendancy of its material well-being through blatantly regressive materialistic enterprises. The recent explosion of nuclear devices by certain eastern nations to gain quick material ascendancy and respect in the fellowship of nations may be seen as such naive materialism.

Inadvertently, the East has activated the demonic aspect of the Shiva archetype, that of destruction. The dance of these light and dark, material and spiritual, eastern and western, masculine and feminine, dynamic and static forces continues as an undulating rhythm of time and history for individuals and cultures. When these forces are seriously out of balance, the dark feminine, the apparently negative dynamic feminine archetypal aspects of the latent code constellate to restore the homeostatic balance. This takes the form of the great dark goddess Kali.

In the preceding chapters, we explored the latent code of the goddess Shakti in her various profiles. Relational profiles of Shakti archetype include Parvati, Saraswati and Laxmi. Non-relational aspects of Shakti include Kali, the destroyer of the existing dysfunctional order in individuals and cultures, and Aditi, the goddess of void that follows Kali's clean up of the personality. Later Aditi becomes the harbinger of new beginnings. We have also explored how the latent code of the goddess Shakti guides the collective consciousness in the story of the MahaLaxmi temple and the building of the city of Mumbai. I hope that this chapter has introduced the readers to the potential of the latent code to guide not only an individual but a whole community and a collective enterprise, which may have profound impact on the life and history of our civilization. In the next chapter, I will discuss the latent code of our relationships, which may guide us to establish informed, vital and soulful relationships.

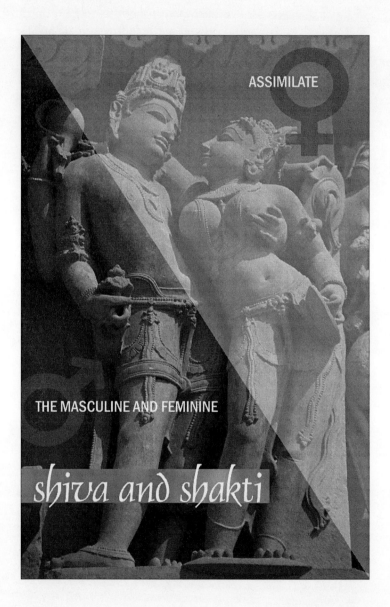

RESCUE FROM

...LY SWALLOWING THE POISON

neel kantha

CH 10
The Latent Code of Relationships
Why Shiva Holds Poison in His Throat

In the preceding chapters, we have explored how the latent code guides individuals and communities in life transitions and new beginnings. In this chapter, we will explore the latent code of the relationships that is relevant to our culture at the present time in our history. Men and women can move their relationship from the mundane to the sacred threshold of their potential if they honor the latent code of the relationships. The story of Shiva holding the poison in his throat with the help of his wife Shakti is the embodiment of this latent code of relationships. Join me now in unraveling the mystery of this story and how it can guide us not only in our relationships but also a meaningful relationship with our own soul.

One of the highest achievements of the human psyche is the process of assimilating the masculine and the feminine, shadow and light, superior and inferior, profane and sacred and all the opposite aspects of our soul potentials together into a whole. There is nothing redundant in the psychic economy. Every aspect of our personality has a purpose in the bigger picture of our life and the order of the universe. When the sacred marriage of these opposites in our personality is consummated, the highest potential of our personality emerges. We come into our essence. We are at our personal best in living out the latent code of our soul. Each individual and every culture has its own framework to synthesize these divergent aspects of their potential at different times and in different places. The myth of Shiva with the blue throat (poison throat) is one such myth, which is very relevant for our culture at this point in our culture. It is a story of how the great goddess Shakti rescues Shiva and the world from its self-destructive tendencies. It is a myth that to me best describes the relationship between

Shiva and Shakti, men and women, the masculine and feminine aspects of our culture at the present time.

The Sacred Marriage

Carl Jung described the heirosgamos, or sacred marriage, as "earthing" the Spirit and spiritualizing the Earth, the union of opposites and the reconciliation of the divided.[72] This is akin to the romance of Shiva and Shakti, the masculine and the feminine aspects of our personality. When they collaborate, the divine child, the soul within, our creative potential emerges. This may begin with a purely intra psychic *union* of intellect or reason with Eros or feeling.[73] The crowning essence of Jung's work was his concept of the *coniunctio (connection)* between the various aspects of the psyche at progressively higher levels of repetitive differentiation and uroboric (a serpent biting its own tail) reintegration towards evolving wholeness of the personality. In this union, ego and shadow, consciousness and complexes, anima and animus, superior, auxiliary and inferior functions, extroverted and introverted attitudes, mind, body, soul and spirit all gradually integrate at progressively more conscious levels, and ultimately rejoin the Universal or spiritual consciousness. The goal of such a sacred marriage between the Ego and the potentialities of the soul was wholeness of personality, not perfection.[74] The ultimate goal of such a sacred marriage between different aspects of the personality was a democracy between the Ego or consciousness and the unconscious and its archetypes.[75] I believe that in his views on the hierosgamos Jung laid out the foundation of a framework for integration of the masculine and feminine aspects of the individual personality and the collective culture, a mode in which both archetypes are available to an individual and the collective (human civilization) in its quest for connection with its highest potential.

In the Latent Code, I have explored many facets of the code with the back drop of the Goddess archetypes. In her Aditi aspect she creates new life out of the void, just as her

Olympian counterpart Gaia creates her own consort Uranus
to mate and thus create the cosmos and set in motion the
eternal dance and conflict between the Masculine and the
Feminine. Shakti may manifest as lover (Laxmi), mother
(Parvati), daughter (Saraswati), creator (Aditi) or destroyer
(Kali). But what aspect of the latent code is most relevant
in a contemporary patriarchal civilization? To amplify the
answer to this question, exploration of the myth of Shiva of
the Blue-Poison Throat has proven valuable. I have been
touched by this myth in my own marriage. It may also be
relevant in the present patriarchal culture in its dangerous
race towards self-destruction. Here is the story of Neel
Kantha- Shiva of the Blue-Poison Throat.

Neel (Blue) Kantha (Neck):
Shiva of the Blue-Poison Neck

As the lesser gods and the demons were fighting their
ongoing war, they found that the war was at an impasse.
Deadlocked, they went together to Brahma for guidance
as to how both sides might manage this impasse. Brahma
said that instead of fighting each other they could churn
the cosmic ocean and that by doing so they would get the
ambrosia or nectar that gave eternal life. The gods and
demons were pleased with this suggestion. Perhaps, they
thought, they could share the ambrosia, and everybody
could live together happily thereafter.

They decided to use Mount Mandera, the holy
mountain, to churn the ocean. Vishnu incarnated as the
tortoise supporting the mountain. The lesser gods and
the demons took the holy serpent, Vassuki, and wrapped
him around the mountain as a churning rope, the demons
taking one end of Vassuki and the gods taking the other.
But when the Serpent Vassuki got tired, he began to spout
venom. The gods and demons knew that if the venom fell
in the cosmic ocean, all of creation would be destroyed.
The problem was to find a storage receptacle for Vassuki's
venom.[76] Neither the gods nor the demons had an answer,
so as a last resort they decided to wake up Lord Shiva and

seek asylum in his precinct. Lord Shiva is an altruist. One can wake him from his trance and ask for his help, and as altruistic individuals (codependent types) generally do, he complies without regard for his own well-being or survival. Shiva said, "I'll solve the problem. I'll die, so that all else may live. Better that one dies than risk destroying all of creation." He then swallowed the poison to rescue the universe from its predicament. However, his wife Parvati came to his rescue out of love and concern. She said, "I can't stop you from swallowing the poison, but I will not allow you to die." She held him by the throat, saying to him, "You can swallow your throat full, but keep it up there; you cannot swallow it all the way down."

Thousands of years have passed since the churning of the cosmic ocean, and Shakti has been holding her husband, Shiva, by the neck. This is how Lord Shiva got the nickname 'Blue Neck,' Neel Kantha. Parvati has to protect him because if he swallows it, he will certainly die. Her trick is to choke him enough to keep the poison up in his throat, but not so much as to strangle him to death.

Don't Swallow the Poison

I think this story is, in many ways, a story both of the modern relationship and of the challenges facing us in a world in which the masculine enterprise rides rough shod over the feminine concerns for the survival of our civilization. Many people, driven by the unbalanced masculine enterprise without factoring in the impact on our civilization and future, look to their partners or lovers (or, alas, both) to rescue them from fully swallowing the toxic products of their aggressive and competitive strivings. How often people symbolically grab their partners by the neck and say, "We've got to have more quality time together to talk and reconnect! Relationships do not live on promises alone!"

The myth of Neel kantha has been very palpable in my life and marriage. Like the lesser gods and demons, in the first half of my life, I had been busy churning the collective ocean to claim my ambrosia. I emigrated from India to England and then to America for a better life and opportunities; I kept churning my professional life for more success and acclamation, I kept undertaking yet one more ambitious project after another. However, in this churning by my heroic masculine drive, I marginalized the feminine aspects of my relationship with my wife, my family, and my own soul. Precious relationships with my wife and children often took the back seat in the medical marriage. My creative and spiritual life was relativized to the rigors of the more glamorous professional drama. While I was lost in the world of masculine enterprise, initially it was my wife, Usha, who often got to my throat to reset the priorities of our life together. With her help and encouragement, I started to attend to my inner life and precious relationships. She fully supported the sacrifices we would have to make as a family for me to shift my work from relatively lucrative medical psychiatry to a more austere analytic and spiritually based psychiatric practice. As I internalize the latent code that my wife, Usha, helped me understand, I am learning to stay more at my own throat in a reflective mode rather than my wife having to monitor the balance of the opposites within my psyche. Consequently, she is freer to carry her own masculine drive, her own latent code, her sense of adventure and enterprise in the outer world as a restaurateur.

I have observed a similar pattern in many relationships of successful professionals. When such people are busy churning their professional lives in the hopes of material and professional ambrosia, they rake up a lot of karmic toxicity. Their relationships, families and inner lives are ignored. They engender relationship problems, workoholism, and often alcoholism. The hoped for ambrosia doesn't materialize. Either they end up as spare parts in corporate or professional waste heap, or if successful, the outer success does not nourish the soul. In such relationships, it is the partner who gets to the throats of their masculine driven partners to prevent them from swallowing the toxicity of their own making. Often, the masculine driven partner refuses to throw out the toxin and the other partner refuses to let him/her swallow it. This is experienced as a relationship problem, and such partners (initially reluctantly) seek therapy or else their relationship would end. In retrospect, most such patients are grateful that their partners had the love and integrity to confront them. It is very gratifying for me as a therapist to see such people take ownership of their own karmic consequences and attend to their spiritual life and precious relationships.

The latent code of the goddess that many contemporary feminine driven individuals carry for their partners protects these masculine driven people from becoming victims of the toxicity of society, yet it does not choke or restrict their activities so much that they die from overprotectiveness. This is a very burdensome task for a relationship to sustain. People caught in the masculine enterprise need to respect the preventive-mothering that their partner can provide them to protect them from their own misguided heroism and Maya (pursuit of wealth and affirmation). At the same time, these Shakti embodying individuals need to be able to mother without choking the other to death.

But this is not the best possible solution. When we see first in another person what actually is a facet of ourselves that we either cannot or will not recognize and own, we make another person responsible for our wholeness. In psychological language, we project what we cannot or will not see in ourselves to another who "carries" it for us. Projection of the unlived universal energies to the other partner tends to keep both women and men imprisoned in stereotypical gender roles: men being "all masculine" and women being "all feminine." The dance of Shiva and Shakti is more rhythmic when an individual develops all four phases of the feminine and masculine potentials in themselves: dynamic Masculine (enterprise), static Masculine (order), dynamic Feminine (creativity), and static Feminine (mothering). Cultivating all four phases of these energies in oneself is one of the great tasks of becoming a whole person.

The task of becoming whole falls to couples especially in the second half of life when they no longer wish to have a relationship structured according to the traditional or stereotyped gender roles. Then the relationship has the opportunity to become both a psychological relationship and a path to individuation, and to the individual wholeness of two persons bonded to each other. This accomplished, both women and men can look back on a life well lived.

Just as couples need to balance their mutual masculine and feminine role assimilations and projections, the culture as a whole needs to work on the assimilation of its potential for wholeness and soulfulness. Presently, our culture is caught in the masculine and patriarchal mode. We are in the process of mastering our environment at the expense of the integrity of mother earth. The answer is a soulful and responsible use of the resources of the planet with respect for the environment while we make responsible use of its resources. We are in the process of harvesting the mysteries of nuclear energy. We need to do it without raking up the poison of nuclear waste, which needs to be stored for thousands of years. We are in the process of understanding the mysteries of our inner life. We need to do it with respect for our souls, not by creating a mechanized super human race where the psyche is reduced to a sophisticated computer program. We need to work towards a human nature and civilization, where the material and the spiritual both have a vote on our deliberations and enterprise. We need to aspire to a civilization where the values of the East and the West, of modern and ancient cultures, with respect for welfare of the body and the welfare of the soul, and where the masculine and the feminine values all have an equal vote in managing of our lives.

In a committed relationship, each person realizes their own *latent code* to the fullest, yet both cherish and celebrate each other, themselves, and their relationship. This paradigm of an optimal relationship between committed individuals may also be a framework for the mature masculine and the sacred feminine to establish their marriage in our psyche. While the gifts of patriarchy are many, this "at Shiva's throat" attitude of the feminine may be necessary not only for the redemption of the masculine but also for the survival of our entire civilization.

CH 11
Attending to the Latent Code

Our life is like a spring. It needs constant renewal at its source. The latent code of our soul constantly renews and replenishes our life by the healing waters of the archetypes and their guiding code. Ultimately however, it the task of our ego or consciousness to undertake the task of tuning into the latent code of our soul under the auspices of the relevant archetypes and implement this code into our daily and lived life. This chapter will focus on the ego's responsibility to implement the guidance of the latent code and embody it in our life, work, play, creativity and spirituality.

To attend to the latent code, first we must get the basic map of our psyche in place. This involves acknowledging the presence of our consciousness and our personal unconscious. Our ego is the center of our consciousness, while the soul is the center of our total personality. The personal unconscious is in continuum with the collective unconsciousness or ancestral unconscious, which is embodied in the cumulative wisdom templates of our civilization, the archetypes. Our soul is the central archetype of our personality, and it synthesizes the energy from the latent code of different archetypes to transform it into the latent code of our individual personality. This is specific for each individual, like finger prints. The latent code of our soul connects our individual destiny with the flow of the universe and our place in the bigger plan of the Great Spirit. If we tune into our personal latent code, we join the symphony of the divine. If we stay disconnected from our latent code, we must return in different life forms in this universe, until we get it and fulfill our destiny. Additionally, we may leave our unfinished work, our karma, for our children and grandchildren to retire.[77]

In the first two chapters, I laid out the fundamentals of the latent code and how to decipher it. In this and the next chapter, we will discuss some pragmatic methods to attend to the latent code in our daily lives.[78]

Fig. 6

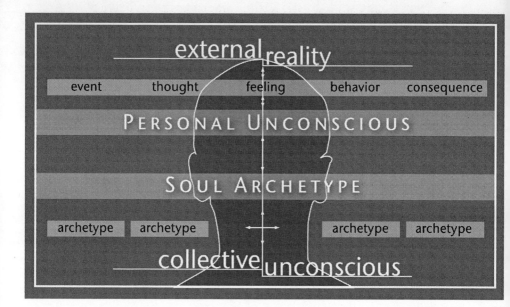

Now that we have established the tripartite structure of the latent code, consisting of the Ego, the Soul and the Archetypes, we will now focus on the interventions our ego consciousness must make to implement the latent code.

How can we attend to our souls and their connection to the primal soul in the hustle and bustle of everyday life? Short of seeking professional help, how can we honor the whispers of the soul day by day? How do we make our life a vessel that can contain the sacred and transform the profane raw stuff, the lead of routine, the dross of old habits, the scars of old wound, into the gold of the soul?

The individual soul, the *atman*, in Hindu terminology,

is a fractal of the primal soul, the *Brahman*. The individual soul, moreover, is capable of spiritual, psychological and physical experience. It is both our window to the primal soul and the "organ" that registers the quality of our lives. When our individual soul is afflicted, it whispers to us via our dreams, day dreams, fantasies, accidents, synchronistic events, hang ups or complexes, medical and psychiatric symptoms and relationship tangles. Moreover, our connection to the primal soul is obscured, sometimes to the point that we need to be vividly reminded that there is such a thing as a soul's latent code.

The Starting Point

The prerequisite and foundation for attending to the soul's latent code has three components: being in the present, noticing the whispers of the soul, and making time to reflect. The human mind chatters. There's always something going on in our minds. It's like a busy street corner in a metropolis: all kinds of emotionally-toned thoughts, hopes, fears, and memories crisscross and bump into each other that tug on our attention and distract us from what we intend to focus on. In order for us to be in the present, we have to do two things simultaneously: pay some attention to the chatter and maintain some degree of detachment. Our routine ego consciousness is in the experiencing and managing mode. The task of attending to the latent code calls for the cultivation of an observing ego, a detached consciousness that can become the reflective witness to its own experience. This moves the compass of the ego from action to reflection, the *measure twice cut once* approach to life.

We have to pay some attention to the chatter, because it is a signal from the soul. Each of the memories, fears, hopes, regrets, fantasies, and so on that scurries about has some degree of emotional charge of one kind or another. The emotional coloration and intensity tell us the significance of the specific content of consciousness and the content often identifies or symbolizes the area of life concerned and its potential to connect us with our latent code.

We also have to maintain a degree of distance, an "observing ego," as it is called. Total disconnection from emotion leaves only our rational minds on the job. Feeling is a function of the incarnated individual soul, and we need to be aware of our feelings if we are to attend to our souls. Only when we are able both to observe and to feel at the same time do we have the possibility of understanding the messages of the soul. If we let the heavy traffic that sometimes fills our minds run us down and carry us away, we have lost the necessary degree of detachment.

The second necessary element for attending to our individual souls is noticing the whispers of the soul. We must take time to actively reflect on what is going on in our lives, outer and inner. We must also make space in our busy lives for active reflecting. It's as important as regularly brushing our teeth. Actively reflecting is a habit we need to form, and it means that we stop, look, and listen *before* the alarm goes off, *before* a complex erupts, *before* a relationship goes sour, b*efore* we fall ill.

I have already mentioned the importance of paying attention to our emotions and to the traffic in the mind that disrupts our tranquility. As I will discuss below in detail, our complexes, our relationship fascinations and antipathies, our dreams and fantasies, synchronistic events, and medical and psychiatric symptoms are all important messages from the latent code of our soul that offer us information on the condition of our souls. It is important that we *actively reflect* on these messages the soul sends us.

The third prerequisite for attending to our souls is time. We have to take time to notice what is going on. We have to take time to reflect on what we notice. When an emotionally colored thought or image or experience of whatever degree of intensity completely fills our consciousness, we do not have the degree of detachment necessary to reflect on it. Setting aside time to reflect, safe from intrusion and distraction, creates the sacred space in which we can ponder the whispers of the soul and explore their meaning for our life.

The three part foundation—being in the present, noticing the whispers of the soul, and making time to reflect— is an ongoing challenge. We don't get it perfect the first time. All three elements demand our patience and discipline. With practice, we can steadily improve our skills and increase our harvest of insight. Let us now very briefly review specific whispers of the soul and consider techniques for working with them.

Fascinations and Antipathies

Wherever we experience fascination or antipathy we are reacting to a reflection of some part of our soul's latent code that is not adequately integrated into our conscious personality. Attraction tells us that we want what we see; repulsion tells us the opposite. Either way, our soul is reacting to a reflection of its unlived potential. For one reason or another, this unlived potential of our soul has not been ennobled in our lived life. A fascination or antipathy is a signal from the soul that the present situation offers optimal conditions for incarnation of this potential. We do not fully control this fascination or antipathy, this attraction or repulsion, since it emanates from the depths of our soul rather than from our waking consciousness. The fascination or antipathy can be in response to another person, an idea, a possible experience, a memory. The list is nearly inexhaustible.

How to Work with Fascinations and Antipathies

Carefully note the content and the emotions you experience. Every detail may be significant, so do not edit, and do not elaborate (yet). Get the facts. Systematically review the content and emotion. For each image in the content, and for each emotion, note down what spontaneously comes to mind.

What or whom does the image remind you of? Where or with whom have you felt these emotions? What was or is the significance of the image or emotion? What role did the image or emotion play in your life in the past? What role does the image or emotion play now? If you are exploring a fascination, what is it in the content of the fascination that you want as a part of yourself? How would incorporating the content of the fascination change your life now?

If you are exploring an antipathy, what is it in the content of the antipathy that you want to disown? How would eliminating the content of the antipathy change your life now? List and prioritize the steps that you can take to effect the changes you have identified. Chart your progress.

Dan is a physician in his 40s, a surgeon, who consulted me for depression in the midst of his divorce. He reported that he was a very inartistic, left-brain individual with little interest in art, literature, and the lighter side of life. However, he was very disturbed that he found himself aimlessly wandering in the evenings, and invariably ending up at a toy shop, gazing in the window with no conscious interest in anything in particular. He was concerned that this was some kind of obsession, his interest in science toys. I invited him to honor this fascination rather than be critical of it. I inquired of him as to how he would see the science toys fitting into his life style. He said that was the last thing on the planet he would want to do, as he already had a basement full of toys except a telescope. He was unconsciously fascinated and consciously antipathetic to this telescope. I proposed to him that perhaps this was precisely what he needed to do to honor his interest in astronomy in some way, perhaps by taking some classes at the local university in astronomy. Dan undertook this enterprise mostly to placate me and to get me off his back. I am glad to report that he is now an adept amateur astronomer, using a specialized computerized telescope, and has received considerable acclaim for his blossoming talent. This interest in astronomy was a childhood dream that was strongly discouraged by his physician father, who wanted his son to follow in his footsteps. Astronomy

now embodies feeling and aesthetic aspects of his soul.
Additionally, getting touch with these finer aspects of his
soulfulness, he has been able to repair his marriage. The
fascination with the stars put him in touch with latent code
of his soul to engage his creative psyche.

Relationships and Projections

Relationships are an important area where we can
attend to the soul's latent code. These are best navigated
by the latent code of relationships discussed in the chapter
on Shiva and Shakti. More focused than fascinations and
antipathies, close relationships bring out both the best and
the worst in us. Close relationships can be a crucible in
which the fire of our intense emotions transforms us. The
old saying, "opposites attract," is often true. Frequently we
are attracted to somebody who seems to us to be our "other,
missing half." When this is indeed the case, the half we are
missing is usually difficult to develop, and often at odds
with a more developed facet of our personality, so that after
the initial phase (the "honeymoon" of the relationship),
we experience disappointment and "disillusionment." We
discover that the other is not all we had at first experienced:
"You're not the person I thought you were." This realization
tells us that we were seeing only part of the other person,
the part that was our own unknown face reflected to us,
and that made us feel complete when we were with the
other.

An overwhelming attraction is pretty good evidence
that we are experiencing the other person as an opposite to
ourselves. Although we don't recognize it at the time, the
"overwhelming attraction" is a measure of the gulf between
us and the other, but also between our conscious view of
ourselves and our unlived soul, as well as the amount of
energy needed to bridge that gulf. If we can learn how to
deal with the difficult and attractive aspects of relationship,
we have the opportunity to access and make our own a
facet of our soul that has always been carried by some other
person.

How to Work with Relationships and Projections

Take careful note of the thoughts, fantasies, and emotions you have about the other. Identify both the qualities, characteristics, and habits in the other that: a) you desire, like, or love and b) you dislike or hate. Who in your earlier life have you desired, liked, or loved with feelings similar to those you have for the other in your present relationship? a) How did that person (those people in the past) respond to your desire, liking, or love? b) How did that person (those people in the past) respond to your dislike or hate? What developed qualities in you does the other person in your present relationship enhance? Which of your underdeveloped (inferior) qualities or skills does the other person alert you to or criticize you for?

Work out a plan of action to develop your inferior skills and abilities hitherto carried by your partner. Monitor your progress as to how much of what was carried by the other is now managed by you, using your own skills and potentials.

Rachel and Steve have been married for two years. Steve is a quiet, caring, devoted husband, and engineer by trade. Rachel is a vivacious, beautiful, attention-seeking hysteric. When they would go to a bar, she would socialize effervescently with other men, often get drunk, and want to stay there till the wee hours of the morning, while Steve would be tired and insist on leaving in a timely manner to be prepared for his work the following day.

Rachel's father abandoned her mother when her mother was still pregnant. She never met her father, nor has she ever seen his picture. Consciously she found strength and security in Steve's rock-solid personality, but unconsciously she kept provoking him. On closer exploration of their relationship, it was apparent that she had a hostile-dependent attachment to Steve, attempting to reincarnate the missing father, provoking him to set limits on her as if he were her parent and simultaneously behaving in a provocative and contemptuous manner to metabolize her rage at an abandoning father.

In a session, I invited Rachel to explore what she would do if Steve left after offering to take her home and agreed to come and pick her up from the bar when she was ready. She commented that she would be enraged and get drunk just to get even with him. I deepened this image. She reported that she would get drunk several times and be there till six in the morning, hoping that Steve would call and come looking for her. "What if he didn't?" I inquired. "Then reluctantly I'd call my friend Mary to come pick me up." I exclaimed, "So finally you would take care of yourself!?" Rachel was amused and amazed that she could parent herself and did not need to project this need for a father onto her loving husband all the time. This is one vignette from a multitude of such interventions that gradually helped Rachel recognize that what she was seeking in her marriage was a father who would take care of her and with whom she could retire her anger at father for abandoning her. Gradually she has learned to parent herself. The marriage was unburdened of this dynamic of hostile dependency. Her own capacity to be her good parent and a loving wife was reincarnated in the sacred vessel of the marriage. The hostile dependency on her husband became the channel for Rachel to activate the latent code of her soul to engage the archetype of father within, the missing father she had projected onto her husband all her married life.

Steve had always wanted to be a playful, carefree bohemian person, but his rough and tumble childhood with an alcoholic father and a depressed mother did not permit such a luxury. He projected his bohemian life onto Rachel, who lived it out in a hysterical lifestyle. As Rachel took ownership of her self-parenting, Steve gradually started to relinquish his heroic adaptation and made room for the more laid back, relaxed, and playful aspects of his soul.

Complexes or Hang-ups

Complexes are a normal part of our human psychic make-up. Not all complexes are troublesome, but the troublesome complexes are the ones that we most often notice. Complexes are our emotionally vulnerable spots. We "go ballistic" or "fly off the handle" when somebody triggers a volatile complex by word or deed.

Complexes take shape around typical human experiences: birth, death, marriage, transitions, parents, siblings, and so on. The core pattern of the complex is archetypal (that is, typically human, and not a personal acquisition); the specific content, or shell, however, derives from our life experience. Together, core and shell constitute the whole complex.

Complexes manifest in several ways. Perhaps the most frequent are in our relationships (as fascinations, antipathies, and other strong emotional reactions); in "spontaneous" floods and (sometimes) discharges of strong emotion; and in dreams and fantasies (that I will discuss below). When a complex is activated, our behavior changes in four ways: our adaptation regresses to that of an earlier developmental level; we become (much) more emotional; we blame the other for "making" us react; and our emotions tend to rumble about in us for a long time. Learning to understand the soul's message sent in the form of activated complexes offers us a stepping stone to fuller actualization of our latent code.

How to Work with Complexes

There are several ways to work with complexes, starting with recognizing when we have become unusually emotional.

Identify the current trigger event that activated our emotions (in case it is not obvious). Identify and note down: a) our emotions; b) our fantasies; c) our memories of similar experiences (people, places, events). What unresolved issue or undeveloped potential does the complex represent? How effective is our usual way of dealing with the activated complex? Work out a sequence of different behaviors (in increasing order of difficulty) to address the core issue in the complex. Chart your progress by noting contra-habits

and behaviors contrary to your own nature in situations
and with individuals that activate your complex: increased
lead time; more rapid recovery from complex discharge;
less frequent activation.

Trudy, a mid-level executive, was referred by her
employer because of relationship problems with her
peers. In her first session Trudy took control and spoke
incessantly, giving me little window to get in on the
conversation. When this pattern continued for a few
sessions, I confronted her. She broke down in remorse,
tears, and a long silence. I invited her to share the image
in her mind. She recalled an incident on Christmas Eve
when she was eight years old. Trudy's father was drunk
and watching T.V. Her mother was depressed and had
retreated to her bedroom. The oldest two siblings were
trying to manage the household. Trudy was the second
youngest of ten children. The younger children were in
chaos, and Trudy remembered darting first to her father,
then to her mother's room, chattering incessantly, trying
to revive them from their alcoholic and depressive stupors
above the din of the chaotic family. Trudy had learned
this anxious, excited, talkative method to resuscitate
her emotionally dead parents. This became an intrusive,
overbearing complex, which regularly got activated in her
staff meetings. We worked on the dynamic roots of this
complex. Through a long process, Trudy learned to honor
and hold her anxiety and to hear others out. Paradoxically,
people now sought out her "chattering", her views and
opinions with respect and reverence for her creativity.
She has been steadily climbing the corporate ladder and
has made substantial contributions to the success of her
enterprise. Her overbearing complex offered us a path
to her latent code. When she worked out the childhood
dynamic that created this overbearing complex, she was
able to claim her authentic authority and well deserved
affirmation at work and in her personal life.

Dreams

Dreams show us the soul's view of our life. As a general rule, a dream supplies the information that consciousness either does not have or does not adequately perceive or value. The following very general rules of thumb will help you orient yourself to your dreams.

Typically, dreams have a recognizable *dramatic structure*: setting, development, turning point, and resolution. Sometimes one or more of these elements is missing, in which case we have an unfinished dream. (Don't worry; from time to time we all get dreams that are or seem incomplete. We can still work with what we have.)

When *known people and places* appear in your dream, they refer either to the actual people and places or probably to something in us that resembles those people and places in our unconscious. For example, when your mother or father appears in your dream, the message may be about the mothering or fathering capacity in yourself. When a known person or place appears in your dream but differs from reality in some way (age, looks, actions, attitude), you can be pretty sure that the dream is talking about a part of your psyche that functions like that person or place.

Dreams do not tell us what to do; rather, they provide a different view that may augment, modify, correct, complete, or contradict our conscious position. As a rule, when a dream presents an extreme view of a situation, it is counterbalancing an equally but opposite extreme conscious position. In other words, the truth lies somewhere in the middle in this case.

Working with one's own dreams is challenging because the dream presents the view that we do not consciously see. In other words, the dream fills in what our blind spot misses. (Often it is expedient to work individually or in a group with a therapist or analyst skilled in dream work.)

One last word: Our dreams can tell us a lot more than we know. Other people will often see meaning in our dreams where we see nothing but the images themselves. Take care that the person(s) to whom you tell your dreams is trustworthy and bears you no ill will. In telling your dream, you are exposing sides of yourself that even you don't see to the view of others.

The second last word: Working on one's own dreams is about the process of dream work, not on the outcome of the work. It's amazing. The "product" you end up with may not look like much, but the process you have engaged in works on you and will subtly deepen your consciousness and informs your consciousness of the intentions of your soul. Here are the basic elements of dream work you need to know; with practice you can acquire the fundamental skills.

How to Work with Dreams

To catch your dreams: Keep your dream notebook and pen or pencil next to your bed. When you go to bed, suggest to yourself that you will recall a dream *and* that you will write it down.

Write down your dream as soon as you awake. To work with your dreams: Review the dream you want to work on. Re-visualize the images; feel the emotions again; re-experience the dream. This brings the dream back to life. Consider the structure of your dream. Does it have a setting? Does the action develop? Is there a turning point? Does the dream reach a conclusion? (Often our dreams end before the turning point or the conclusion, which implies that the development cannot go further at the time.)

Contemplate each image. Note down the feelings, memories, and impressions that arise when you contemplate each image, situation, person, etc., in the dream. *Stay with the image; circle around it; don't let your associations lead you far afield.* What does the dream appear to be commenting on in your life or your relationships? How you get around in the world? The (emotional and mental) space you inhabit? What is opposing you or assisting you?

Compare the current dream with other dreams in which the same or similar persons, places, themes, and images have appeared. What changes do you notice? How

216   is your presence in the dream now different than it was in the past?

After working on your dream, note how your emotional state has changed in the course of your dream work.

Honor your dream by carrying out some action or ritual in your waking life that honors the images and intent of the dream. For example, if a long-forgotten friend appears in your dream, first understand what aspect of quality of this friend you need to activate in your present life to deal with a present situation. Additionally, pick up the phone and call your friend. If you honor your dream and its images by some sacred ritual, the dreams will honor and reward you by continuing to send helpful, guiding messages. It establishes a positive feedback loop.

In one of my recent dreams, there was a huge, gray garbage truck that I was using to deliver food for my wife's catering business. I inquired of her why we needed such a big truck, and would a small, cute, yellow delivery van with her restaurant's logo on it not be more practical and functional. Then my friend and mentor, Dr. Terrence Lear, was visiting us from England. Terry and I took this garbage truck for a ride, and to my amazement, he said that he had a one-day lesson in how to use this garbage truck as an amphibian vessel; we sailed off to a small island off the Milwaukee coast with our families and spent a day picnicking on the beach of this island. We had a small condo for the day, which had a magnificent view of the Milwaukee city skyline. I realized that this was no ordinary truck, and I just needed some brief instruction to explore its amphibian wonders. Consciously I had been trying to simplify my life, like the elegant little yellow delivery van, but it always gets complicated and burdensome like the large gray garbage truck. I decided to accept the cumbersome complexities of my life, including acceptance of my wife's restaurant business that encumbered my conscious life while deepening my soulfulness. I am honoring my spiritual calling in that I must navigate this truck onto the waters of my unconscious and get a view of life from outside-in, from island to mainland, and relinquish my wish to be mainland and mainstream. Paradoxically accepting my *karma* of complexity in my life is actually starting to make it simpler. To honor the dream, I went to the toy store that weekend and bought a cute yellow delivery van and a huge gray garbage truck, and I have laid them side by side in my study. The dream instructed me about my latent code. My life was not going to be quaint and simple; I must honor the cumbersome, chaotic complexity of my life and keep cleaning it up regularly with the help of the garbage truck! This garbage truck was an amphibian vessel, which could navigate land and water. As a psychoanalyst, I must engage the challenges of the conscious outer life symbolized by land and stay reflective about the mysteries of the unconscious life—the waters of the psyche.

Synchronistic Events

Synchronistic events are those meaningful coincidences that we notice. For example, dreaming about somebody you haven't seen or talked to in months and getting a postcard or letter from them the same day, or the occurrence of similar or identical thoughts, ideas, dreams at the same time to different people in different places. Neither the one nor the other coincidence can be explained by causality. Synchronistic events are evidence of a close connection between the two or more parties or things involved. They are a kind of "heads up!" urging us to pay attention.

The soul arranges synchronistic events to draw our attention to the constellation of the energies, events, people, and circumstances in such a way that some aspect of our soul potential can be embodied in our life at that moment. It is a mysterious and sacred moment when cosmic forces, our soul energy, and events and people in our outer life are in optimal alignment for some invisible aspect of our soul to become visible, if only we acknowledge it, attend to it, and act upon it in a conscious manner.

A colleague of mine and I decided to meet one day to discuss a possible research idea. With our busy schedules we both decided to have a brown bag meeting. To our amazement, we found that both of us had, independently, brown bagged a grilled chicken sandwich on whole wheat bread with dill pickle and bags of potato chips (of the same size bags). Immediately I knew that our souls had spoken and that the outcome of our cooperation would be numinous. We wrote an excellent little article as co-authors, which was published in a reputable journal, received broad acclaim, and made a small but significant contribution to improving a certain treatment method. This synchronistic event activated the latent code of twinship and collaboration with the friend.

Medical and Psychiatric Symptoms

Medical and psychiatric symptoms are the soul's most urgent distress call and the most clear cut message from the latent code. If you are experiencing any strange physical symptoms (e.g., shortness of breath, or difficulty breathing; dizziness; chest pains; chronic headaches; blood in your urine or stool; etc.) or recurrent bouts of depression, anxiety, hallucinations, loss of time, or severe relationship difficulties, you should consult your primary physician and ask for treatment or referral.

Once your symptoms have been professionally diagnosed and the appropriate treatment regimen begun, it may be worthwhile to explore the message the soul is trying to communicate to your ego consciousness. The depression and the panic disorder may be the call of the mother archetype inviting us to mother ourselves more adequately and establish a ground of physical safety and psychological security. The problems of prostate or endometriosis may be alerting us to attend to the latent code of the father archetype and attend to our needs of self-parenting, establishing a fertile ground for generativity and healthy ambition. Stomach and gastro-intestinal problems may be the call of the latent code of the warrior archetype, calling us to attend to the inner hero or heroine within us, to step up to the plate to attend to the challenges and opportunities of life. Heart problems are often the activation of the latent code of the lover archetype. It calls us to attend to our feelings, relationships and reassess what is really of value in our life and reset our priorities. Thyroid and throat problems may be the call of the latent code of the divine trickster, the Hermes or the Krishna archetype, calling us to attend our capacity to communicate with compassion and wisdom. Migraine headaches may be the call of the latent code of leadership, inviting us to wear our crown around our head and establish leadership in our community by altruistic endeavors. The problems of autism, schizoid personality and other disorders of social withdrawal like social phobia, avoidant personality, etc. may be the activation of the latent code of guru, mentor, wise man and wise woman archetypes inviting us to honor the crucial dimensions of spirituality by relativising social entangles. Medical and psychiatric symptoms are a final distress call from the latent code of our soul to alert us to the danger of suffocating, alienating, or losing our soul. On the other hand, if we respond to this call, we have one last opportunity to join the bridge that leads us back to the soul. A hard-driving, controlling, logic-driven outcome-oriented, emotionally distant executive gets chest pains as a prelude to an impending heart attack. Symbolically this may be a call from his soul to address and honor his heart chakra, the feeling realm before he loses his soul-and perhaps his life.

These are ways to honor the whispers of the soul, to attend to its message, and to implement its intent to establish healing of our wounded lives, and wholeness of our incomplete existence. Such a life then becomes a sacred temple for our soul, and all aspects of our being have the potential to manifest and enhance our life in countless ways. More importantly, we now have the opportunity to live out the meaning and the mystery of our own unique latent code on the stage of our life and of the larger human community.

More Ways to Listen for the Soul's Latent Code

In addition to the ways of responding to the Soul's whispers (by working on our dreams, dealing with our complexes, attending to our relationships, noticing synchronistic events, etc.), there are several other approaches that are of value: silence, meditation, spontaneous writing, journaling, active imagination, and divination. I will briefly discuss each.

Solitude

Philosophers have aptly noted that solitude is the food of the soul. I have found that the capacity to invoke and honor solitude is crucial to attend to the latent code of our soul. When we regularly maintain some amount of solitude in our lives, we create the indispensable precondition for opening consciousness to the invisible unconscious background, the ocean whose invisible currents carry the ego and inform our individual soul. The wisdom of the universe is now available to us.

In the hustle and bustle of modern materialistic society, it is not easy to cultivate a daily period of solitude. If we recognize our need for solitude and protect it, however, it can become a bridge connecting us to our individual soul and, further, to the primal soul. The triangle of the latent code is now completed by connecting the three dots; ego consciousness, soul reflection and universal flow of wisdom. For example, you can devote some regular daily time to retreating within yourself when you do nothing but sit quietly and see what emerges into your consciousness. Later, after this period of solitude, record what emerged in your journal and reflect on it to get in touch with the deeper feelings and images that arose.

On occasions when you cannot create the space of solitude, improvise. I have often counseled individuals who, when commuting to and from work, instead of turning on the radio should maintain quiet and silence, converting the commute time into a time for solitude, silence, and communion with their souls.

Silence

Silence makes room for the whispers of the soul to become audible to our monkey mind. In many of the great spiritual and cultural traditions of the East and the West, the importance of silence and solitude has regularly been emphasized. Examples include the Roman Catholic tradition of retreat, daily silence, solitude, prayer, and meditation; the great Buddhist tradition in which monks maintain silence and solitude to experience the inner spiritual ground; and the Zen practice of sitting in silence.

Mahatma Gandhi, the great Indian spiritual leader, followed a ritual of maintaining total silence one day each week. He participated in all activities of life but remained essentially nonverbal and quiet. This was a day when he allowed the outside world and his inner spiritual world to affect him, without mediation or verbal intervention on his own behalf.

This mode of ritual silence is referred to in Indian holy scriptures as the maun wratha, the silence ritual. It is often fascinating to see what emerges when we do not interact verbally with the world around or within us, but rather watch what unfolds on the stage of life. When we do not try to modify what is going on through speech, we gain a unique opportunity to palpate the pulse of our inner and outer environments.

Language and speech, among the higher achievements of evolution, not only express, but also limit, consciousness. Because our intuitive images come from the deepest source of being, language often cannot translate them into any known concept. When we become too earthbound by conditioned consciousness and by the use of language for self-expression and communication with others, we limit what we can experience and perceive to the bounds set by the spoken word. So when we maintain total silence for a period of time, we temporarily abandon language and free ourselves to explore the territory of our inner and outer worlds, unfettered by linguistic maps.

When we combine solitude and silence, we shut out

the external world, as well as our linguistic interaction with it and our filtering of it. We then have the opportunity to perceive and experience inner images and riches because we are not trying to force them to fit the procrustean bed of our vocabulary. These conditions of silence and solitude are most conducive to tune into the latent code of the soul and the wisdom of the flow of the universe.

Meditation

The great Rishis, the holy men and women of the east, have long postulated that we live in three states of consciousness: awake, asleep and dreaming. But the transition between these states involves engaging the "gap" in our states of consciousness. In this gap, we are tuned into the flow of the great energies of the universe, its timeless wisdom, its infinite void, its immense potential for new creation and countless possibilities. It is also a realm of great danger, where the uninitiated can get lost in the dark side of the cosmos and not find the way back into human consciousness. Different meditative traditions of all the great cultures have some guidelines to soulfully engage this sacred space. Transcendental meditation is one such tradition of the East. The latent code of Aditi guides us in this realm of the gap, the flow, the void, and paves the way to tap into the vast potential of the wisdom of the universe.

There are essentially two forms of meditation: directed meditation that focuses on a mantra (a sound, syllable, word, or phrase, usually drawn from scripture or the sayings of a teacher), and undirected meditation that observes whatever floats through consciousness without holding it in focus. Both forms are valuable. Focused meditation disciplines the mind to attend to only the object of choice, ignoring all distractions. Undirected meditation disciplines the mind to detach, to let go.

A variation of directed meditation (useful in dream work) involves circumambulating an image. Choose an image (from a dream or a fantasy), focus on it, and note what comes to mind, always maintaining the chosen image as the center point around which your associations gather. The challenge of circumambulatory meditation is to keep returning to the chosen image and not follow your associations away from the image to which you chose to associate.

In the section on active imagination later in this chapter, we will discuss a special meditative, which was formulated by psychologist Carl Jung.

Studio Time

Studio time is that part of our lives that we devote exclusively to expressing and getting in touch with the creative flow of our soul and the underlying creative rhythm of the universe. It is time we regularly set aside every week when we exclude all other agendas, responsibilities, and distractions, and place our skills of expression exclusively in the service of the creative spirit. It is a tree house for the inner child in us. One may find it on the lake fishing, walking in the wilderness with your journal or drawing tablet, or a while sitting in a quiet nook in the basement of your home.

This morning, I decided I would write something about the creative process without making any outline ahead of time. Of course, once I capture the ideas in whatever order they occur to me, I then subject them to the academic process of restructuring, rearranging, and adding references, life experiences, case examples, and other materials.

Working on what comes to me spontaneously establishes an appropriate partnership between the creative source of my latent code and my outer ego consciousness. Their dance will become apparent in the ultimate outcome of my creative endeavor, which I hope will be an intelligent, well-written essay that respects both the unconscious source of the ideas and my accumulated knowledge, experience, and judgment on the subject.

To make optimal use of studio time, try to set aside the

same time every week, or several times a week. It should be a quiet time without intrusions, as studio time is spent in solitude. You also need to have the tools and materials for your mode of expression. If you are a painter, you are in your studio where you have your canvas and your paints. Choose a quiet time when you can draw from inner inspiration, images, and ideas. Because I am interested in writing, I set up my tape recorder Saturday night so that on Sunday morning I am ready in my studio time to start writing some of my ideas on whatever subject I have chosen beforehand.

Occasionally, no inspiration emerges. You should honor that, too, because the unconscious may be incubating some particular idea of which you are not aware at the time. Nevertheless, it is essential to set aside the studio time on a regular basis to give the unconscious and the ego consciousness an opportunity to enter a partnership that may bring forth something unexpected.

The value of this exercise in studio time is to let nature speak— to let the latent codes unfold on the stage of consciousness. People who give themselves studio time have discovered that this exercise, when regularly practiced, opens the floodgates of creativity.

Journaling

Journaling is more structured than spontaneous writing or painting, or whatever your medium of expression may be. Perhaps the best-known journal format is that developed by Ira Progroff. You can, of course, create your own journal format. For example, you may have sections on daily life, dreams, meaningful personal encounters, synchronistic events, or activated complexes. As you work the various parts of your journal, look for recurring patterns (between dreams and daily events, or meaningful encounters and activated complexes). When, for example, a dream figure reappears several times, try to discover more about that figure by practicing active imagination.

Yantra Meditation

In earlier chapters, I have discussed the basics of the Yantra and the structure of their sacred geometry and their function in helping us focus the energies of the latent code of specific archetypes in amplifying the healing energy of the code. Once your soul work and life stage assessment have helped to establish what archetype you need to guide your present life path, you may meditate on the corresponding Yantra and supporting Mantra (sacred word) to help you center your self in the matrix of that archetype. If you are a student, you may benefit from Saraswati Yantra; if you're embarking on new project, you will need the support of Ganesha Yantra; if you are aspiring to peace, prosperity, plenty and marital and domestic bliss, you will do well in connecting with the energies of Sri Yantra. If you need to untangle a messy life situation, you may need to contemplate on the Kali Yantra. Sometimes, it may be helpful to draw the Yantra with love, devotion and reverence, and it may impart its energies to your ego to do the necessary work to implement the latent code of your soul. Since these techniques have been discussed in individual chapters where relevant, I will refer the readers to individual chapters to explore these methods.

Advanced techniques and practices

There are several additional ways of opening yourself to the whispers of the soul, like sand tray technique, divination methods and most importantly the process of Active Imagination. These are advanced practices that you should engage in only under the guidance of a competent practitioner. In the next chapter, we will discuss the process of active imagination as a proactive method to engage the latent code under the auspices of goddess Aditi.

CH 12
Dialogue with the Latent Code of the Soul
Active Imagination

We live in three states of consciousness: awake, asleep and dream state. Each of these states is physiologically distinct as evidenced by the electroencephalographic recordings of the brain during these three states. More advanced brain imaging techniques have confirmed these findings. Rishis and wise men and women in the East have known this for thousands of years. However, the easterners have been greatly intrigued by the process of transition between these states. What happens to our mind, brain, body and soul when we are in transition between these states? Researchers on transcendental meditation have studied these transition modes in great detail, and this phenomenon is the subject of continuing intense neuropsychological investigation. The transitional space is the fourth dimension of our existence, and since we are neither awake, asleep nor dreaming, we are suspended in the void, the realm of the goddess Aditi. When we engage this void, it opens up the possibility of creating new consciousness with the help of the latent code. The meditative and contemplative practices of all the great traditions, including Buddhist mindfulness, transcendental meditation, Christian contemplative practices, Yoga and other methods help to engage this void and its healing potential. When we are suspended in this void, we are in direct communion with the healing energy of the Spirit and the flow of the latent code of the universe. However, most of these practices are a one way street, tuning in and receiving the guidance of the latent code of the universe. Psychologist Carl Jung made a giant leap forward in dealing with this fourth dimension of consciousness when he invented a method to actively engage this void. He coined the term "Active Imagination" to describe this method.

Active Imagination is a conscious, voluntary dialogue between the ego and the unconscious under the auspices of goddess Aditi. During active imagination Aditi helps us to consciously activate a complex or a hang up and modify it. After his breakup with Freud, Jung went through a tumultuous time, his dark night of the soul. He called this a state of disorientation. Jung honored this void – the "not knowing" – and engaged his unconscious in a dialogue. It is my hypothesis that this was his encounter with Aditi. During this confrontation with the unconscious,[79] Jung developed the method of active imagination and encountered the archetypes, including the archetype of the soul. This was his most depressing yet the most creative phase, when he laid the groundwork for many of his later theories. Jung used active imagination to meet his sub- personalities. He encountered the wise old man and the anima archetypes. Philemon, the wise old man figure, was the deep archetypal core of his father complex initially projected onto Freud.

Active imagination is a method of personifying the unconscious. It is a bridge between the conscious and a selected aspect of the unconscious and in this context it can be seen as an activation of the transcendent function or a bridge between our consciousness, our soul and the universal spirit under the watchful guidance of Aditi.

Using the template of the latent code, the process of active imagination is analogous to creating a psychological Yantra. In this Yantra of active imagination, the seeker of the code uses the square or gate of consciousness to enter into the realm of the circle or the unconscious to engage the mystery of the latent code of the soul to guide the consciousness with the help of the present myth of the seeker. The goal is to seek the center or the Bindu which guides the individual on his path of spiritual engagement and life lived in accord with one's latent code. The reader may want to refer to the Yantra basics in the chapter on "Deciphering the Latent Code."

Method of Active Imagination

The starting point of the active imagination can be a dream image, a mood, or any spontaneous visual image.

Von Franz[88] was the first to describe the four steps involved in the active imagination. It is the conscious attempt to modify and temporarily suspend the ego complex to accentuate the faint whisper of the unconscious in the sacred realm of Aditi. Here are the four steps of the active imagination:

1. The Invitation to the Unconscious

This is a term introduced by Robert Johnson[89], which involves several layers of engagement of the unconscious. First, we must empty the mind from the trains of thought of the ego – the "monkey mind." The ego now invites the inner images from the unconscious to come to the surface and make contact with our conscious mind. Rituals like closing your eyes, slowed breathing (discussed later in this chapter) and gradually relaxing your body introduce the relaxation response of the body. This may lead to reduction of self-consciousness. Such an altered state of the ego leads to intensification of the feelings. At this point the consciousness shifts from logical thinking to archaic, primitive or primary process thinking (imaginal, non-rational and images and pictures). Ego's role in this psychic imaginal space is that of the conscious recorder— the scribe of the soul.

My patient John reported in one of our sessions that he was feeling sad, blue, moody and depressed. I invited him to personify this feeling. Gradually, this feeling took the form of his favorite aunt, Mita, a soulful favorite aunt, a spinster, whom he was very close to as a child. John would often go to Aunt Mita's home after school and hang out. She made him feel calm and tranquil. John was diagnosed as an Attention Deficit Hyperactive child. Aunt Mita was an island of serenity in his otherwise chaotic, driven life. Mita was a symbol of serenity and sacred space. Because of his personality and hyperactivity disorder, John would confuse serenity with depression and boredom. Gradually, he was able to tune into the call of Aditi to establish this island of tranquility in this sea of chaos.

2. The Ego's dialogue with the Soul

Von Franz warns of two common mistakes at this juncture. The individual either fixes the image and nothing further happens, or fantasy runs loose and image changes too quickly. In contrast to this passive fantasy, active fantasy is creative, synthetic, and active and requires effort on the part of the ego. Individuals can attempt to alter the course of the experience by becoming the agent of fantasy instead of its victim. One allows things to happen; one does not make them happen. Jung distinguishes between Phanatasia (a subjective figment of the mind) and Imaginatio (an image making, form creating activity). Now emerges an imaginal dialogue between the conscious ego and a personified part of the unconscious. It may be an auditory approach in which the voice of the unconscious is imaginally heard in response to the questions. Alternatively, other modes of dialogue with the unconscious include painting, sculpting, movement, dancing or writing.

My patient John, whom I presented above, learned to have a written dialogue with his long dead Aunt Mita whenever he felt overwhelmed in his driven life. She symbolized the quiet, sacred space he needed to create to compensate for his driven, chaotic life.

3. Embodying the Soul Symbol

Dialogue between the ego and the Soul is not enough. The ego must react to what has been expressed in the dialogue with the unconscious, draw conclusions, and put them to work in life before the process can be said to be complete. Jung emphasized the importance of concretizing the work to prevent the contents of the work from slipping back into the unconscious.

One medium for embodiment is to use the auxiliary or inferior function; for example, the writer should paint or sculpt, the painter should dance, etc. Another approach is to use the superior or the familiar function (thinking, feeling, intuition or sensate) to concretize the work. The

danger is that skill serves the ego rather than expressing   *231*
the unconscious. Mistakes express the unconscious and
interfere with the ego's intentions. Skill interferes with
the mistakes. Mistakes are the cracks in the consciousness
through which Aditi whispers the intentions of our soul.
The next step is an attempt at "creative formulation."
Material is worked and reworked to fit the individual's
aesthetic taste or artistic sense. The danger is that one
may feel that the product is nothing but art. This shows
love and devotion to the gift from Aditi. Jung painted
and sculpted his fantasies and then used the principal of
understanding by amplifying these images through his
understanding of myths and alchemy. Creative formulation
engages the body in the work, which forms a bridge
between the worlds of the spirit to the concrete world
of the matter. Now the individual must invoke the ego's
"principal of understanding" when the individual struggles
to comprehend the meaning of the unconscious product.

My patient John, whom we discussed above, had a
continuing dialogue with the image of his favorite aunt,
Mita, who symbolized a quiet, sacred space in his driven,
chaotic life. However, the image was not enough. It had to
be embodied and lived out. John started to make room for
the sacred space in his driven, mundane life. This included
silence, solitude, studio time, journaling, prayer, meditation,
playing golf and just staying home two evenings a week.

4. Ethical Confrontation between the Ego and the Soul

How the Ego interacts with the unconscious product
is the true essence of the individual. To enter into this
dialogue with a fictitious ego invalidates the process. If
the ego in this sacred space of active imagination is more
heroic or less emotionally involved in the process of active
imagination than the waking ego, it is a red flag as to the
fictitious ego. The image in active imagination must be
treated as if it were as real as the material world for it to
have its healing impact on our psyche.

The ego needs to have it out with the unconscious (Barbara Hannah[90] 1953, 44f). The position of the ego must be maintained as being of equal value to the counter-position of the unconscious. There must be an establishment of democracy between the ego and the unconscious with both entities having an equal vote. A long conflict between the ego and the unconscious may have to be borne demanding sacrifices from both sides. Jung proposes the question, "How am I affected by this sign."

Von Franz recommends the following (1978, 133) guidelines to deal with the image from the unconscious. First, apply the image of active imagination to ordinary life. Show love, devotion and respect for the unconscious by acknowledging it, communicating with it often, and integrating images and insights gained into life and consciousness. Now something physical must be performed to decrease the risk of intellectualization. Robert Johnson emphasizes the need to ritualize the insight. Ritual is symbolic behavior consciously performed. I recommend to my clients that they perform some ritual in the next day or two to honor the image from the unconscious. Once I dreamt that I had to choose between a garbage truck and a well-appointed yellow pick up truck to perform a certain task. I bought two matchbox miniatures, one of a garbage truck and one of a pick up truck to honor the dream. These two symbols continued to guide me for about six months in a certain major project where using a dump truck to simplify the project was more crucial than having fun in the pick up truck!

One needs to assess whether active imagination personified leads to symbolic change, concrete change in life, behavior change, attitudinal change, etc. This may involve horse-trading; some compromise between the conscious and the unconscious image (Robert Johnson). This helps us establish a living relationship with the unconscious.

Some Clinical Observations on Active Imagination

I will briefly present some clinical observations on active imagination technique, and then we may do a brief exercise of active imagination so you can focus on a recurrent nagging problem in your life and look at its healing and "whole-ing" potential. In the first half of life and in our conscious life, ego is the center of the conscious personality. We delude ourselves in the first half of life to assume that our conscious life is the only life we live in and that ego is its center and reigns supreme. And indeed it *must*, so that we might adapt to and master the tasks of the first half of life.

The Ego and the Soul

As we mature in our life and retire the responsibilities of the first half of life, we are initiated into our second life. Here we begin to see that our ego, which reigned supreme and was extremely adaptive in the first part of life, starts to break down. It just does not hold sway over the complex existential challenges of the second half of life. We start experiencing nagging problems in our self esteem, our relationships, and our health, which won't go away. We start getting physical symptoms. The body speaks. We start having dreams and nightmares. We start experiencing heart problems and arthritis. We start feeling down and sad and depressed. On the surface these are nagging distractions that seem like intrusions into the well-functioning machinery set up in the first half of our life.

Soul Fractals

If we pause to tune into these whispers of the unconscious, we might see that there are messages there. This information is what the British psychoanalyst Fordham[80] calls "de-integrates" or parts of the soul that satellite off into the realm of our consciousness. These are really fractals of our soul, trying to inform us of our depths, our potential, and our heights. Life in the first half is lived in a horizontal plane, skating on the ice rink. Life in the second half is lived in a vertical plane, up and down. But to reach the spiritual heights, we first need to go down to our psyche's depths. It is part of the journey, the preamble to rising to our own potential. This is indeed the most difficult task and one which our ego would like to avoid. But it's a matter of going down before you can go up. It's like a tree. It must send its roots down into the bosom of the earth for its leaves and flowers to reach the skies. And that's the human dilemma: how do you access the depths without getting stuck and lost in these very depths?

So all these nagging problems—depressions, marital problems, medical problems, psychiatric problems—are the meanderings of the soul, like a tree trying to find its own ground before it can grow towards the skies. We have two choices about this. Our first choice is to suffer and let these symptoms gradually tell their own tale. We may experience life, and we burn in the fire of life experiences—a burning and drying out process—before we reach our ground, the residue of which is solid and substantial. And that's fine, if that's our chosen path. But those who want to brave the journey to the depths consciously and voluntarily rather than to wait for the symptoms to come to the surface must engage the unconscious proactively. If you choose to do that, you have established a conscious contact with the unconscious. And that is a risky business. Such a proactive engagement with the unconscious is the goal of active imagination.

Carl G. Jung's Encounter with his Soul

Jung broke from Freud around 1912 when he wrote his book, *Symbols of Transformation*. The major hypothesis presented in this book was that neurosis and other emotional problems are not just an expression of repressed sexuality as Freud postulated but rather unlived spiritual and creative potential of our soul which seeks expression symbolically via our the whispers of our soul. After this final divorce between two great men, Jung went into a very serious depression for several years between 1912 and 1919. In 1913 and 1914, he was at the brink of psychosis; he was looking for some way to make sense of his despair, his imminent breakdown. And he started regressively going out and making images made of stone at his lake house in Zurich. And then he started drawing the images that came from his mind. He started drawing mandalas (circles representing our soul). Slowly a pattern started to emerge. And that journey within himself is really the most fascinating and courageous account of an active confrontation with the unconscious that any human being has made and has been able to come back and record for posterity for the rest of us to learn from.

From that experience he came up with the organizing principle of his philosophy. He understood the theory of archetypes and the central archetype of the Self. He found that for him, his hallmark, his contribution to human consciousness was the concept of the archetype of the Self (Soul), which is the bigger center in our unconscious that guides and directs our life and destiny. A critical task of any lived life has to do with establishing a bridge between the ego, which is the center of our conscious life and the soul – which is the center of our unconscious life—establishing what Neumann calls "the ego-Self axis."

Principle of Reciprocal Action

Now, "active imagination" is a method to consciously walk across that bridge. What it does is to make a voluntarily and conscious contact with an emissary from the unconscious and start a dialogue with it. What happens? How do you make that contact? First of all, to be able to make the bridge, you need to create a space, a vessel, a container worthy to invite such an esteemed guest. It's like a simple man inviting the Dalai Lama or the Pope to his home. What sort of preparation do you make? It will take a tremendous amount of reverence and preparation to be able to prepare for such valuable guests. Similarly, when you're practicing active imagination, you're really inviting very precious and valuable guests into your consciousness. There are people who take it very lightly. They are flippant, they just light a candle and a little incense, and then they go. Those are important rituals, but they should be done with devotion and reverence. There is a principle called the "principle of reciprocal action,"[81] which means that the unconscious will treat you the way you treat it. So if you treat it with reverence, it will guide you and heal you. If you treat it flippantly, it will pull you in the abyss of your own madness, your psychoses, and you may get lost. So it's crucial to have the right attitude when you start dealing with such a powerful entity as your own unconscious. It's like going to an ocean. You don't just go to the center of the ocean and dive down there for a swim. You need to be well prepared with a submarine and with the communications you need to keep contact with the outside.

The HALT Paradigm

So, first of all, to practice active imagination you need a prepared psychic space, free from all distractions, when you are not in any mode of distraction. The four major distractions for human consciousness are **H-A-L-T**—meaning if you are Hungry, Angry, Lonely and Tired, don't do it. If you feel sleepy during your meditation, then you need sleep; you don't need yoga or meditation. So to do this, take a good night's sleep, be well fed, call a couple of friends so you feel connected, and make sure you are not angry at your boss or your spouse or a significant other. When you are in a good state, when you really don't have a major problem to deal with in the outside consciousness, it is a good time to practice active imagination. So it is important to create a neutral enough mental state to welcome these guests.

So to create that space, of course, it is helpful to have a quiet place, and it's helpful to undertake any ritual that creates a sense of transcendence for you. Much of the preparation for yoga and for active imagination is identical, actually. The preparatory stage of invitation to the unconscious is identical in both traditions.

The Parachute

Once you have created this space, when you are rested and you are assured of no disturbance for an hour or so, then it is important to have some mechanism to get you out of that space once you get in it. Once you are in this inner place, you are in a timeless zone; one can get lost in it. This engagement of the eternal space for us humans who are caught in the temporal dimension is a quantum leap of consciousness. So it is very important to make preparations for someone to get you out of this place in the event your mechanisms fail. I always ask my wife. She's my parachute in this, as in many other endeavors! And so I arrange that when I go in my room, in my study, if I have not come out in two hours, I ask her to come and get me, but I tell her, "Don't barge in. Get me out gently." In this way we have worked out an emergency rescue plan in case something catches me down on the floor of the ocean.

The Centering Mantra

You may have your own system of creating this space. Some individuals use a japa (repetitive chanting of a sacred word) or mantra that is helpful to you. I use the OM (AUM) mantra to get me in that place. Of course, you can use other chants or repetitive activities. OM is the holiest of Hindu mantras. It encompasses the quarternity of wholeness as experienced in sound.

A Creation - the creation of sound in the throat,

U -Maintenance of sound resonance in the oral cavity,

M- Containment or Destruction of the sound by closing the mouth, followed by

Silence or Void; this is a prerequisite for creation of yet another cycle of OM and creation. Aum is the cosmic sound which is the root of all creation of spoken words in

Sanskrit. This silence is the realm of goddess Aditi.
AUM.

You can have your own mantra, but I think it's important
to evolve a consistent mantra because then it conditions
you to quickly access that space whenever you are prepared
to go there. Consistency is important; stick to one if you
can.

The Relaxation Breathing Technique

There are many valuable relaxation methods you can
use. You could use the "1, 2, 3-1, 2-1, 2, and 3 technique."
It's a very simple breathing technique, based on yogic
breathing or pranayama (breath control) principles. Sit in
a very relaxed posture. Remember there are two types of
breathing: chest breathing, which is breathing through a
bony rib cage and tummy breathing, which is breathing
through a tire-like flexible abdominal cavity. A tire is
always better for breathing than a cage, so always breathe
through your tummy when you're going to relax. And
put your dominant hand—your right hand if you are
right handed—on your navel. Remember this is not *deep*
breathing, it is *slow* breathing. It is not essential to do deep
breathing because deep breathing will actually distract you.
This exercise is merely to slow your breathing down. And
as you count 1, 2, 3 slowly, feel your tummy rise and hold
for two counts—1, 2—and gently breathe out counting 1,
2, 3 as you breathe out. So, 1, 2, 3...1, 2...1, 2, 3. Do this ten
times. As you are breathing out each time, focus on the
object you may have chosen in your meditation to focus
on. It may be a flower or a crystal or an image or a stone.
That is the focus for your relaxation. You may use the word
"relax" or Shanti (goddess of peace) if you can't find a focus,
if you are out some place in a new community or even in
a hotel room; just think the word "relax" as you breathe
out. You'll find that just doing ten of these will center you
tremendously. The navel centers you, too—being in touch
with the navel. The navel chakra is the control chakra, so

once you are there you get hold of your consciousness.

Ego's Dialogue with the Soul

The next step is to have a dialogue with the unconscious. This is a very difficult step, but if you stay with this process, it will emerge. How do you dialogue with the unconscious? What part of the unconscious do you dialogue with? Well, for this you can dialogue with anything that is unfinished business of the day for you, something which catches you. It could be a dream that you had last night which is unfinished business; then it would be a matter of dreaming the dream forward. It may be a dream which keeps you hanging in mid-air. Actually, those are good dreams. Completed dreams are like novels which you have read and you already know the ending. But it is the mystery of the ending that you do not know that you provide the goal of active imagination. So it's good to take a confusing dream which keeps you hanging out there. Or you can take any nagging problem in your present life and treat it not just as a problem but as a handle to reach the depths of your psyche. You need to change your attitude about it and then enter that space. Or you can take any body symptom as a starting point of active imagination.

I often do active imagination with patients—this is "guided imagination" since a third party is involved. "Active imagination" is always done alone. But what I do in my office will be guided imagination and that's fine. It is a good teaching technique: then people can go home and use it themselves between sessions. So you can take a body symptom like a backache or headache; in fact, I am using this technique with patients with cancer—they can dialogue with the cancer itself and see what comes from the dialogue. Why has the cancer visited the patient?

Emissary from the Soul

The next thing to do, once you have chosen the emissary from the unconscious, is to invite it out for a dialogue. And invite it to take a human form or animal form or some other form. Now it will resist because, you see, if it becomes personified, it loses its power. This will be the most difficult step. One of my patients recently was working on shadow issues. She's a white woman; very spiritual, very upright. But in her active imagination she has constellated this dark shadow which eventually took the form of a black woman who wanted her to loosen up and "have fun." The dark woman was like the goddess Kali, who had appeared in my patient's life to guide her in the mystery of Eros. It is very important to insist that the emissary from the unconscious take a form: because only a *form* can *inform*. Otherwise there's no information when the form remains obscure.

Only a Form Can Inform

Let's say you tried your best, and there's no way this image is going to take a shape or a form. Then what do you do? Well, then you *give* it a form. You may do it by drawing it or sculpting it, if you know how to. You can take silly putty and create an image. You can use the sand in a sand tray and create an image in sand. Use whatever toys you have. But create a form for this image. If it still resists you, if it is so obscure that you just can't project any image even in sand or even with sculpting or drawing, then write a brief paragraph describing this form. In this way you've given it a written form. These then are ways to counter its resistance to taking form.

The Inferior Function and the Dialogue with the Soul

If you are going to write or draw, use an inferior function rather than a superior function to objectify the unconscious. If you are a right handed person, write with your left hand. If you are very good at writing, then draw. If you are very good at drawing, then sculpt. If you are very good at sculpting, then dance and let your body incarnate

the form. If you are a thinking type and are always in your
head, then actually dancing the form out is important.
That's why in Eastern traditions like Bharatnatyam (a ritual
dancing tradition of India) have a very highly ritualized
form of dancing, with very clear postures. These postures
embody the moods and inner images. They are much
systematized. They are not established at random; they are
meant to capture and form the unformed.

So now you have personified the unconscious. You have
used your inferior function because the superior function
is always used in the service of the ego. There are four
functions: feeling, thinking, intuition, and sensate. These
include the Thinking types, feeling types, intuitive types,
and sensate types—people who feel in the body or feel
the body of the environment. They are very aware of the
textures, and the colors, and the environment. So of these
four types, you must use the type which is opposite your
superior function. So for thinking-function people, the
feeling function is the inferior function. And for intuitive
types the sensate is the inferior function and vice versa.
Always use your least comfortable function because then you
are most likely to make mistakes, and as you know, it's the
mistakes, the errors, the slips of tongue, and the accidents
which come from the unconscious. Consciousness does
not make errors. The unconscious makes you make errors.
It trips the ego consciousness and slips through the crack
of the error. The unconscious, announced by mistakes,
errors, slips, breaks, goofs, tells us a real story about our
soul. That is why they are so valuable—people who have
made no errors have had no problems, make no mistakes,
suffer no accidents, and are indeed very deprived. They are
deprived of a connection with their unconscious; it never
slips through. Then when it does, it explodes in a major
illness or major catastrophe. We are fortunate if we have
small problems, little aches here and there, even a minor
health problem. That's much, much better than people
who have very smooth sailing and do not permit the depths
to speak in a timely manner. It has no choice but to come

down with a vengeance. These are people who drop dead unexpectedly from heart attacks. So leave room for errors in life. It's crucial to permit the unconscious to speak and not to be too harsh with it. So when all this has happened, you begin a dialogue. A dialogue with the unconscious will inform you and will dream the dream forward. You will get the meaning of the symptom. It will inform you of what is missing in your conscious attitude and adaptation to life.

My Encounter with Aditi

In one of my first active imagination exercises I went back to this very numinous space. I went back all the way to my college days, pre-medical school days, when I had two heroes. One of them is Abijit, who is one of the leading physicists in India. He is a very solid person. He is my ego ideal! When he speaks, Saraswati flows through him... My other hero was—and probably still is—Sajan. He was a playboy. He had plenty of women, fast cars, and a red convertible. So I said, "Well, that's strange." I thought I had forgotten about this guy! It was such a long time ago, but here he was, alive and well in my unconscious.

So then I said, "Well, what is going on?" And the images said, "We are two of your closest friends, and you have not talked to us in a while." So welcome back. And from Abijit, the scholar, I got a lot of praise. He said, "You have carried my traditions well in your life. You are well achieved. You are a solid psychiatrist doing well, etc." I got a lot of affirmations from him. And I was thankful to him for that feedback. Sajan on the other hand said, "Well, friend, you have been ignoring me all these years. We've got to talk." I said, "Well, I'm a married man. I've got two lovely children. I've two lovely grandchildren. Your days are gone," I said. "You can't come back." That shadow part of me was alive and well and flourishing in my unconscious, unbeknownst to me, and ready and poised to lead me if I do not pay attention to it. Fortunately, I got to him in good time and established dialogue before he could take over my life. I had nurtured all these fantasies of India's Bollywood actors— call it a day, go to California, and take a nice job, be a beach bum someplace in Los Angeles. I always had this fantasy of running off to California. So that part was there, but I thought it was a harmless fantasy; I did not know it was a really powerful image lurking back there waiting for its opportunity.

When you have begun this dialogue, then what you do is what Robert Johnson calls "horse trading." Now starts the ethical confrontation or the serious negotiation with this image. And in serious negotiations, there will be a lot of give and take. The unconscious will be unwilling—I told Sajan, "I can't be unfaithful to my wife, and I can't run off to some place. I won't be a womanizer. I won't become a Casanova. I'm a very happily married, spiritual guy, so leave me alone." And he says, "Well, you really think you're happy, but you're not happy." So I said, "You're not going to succeed. This is just not my style, but I enjoy your energy, your power, your red car."

When I continued to dialogue with this image something interesting happened. The image started to transform a little bit. Just a little bit. But I stayed my ground, and this was the longest part; I was just about crossing the alarm threshold before my wife would rescue me. This was the time I got closest to the danger point! And, of course, she has rescued me in more ways than one at such times. So then the image started to transform and this playboy started to get darker. Sajan has a very fair, northern Indian complexion, handsome guy in real life, but this image started to get darker. I said, "Well, that's interesting. It's the shadow." But I said, even though you are showing your true colors, we still haven't negotiated; I can't still act out. And then, amazingly he took out a flute... and...He became the image of Krishna! It was the trickster archetype of Krishna that was alive in the unconsciousness. Then of course I knew who Sajan had been all my life. It wasn't a playboy. Krishna, although he's a diplomat and a trickster; in Indian folk mythology, he's considered to be the playboy, the Eros of Indian psyche, the mediator with the unconscious and the spiritual core of our psyche. He is also a tantric god, connecting you with the feminine principle. What was emerging in this encounter was a redeeming bridge to my feminine, not the playboy. The Krishna image had constellated to mediate my connection with my femininity, my feelings and my creativity. So it opened up the channel. And since then, Krishna and I have been having regular chats. Whenever I get lost in my logical lopsidedness, Krishna guides my path to wholeness. I am an intuitive, thinking type of person. For me, wholeness usually involves attending to my feelings and my sensate functions, which sometimes leads to a creative resolution to the problem at hand.

And that became possible only when I stayed my ground and continued the horse trading: "I'm not giving in; just show me another way that you can live in my life." If you confront the personified unconscious, it will show you its divine archetypal intent. And if you are ready to contact it down in the depths, it will show you the way out. But the big key here is to insist on a kind of *democracy* between the ego consciousness and the Soul-consciousness or the unconscious. And I can dare to say that's a big debate for my own personal psyche. As a Jungian in my philosophy of treatment, I'm becoming very astute with the concept of the democracy of your ego and soul. Both of them must be on a level field. When either the ego or the soul establishes a dictatorship over each other, then you are psychologically lopsided. It's like if you are a little ship in the ocean, you must still maintain your sense of mastery in midst of a ferocious ocean. The little ship must do what it takes to stay afloat, to stay connected with the ground control of the harbor, to stay connected with its sister ships in the vicinity. It's important to maintain whatever it takes to maintain the integrity of the ego in the face of the ferocious forces of the unconscious. Perhaps the biggest contribution of Jung and his analytic movement is the sense of democracy between the two.

Democracy between the Ego and the Soul

I agree with Carl Jung that the optimal way to honor the latent code of the soul is to establish an attitude of democracy between the ego and the soul. As a Hindu, I believe in the supremacy of the unconscious and its forces in guiding our course and path and destiny. These are very divergent philosophies of life. Who should be in the driver's seat? The ego, the democratic government of the ego and the unconscious, or the varying forms of timeless forces of the unconscious? I have to report that up to this date I have not resolved this dilemma and in my fragile container I'm holding the tension of these opposites. And perhaps that is my karma: to hold these opposites and stay with this tension of not quite knowing whether as a well trained western medical man, I want the ego to be in the driver's seat; it's so elegant, so organized, so systematic. I like Jung's seductive notion of the democracy of the two, but my soul as an Indian, as a Hindu, is ready to give it over to the divine forces. And on any given day I go through all three cycles. On any given dilemma in life, I go through all three epicycles. And I will continue struggling. But for sake of discussion, in active imagination, it is the democracy between the two that claims the terrain.

Concretize the Dialogue with the Soul

To return to our description of the work of active imagination, we have established the form and entered into dialogue with the image, which in turn has responded to you. Now before you close this process you must concretize the dialogue in some way. It's not enough to have a dialogue; it must be concretized. It must be put in some form once again, in a finished form. And that again could be done as a paragraph about your understanding of the problem—this will appeal to thinking types. Or it could be drawn as an image of some kind—this will appeal to the sensate and intuitive types. But whatever you do, it should be done aesthetically. The final product of your dialogue should be understood in some intellectual manner even if it is a crude or rough or preliminary understanding. **It should be *felt*.** Where do you feel it? In which chakra of your body do you feel it? Do you feel it in your genitals? Do you feel it in your guts? Does your heart palpate? Do you feel it as a burning sensation in your throat if you want to sing or speak? Do you feel the sensation in your head? Do you have a headache? I think it must be felt somewhere in the body for it to be a complete exercise. And finally it should be given some symbolic, concrete form in terms of drawing or writing. All four functions should honor the outcome of this dialogue for it to be a completed exercise. Some people will have this dialogue and will create a very good picture. They will paint a wonderful painting. And they will get so seduced by the painting that they will not understand the meaning of it. Or someone may understand the meaning of the dialogue but may not honor it by some visual image. It is just a head dialogue. Then there is no life in it. So you must attempt to honor the final product in some way. You might just cut some pictures from a magazine and create a collage, if that's all you can do. But something must be done.

The Ritual to Honor the Encounter with the Soul

And then, after all this has been done, comes the most important moment of active imagination. And that is to perform a ritual act of some kind or initiate a real change in your life which honors this insight.

What I did was install a Krishna idol at my meditation altar. At that time I did indeed buy a toy red car, I should admit! That was the most benign way I could honor Krishna. But it had to be honored. You can't bypass that energy, otherwise it will get you. So there must be a concrete change in life which will honor that image, or there may be a behavior change. If you have a palpitation in your heart region after your exercise and you know your heart is in trouble, then get up every morning and start taking a walk for forty-five minutes. Additionally, you must attend to your heart charka of relationships and feelings. By honoring that image in some way, you establish a living relationship with the unconscious. Once it knows you take it seriously, it will start taking you seriously. So then you have completed the Uroborus – the reciprocal action with the unconscious. Uroborus is a serpent biting its own tail; when you catch this serpent from the unconscious and bite its tail, then it completes the mandala, the circle of life. It is a closed space. And only a closed circle can have a center. You will not have a center in your life—a headquarters, the capital of the democracy between the ego and the unconscious—unless you complete the circle. That is a very important part of the process.

Some Common Indications for Active Imagination

There are some clinical indications for practicing active imagination. In therapy, if you have a patient who is getting too many dreams which have no form or structure that means the unconscious is sort of overflowing, bursting at the seams. So rather than let the unconscious abscess burst, you pierce it. You cut and drain it consciously by doing active imagination. Or you do it when there are too few dreams. There are patients who just can't dream. The body speaks for the unconscious. So it is a very valuable tool for that group of patients or individuals. For other individuals, it is in an impenetrable complex or life problem that becomes the focus of active imagination. They keep making the same error time and again. That is an important time to take them into that place and to personify the complex. They just don't learn from their own errors. Then you visit this problem. Of course, it is a very useful technique for self-help and establishing an inner guide in the journey on this transcendent path.

The Dark Side of the Soul

One question that the reader may have is that while the unconscious invariably has the welfare of the entire organism in mind, is there such a thing as an unconscious that's trying to do something destructive? Unfortunately, the answer is "Yes." We need to confront the dark side of the unconscious. Although it is essential to acknowledge and honor the dark side of the soul, it is crucial not to yield to it. You must go eyeball to eyeball with the image of the unconscious. The ego and the soul need to negotiate a deal. Both parties gave and took some. The crucial part of this process is the ethical confrontation with the image of the unconscious. If you don't confront it, it's like John Kennedy said, "Those who ride the back of a tiger end up inside." So if you try to ride this unconscious, you will end up inside its stomach. Jung was very clear about this aspect. The only difference between a psychotic and a person whose active imagination work is effective is whether you have enough ego strength, enough integrity to stand up to this image and force it to negotiate actively with you. I had the theoretical knowledge to understand that Krishna was a symbol of mediating creatively with the contra-sexual. It's not about affairs with 16,000 women like Krishna in his myth; it's about attending to my multiple feminine potentialities.

The Story of Alexander and King Porus

The story of Alexander and Porus is instructive in this context. Alexander the Great was a very brave warrior who won many wars. His dream was to rule India. He was only thirty-two when he reached the outskirts of India near the Khyber Pass, and the Indians knew that once he crossed over it, there was no other protection because the people were splintered into small kingdoms. So the old, wise king who was ruling the Khyber kingdom—a small, little kingdom—was King Porus. And, of course, Porus put on his armor, marshaled his men and went out to fight Alexander. In less than a few hours the war was over and Porus was in chains and thrown into a dungeon. And the next morning Alexander was sitting in his improvised court in the mountains and sitting on the throne high up there with all his chieftains and his men around him. And then they brought into the middle of the court King Porus, in chains, without shoes, without clothes, looking entirely miserable. So Alexander was sitting up there and looked at this wise, old, brave King Porus whom he had heard so much about, and he chuckled when he said, "So you are King Porus?" He said, "Yes, Secunder (Alexander)."

"Well, I have heard a lot about you. Look at you. Your army could not even last twenty-four hours against my mighty army. Look at you now. You are the guardian of the door to India, the gateway to India. Look at you right now." So Porus says, "Yes. You're right. Here I am." So then Secunder asked him a second question. "So now tell me old, great King Porus, how shall I treat you?" So Porus thought for a minute, and he looked up at Secunder and said, "Well, Secunder, it depends upon what kind of person you are. If you are just a barbarian, then you must put me to death as soon as you can before the word of my defeat and disgrace spreads and the Indian people get organized to fight your army and cause trouble for you. So as a strategist and as a barbarian you must instantly kill me. But if you are truly a king, then you must treat me as one king treats another, whether a victor or vanquished." And that of course was what Secunder did. They became the closest friends, and Secunder stopped his march into India. Ego and soul must treat each other with honor and dignity, irrespective of who has power or ascendancy at any given fleeting moment.

I hope this brief rendering of the important technique of active imagination has inspired you to establish an active collaboration with your unconscious and a vital bridge between your ego and your soul. At a pragmatic level, I recommend to my patients that they maintain the practice of active imagination at least weekly and as needed. Whenever there is a dangling dream or pervasive mood, a physical or emotional symptom, a fantasy image, one may consider a dialogue with the unconscious proactively via active imagination. It is this bridge that is the source of our health, healing and wholeness. This bridge between the ego and the soul is the precinct of the goddess Aditi.

Now that we have discussed the important techniques for the ego to implement the latent code of the soul, let me now present the fruit of my labors – a Symbolic attitude to life.

The Symbolic Attitude

A symbolic attitude embodies a belief that a deeper center of consciousness– the soul– guides our inner life and the overall trajectory of our life. While our ego manages our dealings with daily responsibilities and the outer conscious life, the soul, what the Hindus call the Atman, is connected to the universal consciousness that we may call the spirit, the primal spirit or Brahmana. There is constant dance between the body, the soul and the spirit. Body embodies the soul's program. The soul gets its instructions from the primal spirit in guiding our life. A psychological mindedness implies that we are open to the whispers of our soul in guiding our life path into its soul groove in accord with our latent code. It involves a reflective attitude towards life in which one is able to reflect on life problems as a password that connects our outer life with the latent code of our soul and connects our individual soul with the code of the primal spirit.

A symbolic attitude respects the unknown. Our soul lives at the boundary between what we know consciously and that which is not yet known. The unknown is the boundary where the precinct of the soul and the spirit merge. It honors the void. It sponsors the capacity to deal with the uncertain until one is able to reflect on and understand its symbolic meaning. It establishes the context of how this voids incubates our soul and intentions of the primal spirit. It respects the symbols of our soul's latent code and how these symbols inform our life and align it with the spirit's intentions for us.

To honor the symbolic attitude, we need to establish a personal framework, to maintain a dialogue with the

soul and the spirit. This includes a personal system to
decode, honor and implement the intent of the symbols
that emerge from our soul to guide our life. Through the
mist of time, our collective wisdom has accumulated in our
myths (archetypes). These myths manifest as life patterns,
dreams, medical and psychiatric symptoms, art and
creative products. Archetypes are modulated by the primal
spirit. Archetypes are activated to guide us through major
life issues, initiations, developments, crises, transitions
or catastrophes. A symbolic attitude is respectful of the
guiding wisdom of these archetypes.

We live in several realities. These include the body, the
psyche, the soul and transcendence with the spirit. The
body is the monitor, psyche is the hard drive, the soul is
the program and the spirit is the purpose. The purpose
of the body is to be a vessel for the soul in this life time.
When we die, the body merges into the elements and the
soul merges with the divine. The purpose of the soul in
this incarnation is the achievement of four dharmas or soul
potentials. These include sva or self dharma – honoring
our innate skills and talent; ahsrama or family dharma –
attending to our responsibilities to our loved ones; varana
or community dharma –playing our personal best role in
the matrix of our community; and reta or spiritual dharma
– honoring our relationship with the divine and preparation
for merger with the spirit. As a river flows into the ocean, a
purified soul merges into the spirit. The soul is the pilgrim,
the spirit is the destination. Many paths lead the soul to
the spirit. All great religions and traditions of the world
offer "A Path." A path must not be confused with the
destination.

The purpose of this lifetime is a preparation for the
merger of our soul with the universal, primal spirit. Hindus
call this union of individual soul or atman with universal
spirit or Brahamana. In this lifetime we have the task to
make our soul worthy for merger with the spirit, for a
young soul to become an old soul. If we do not complete
the task in this life time, we re-incarnate to complete the

process, and we leave un-retired karma for next generations to retire. This becomes our family or clan karma.[82]

Mahatma Gandhi differentiated the young souls and old souls thus -

Wealth without Work
Pleasure without Conscience
Science without Humanity
Knowledge without Character
Politics without Principle
Commerce without Morality
Worship without Sacrifice

Let me conclude with some of my favorites quotes adapted from Bhagwad Gita.[83] These embody the characteristics of the old soul.

Re incarnation of the Soul

Just as the soul acquires
A childhood body, a youth body, and an old age body during this life similarly,
The soul acquires another body after death.
This should not delude the wise. (2.13)

Soul–Enduring Energy

The physical body is perishable
But the Soul is eternal, immutable, and incomprehensible. (2.18)

Reincarnation

Just as a person puts on new garments
After discarding the old ones
Similarly, the Soul acquires new bodies
After casting away the old bodies. (2.22)

Soul–Pure Energy

Weapons do not cut Soul

Fire does not burn it,
Water does not make it wet, Wind does not make it dry.
The Soul cannot be cut, burned, wetted, or dried.
It is eternal, all pervading, unchanging, immovable, and primeval. (2.23-24)

Grief is the Experience of Our Ego

Even if you think that the physical body takes birth and dies perpetually, even then, O Arjuna, you should not grieve this.
Because death is certain for the one who is born,
And birth is certain for the one who dies.
Therefore, you should not lament over the inevitable. (2.26-27)

The Soul Merges with the Spirit

This (Soul merged with the Spirit) is the super conscious state of mind (Nirvana, Freedom from Opposites in Psyche or Mokasha).
Attaining this state, one is no longer deluded.
Gaining this state, in this life,
A person becomes one with the Absolute. (2.72).

CH 13
The Latent Code
Some Concluding Thoughts and Feelings

Why do we need the latent code? How does it enhance our life and make it relevant to the plan of the universe? What does a life lived out of the latent code feel like? Does the latent code guide the individual or benefit humanity? Are we robotic beings meant to live by some mysterious latent code or do we have free will to shape our own future? Does the latent code merely help us fit better in the collective picture of humanity or does it honor our own unique individuality? These are some of the questions that my readers may have raised during the reading of the preceding chapters. By now, most of you must have your additional questions and your own answers to these questions. I will share some of my concluding thoughts and feelings about these and other questions that perplexed me as I engaged the mystery of the latent code.

The central question of our life is what is the meaning and purpose of my life other than survival? What considerations should guide our choices and actions? What role does the latent code play in these choices? The most cogent response to these questions comes from the sacred Hindu text of Bhagwad Gita. Krishna is the guide of the great warrior Arjuna, who is reluctant to lead his army into war against his evil kinsman. He says that he would rather loose the kingdom than to succeed by confronting and destroying those he loves. This ambivalence leads Krishna to communicate the latent code to his protégé Arjuna in the form the epic poem Bhagwad Gita. The central theme of Krishna's counsel is that Arujuna must make his choice as guided by his soul, not for personal gain but to discharge his duty as he best understands it to serve the cause of justice and restore the order of right over wrong. Krishna further counsels Arjuna to do his duty and turn over the outcome to the divine. This is the central theme of the latent code. It instructs us to make the choice and take action in accordance with the guidance of our latent code and turn over the outcome to the universe and the primal Spirit.

You have control over doing your respective duty only, but no control or claim over the results.
The fruits of work should not be your motive, and you should never be inactive. (2.47)

Do your duty to the best of your ability, O Arjuna, with your mind attached to the Lord, abandoning worry and selfish attachment to the results, and remaining calm in both success and failure.
The selfless service is a yogic practice that brings peace and equanimity of mind.[84] (2.48)

I am glad you decided to join me in exploring and honoring the latent code under the guidance of the goddess archetype. I hope your encounter with her is as fulfilling as mine has been. Shakti has informed, involved, guided and presided over my path to the soul, and continues to be my guide. Often we run into treacherous dead ends in our life. When our outer ego consciousness sees no way out, it is the latent code of the soul that steps in to guide our path. The defeat of the ego is the path to the soul and this opens up the possibility for a deeper meaningful and spiritually informed life.

Our conscious life is lived on the horizontal plane of existence. We skate on the surface of life. This gives us breadth and spread of life experiences necessary to sample the possibilities of our potentials. However, sooner or later, we come to a turning point in life when the latent code of our soul is activated to guide us to engage the vertical axis of our life. This is experienced as a series of descents or problems, illnesses, relationship tangles, accidents, disappointments, depressions, etc., followed by experience of ascents or insights into the meaning and purpose of our life. When we engage both the horizontal and the vertical axis of our life, relationship and potentials, we live out our quaternity, our wholeness, the personal experience of our cross to bear.

I hope that I have made you curious about the latent code of the soul and the helpful role it can play in your personal life and also in alerting you to its movement in the collective human consciousness. While we are busy living our manifest life at the outer fringes of our potential, the deeper forces of nature and the wisdom of the Universe are guiding our life as individuals and as a civilization to align us with our destiny. If we tune into this code, we can live our life out at its fuller potential as individuals, as members of our families, our community and in accord with the intentions of our spirit. If we stay disengaged from this latent code, we create negative karma for ourselves and leave a legacy of negative karma for our families, communities and human race. It is our choice – to add to the darkness of the culture or leave this world a slightly better place than we found it. I am sure that at the bottom of our hearts and from the depths of our souls we want to contribute to the well-being of this fragile planet that we call home.

In this preliminary work, I have tried to introduce my readers to the mysteries of the latent code, its tripartite structure orchestrated by the soul, guided by the timeless templates of archetypes and implemented by our ego consciousness. For each stage, transition, initiation, crisis, trauma, responsibility and opportunity of our life as individuals and as citizens of the human race, we have a specific segment of the latent code, embedded in the corresponding archetype that informs us and guides us onto our path. I have chosen a few goddess archetypes to instruct the reader in this process of respectful and reflective collaboration with the latent code of their soul. Interested seekers on the path to their soul must familiarize themselves further with the myths, stories and symbols from their own traditions to deepen their work. This book is meant to serve as a preliminary template. It is to give you some introductory lessons on fishing in the rich waters of the psyche. I urge you to keep on fishing in your own waters and harvest the gifts of the soul and the spirit.

This book also lays out a preliminary map of the latent code and ways to decode and implement it. Not every method will work for everyone. I advise you to assemble your own framework from different methods outlined in this book to invoke and attend to your latent code. For some individuals, transcendental meditation may work, for others it may be dream analysis, working on understanding their complexes, untangling their relationship problems, focusing on a yantra or practicing active imagination. However, the basic attitude of respect for the deeper dimension of psyche, trust in the wisdom of the universe, awareness of the wealth of our archetypal wisdom embedded in the myths and other products of our civilization like art, music, scriptures, fairy tales etc., and finally a symbolic and reflective attitude towards the hidden dimensions of our consciousness is crucial to attend to the guiding wisdom of the latent code. When all is said and done, it is our ego consciousness that must undertake the arduous task of decoding the latent code of the soul embedded in the archetypes and myths of our civilization, make necessary sacrifices in our existing adaptation, tolerate the void that is essential in order to gestate new consciousness and have the courage to make auspicious new beginnings in our life and fulfill our spiritual calling in this lifetime. This transforms a young soul into an old soul, and we are able to reconcile the opposite tendencies in our psyche and become healed and whole. This is no mean undertaking for our fragile human ego, not unlike David taming the giant Goliath. To undertake this Opus Magnus of our life, we must confront our comfort zone. The maximum personal growth comes from the contra habit enterprise.

When our ego runs into an impasse and we cannot wiggle our way out of a difficult situation, when our usual and customary methods of responding yield diminishing returns, the latent code of the soul is activated. The soul may speak through a dream, a fantasy, a day dream, an accident, a synchronistic event, a medical or psychiatric symptom, a relationship problem, a hang up or a personality quirk. These whispers of our soul contain a new symbol to reset our life path in tune with the latent code. When I was in medical college, I met this pretty woman that both intrigued and puzzled me. She had a feisty argumentative streak, and I did not see any real potential in our emerging relationship. I decided to break up from this relationship and decided to relate this to her the next day. The night prior to our meeting, I dreamt that she gifted me a beautiful red rose with a thorn in the stem. I deferred our break up and stayed with the energy of this symbol. A Rose is worthy of a place at the alter of the divine and not to be discarded. Gradually I learned that my girl friend was the Rose, and like any rose, she had an occasional thorn in the stem. Our relationship deepened, and I was fortunate she agreed to marry me. I am blessed that she is a part of my life now for over thirty-five years.

The latent code of the soul gifts us a symbol which points the way to the new myth of our life. I was on the warrior path with my girlfriend, and the rose symbol activated the lover myth, which was more appropriate to my relationship. A symbol is a gift of our latent code. It derives from ancient Greek custom of breaking a clay slate into pieces and giving a piece to each member of a group before their dispersal. When they reconvened, the pieces would be reassembled (Sumballein=to throw together). Like a jigsaw puzzle, the individual's group identity is confirmed. A symbol is an unconsciously chosen expression of the latent code that is a best possible conscious manifestation of a relatively unknown fact that is known or postulated to exist.[85] A symbol is pregnant with meaning. The symbolic value of an expression is contingent upon the attitude of observing consciousness. A symbol has life giving and life enhancing value.[86] Symbols evoke a deep emotion and invoke a felt sense of Numinosum. It fascinates, has a sense of mystery and intrigue. It manifests in a synchronistic matrix and feels relevant to the present life situation and emerging trajectory of life direction. Symbols combine many diverse elements into a unitary expression, tolerate paradox, and are felt. In conventional language a symbol is often confused with a sign. A sign is a representation of something known, conveys specific information and is derived from Latin Signum— a mark. Sign and symbol are often interchanged in daily usage but have specific meanings in analytical psychology literature. A sign is expressed in words and represents logical thinking, while a symbol represents fantasy and imaginal thinking. A sign uses numerous words needed to deal with one thought, while one symbolic image may represent a large mystery of a relevant latent code. A symbol is activated when the underlying archetype is invoked. A symbol is activated at times of crisis, trauma, developmental and initiatory transitions. A symbol is experienced by the ego complex. The conscious experience is the personal pole of the symbol. In the depths of our psyche, the symbol extends into the archetypal matrix of the collective consciousness. This is the collective pole of the symbol. The symbol connects the ego or consciousness to the collective psyche or the wisdom of the universe. This is the transcendent function of the symbol. Hence, a symbol is both personal and collective. A symbol may manifest as a day dream, fantasy, dream, a synchronistic event, a medical or psychiatric illness, a personality hang up, a fascinating relationship, an experience in encounter with art, movies, a favorite fairy tale, and other creative contents of our psyche like a drawing we may doodle when day dreaming.

For many individuals their first conscious encounter with the latent code may be through a series of synchronistic events. I was initiated into the mystery of my latent code by the soulful spouse of a professional adversary, who gifted me a book of dreams by Carl Jung following a dinner table chat at his farewell party. This gift provoked deep interest in Jungian thought and eventually inspired me to undertake a formal training in analytical psychology. The journey has been both perilous and promising. On the way I have met Kali, who beheaded my ego several times in the trials and turbulence of my continuing individuation. This created a sense of void, an Aditi encounter that I was not very well prepared for as a medical type who expected to act and intervene. I gradually learned the sacred art of honoring the void, silence, solitude and attending to inner life. Significant dreams at crucial crossroads, synchronistic events, and the continuing analytic exploration of my own latent code gradually constellated new creations of self-structures.

In the present environment, both young and old must constantly retrain with new skills to stay viable in a fast moving market place. This involves going to school or retraining on a lifelong basis. This lifetime of learning is mediated by the latent code of Saraswati, the goddess of learning and knowledge. Individuals in young adulthood and midlife must find ways to honor their relational ground. This is mediated by the latent code of Parvati. Once we have mastered the academic, professional and relational ground, we are ready to usher in an era of peace and prosperity. This is mediated by the latent code of Laxmi. At repeated crossroads of our life, we must relinquish the old and make room for the new beginnings. The latent code of Kali mediates letting go of the dysfunctional attitudes, the code of Aditi incubates the sacred void, and the latent code of the elephant headed, divine child Ganesha ushers in the auspices new beginnings in our life.

For many men, their wives and daughters carry the burden of the unlived feminine aspects of their latent code. For women, the men in their lives may carry the unlived masculine aspects of their latent code. It is the task of the midlife crisis to gently wean ourselves from dependence on our spouses to carry our unlived life and lay claim to it. For men, this may involve attending to their feeling function, their relations, and their capacity to play and honor their creativity. For women in midlife transition, it often involves reclaiming their thinking function, their sense of adventure and enterprise and reentering the professional or business world and staking claim to their authentic voice, their ground and authority. Many new businesses in America are started by women in their midlife. When we let go of the burden to carry the unlived potential of our spouses, it frees both participants in this relationship to follow their own bliss and collaborate as partners in mutual enterprise.

Retrospectively, I can see why it was not optional but essential for me to undertake the latent code project to achieve a new threshold of individuation. It realigned me with my own depths under the watchful guidance of the goddess. Whenever I have been at an apparent impasse in my work with my patients or my own life, the latent code has appeared either in my dreams or synchronistic events, or those of my patients', to guide and direct us. Several of these examples are included in this book.

As I continued to work on this project, it also bore some additional dividends and insights in many sectors of my professional and personal life. Professionally, it became apparent to me that the different sectors of my interest could not be successfully completed without the inclusion of the feminine dimension in their matrix. The best template to tune into the latent code in myself and my patients is the initial dreams in analysis. They are the best possible representation of the creation myth of our life to guide us in our new beginnings. The creation myth of an individual is a fractal of the creation myth of a culture in which one is embedded. Jung calls this the correspondence between the microcosm and macrocosm. So many of my patient's and my own initial dreams have feminine images in them, which I personally believe are the goddess archetypes that are guiding us as we embark upon a new millennium.

Personally, this project has had a deep impact on my work, relationships, play and creativity. The latent code put me in touch with my auxiliary feeling function. This has greatly enhanced my work. I feel more fully present with

my clients, not just intellectually but also present with my
heart and my soul. A better access to my feeling function
has also deepened my relationships. In managing the latent
code project, I had to massage and access my inferior sensate
function, e.g., the very process of composing this book on
my computer, of taking photographs in goddess temples in
India, and amplifying them on my computer. This was a
challenging but very gratifying experience, and it fostered
my playfulness and creativity in the process. Overall the
most precious gift of this project was a closer connection
to my daughter Ami as we collaborated during our India
visit to the goddess sites in India in the winter of 1999.
Many of my patients have reported similar experiences of
wholeness when they consciously implemented the wisdom
of their latent code in their lived life. Their conscious life
was deepened by the unconscious dimension; their life
had a better balance between love, work, play, creativity
and spirituality. The circle of their life was more fairly
balanced.

The process of writing this book was an alchemic Kali
and Aditi experience for me. My initial rendering of this
book was a highly archetypal and intellectual enterprise. It
was the outcome of an ethereal World-view (intuitive and
thinking mode), loaded with interesting ideas and intuitions,
but short on personal details and feelings. With the help of
my daughter, Ami, who confronted the lopsidedness of the
project and invited me to amplify the personal, experienced
aspect of the latent code. Typologically this added the
experial World-view (feeling and sensate or detail oriented
mode) to the book. Initially this was a Kali experience. I
felt dismembered, destroyed, beheaded! Kali had done her
destructive dance. This dissolved my ego. It was void for a
while. Then Aditi stepped in to help me deal with this void.
She guided me to integrate my felt experiences of the latent
code. I have tried to integrate the personal feelings and
lived experience of the feminine in this book. It is my hope
that the new synthesis is more soulful in its feeling tone
and grounded in experience. My image is that it is like the

child of Shiva and Shakti, Ganesha – the elephant headed god. He has his trunk-raised up to the skies of thought and intuition, and his feet firmly grounded in the feeling and experience of the mother earth. In the true alchemic tradition, this revision was like an experience of "dissolution and coagulation" of the prima materia (soul substance) at a higher level of integration. It involved dissolving the old attitudes and constellating a new synthesis of thinking with feeling, masculine with feminine, clinical with spiritual.

Over the years, I have had the privilege of working with many patients who were physicians, psychiatrists and therapists. Looking back, it has been my observation that it is the guidance of the latent code that finally brings these individuals to the crossroads between the meaning and the mystery of the human psyche and suffering. With the guidance of the latent code, it is more tolerable for them to hold the tension between the search for meaning and mystery, between human triumphs and tragedies, success and suffering. I feel that this is the optimal attitude for a healer and for those who are on a quest to heal their own soul.

My attempt at putting this book together has put me in touch with my latent code embodied in introverted feeling function. This has deepened my work with my male and female patients, my relationships in general, and with the significant women in my life in particular (my mother, my wife, my sister, my daughter and female patients and the feminine dimension of the male patients) and helped me establish a more conscious and fruitful connection with my inner feminine, sponsoring a reflective attitude to life. In my personal and professional life, I now approach it from a more balanced typological perspective rather than the familiar and comfortable intuitive and thinking functions. Some of the most creative work that I have done and have observed tends to come from unfamiliar aspects of their personality. Often this entails attention to detail and to my feelings about the matter. This often happens in spite of me, not because of any conscious deliberation on my part! It

seems that when we make honest mistakes, we inadvertently
seem to make the most beneficial interventions in our life
and work. Perhaps when our consciousness is not standing
guard at the door, the latent code of the soul is able to get
inside the relational space.

This book may give an impression to some that our life
is predestined to live out a certain script, and the best we
can do is to live it out and stay out of the way of the latent
code. This is precisely what I want to caution the readers
against. The highest achievement of the human psyche is
the capacity to make a choice and exercise free will. This
freedom has light and shadow. We can choose to avoid our
role in the drama of life or choose to engage life lived out
of our full potential. When we live out our potential, we
have the capacity to do great good or tremendous harm to
the plan of the spirit. When we live an informed life under
the soulful guidance of our latent code, we are able to play
our part in the plan of the universe. When we live our life
out of our limited manifest consciousness, we may end up
complicating the flow of the universe by intercepting it
with mundane considerations. The latent code does not
limit us to any predetermined script. Rather, it helps us
to live out our innate potentials to their fullest and then
leave this world a little bit better place than we found it.
The greatest attitude change this calls for is to focus on the
right action and turn over the outcome to the spirit. To
quote Lord Krishna's guidance to warrior Arjuna in Gita,

*Acts of service, charity, and austerity should not be abandoned,
but should be performed, because service, charity, and austerity
are the purifiers of the wise. (18.05)*

*Even these obligatory works should be performed without
attachment to the fruits. This is My definite supreme advice, O
Arjuna.*[87] *(18.06)*

The relevant question is the relative significance of the
latent code for the individual versus the collective welfare.
The latent code does not lead to a pre-formatted path to

our fate but rather offers the dynamic of choice. Each of us can choose to engage our destiny or ignore it only to have to either retire it in a future incarnation or leave a legacy for our children, grandchildren and seven generations to retire. When all is said and done, claiming our destiny is a matter of free will and choice. We are not robots living by our latent code but free individuals who may choose from a repertoire of possibilities under the helpful guidance of our latent code to make personal choices that fulfill our personal program of self-development and play our part in the collective welfare of the universe. The greatest freedom is the freedom from preoccupation with the short term outcome of our choices. It may be several generations before the optimal outcome of our choices may manifest. Preoccupation with the short term outcome is the greatest trap of our nature, a remnant of our animal nature. To look beyond immediate gratification, the capacity to make personal sacrifice for altruistic goals is the highest attribute of what is truly sublime about human nature.

What does a life lived in tune with our latent code feel like? There are certain manifestations of a spiritually engaged and meaningful life, which I will briefly summarize here, though these observations are sprinkled throughout the matrix of this book. One of the most significant feelings about a spiritually engaged life lived under the auspices of the latent code is that it is a life of balance. It balances inner with outer life, ego with the soul, engagement of the present moment and awareness of our role in the bigger picture of the universe. It involves balancing our thinking with feeling function, our broad intuitions with attention to details, and our masculine with our feminine psyches. These individuals balance the four important sectors of their life; love, work, play and creativity. When these four quadrants of life are optimally balanced the fifth dimension, the quintessence, the spiritual essence of our life emerges. Life now feels grooved in its purpose and meaning.

Our purpose in this life is engagement with our own mysterious depths. This involves our ego's bridge to our soul, and our soul's maturation for merger with Spirit. Hindus call this union of individual soul or Atman with Universal Spirit or Brahamana the process of Moksha or freedom from mundane existence and union with the sacred dimension of life. In this lifetime, we have the task to make our Soul worthy for merger with the Spirit. In this life, young soul has the opportunity to become an old Soul. If we do not complete the task in this life time, we re-incarnate to complete the process and leave un-retired Karma for future generations to retire.

Medical science is making tremendous strides in offering a biotechnological understanding of the human mind, psyche and illness. However, this is primarily a masculine, logical enterprise. It is precisely at this point that we need the wisdom and the guidance of the latent code of the slumbering goddess. She has the potential to add the feeling perspective and the soul wisdom to our attempts at healing and wholeness. She stands guard at the synapse of the body, mind, soul and the Spirit to inform us about the meaning and mystery of our life and suffering. The latent code can help us navigate our individual path to the soul and align it with the calling of the spirit. Thus the opposites in our nature and in our culture are reconciled in a sacred union to do their eternal dance on the stage of our life and our civilization. This may lead to achievement of our full potential, mutuality with our family, purposeful participation in the fabric of our community and alignment with the flow of the universe. Love, peace, prosperity and celebration of our differences in a soulful mosaic of One seamless World may prevail for the next thousand years.

To the latent code of the goddess
Who initiated my baby steps
Onto the path to the soul
I dedicate this humble rendering
Of the Latent Code
Of the timeless, formless, infinite, ever present
Goddess Shakti.

Acknowledgements

Many thanks to the following authors and publishers for permission to quote from their books: Open Court Publishing Company to quote from Edward R. Edinger's book *Anatomy of the Psyche: Alchemical Symbolism in Psychotherapy*. LaSalle, IL: Open Court Publishing Company (1985), Ms. Anjula Bedi to quote from her book *Gods and Goddesses of India*. Eshwar Publications: Mumbai (1998), pp. 79-82, University of California Press for permission to use material from David Kinsley. *Hindu Goddesses; Visions of the Divine Feminine in the Hindu Religious Tradition*. Berkeley: University of California Press (1986), Copyright 1985, The Regents of the University of California, Donald Kalsched. *The Inner World of Trauma: Archetypal Defenses of the Personal Spirit*. London and New York: Routledge (1996), Gareth S. Hill, M.S.W., Ph.D., for permission to quote from his book *The Masculine and the Feminine*. Boston: Shambhala (1995), Shambala Publications, Inc., for permission to quote from "Creation Myths" by Marie Louise von Franz © 1972, 1995 Reprinted by arrangement with Shambala Publications, Inc., Boston, *www.Shambala.com* , Micha Lindemans for permission to reprint material from Encyclopedia Mythica *mythica@pantheon.org*, American Psychiatric Publishing, Inc., for permission to cite from *American Psychiatric Association: Diagnostic and Statistical Manual of Mental Disorders*, Fourth Edition, Text Revision. Washington, DC, American Psychiatric Association, 2000, Margaret P. Johnson, Ph.D., to quote from Psychological Perspectives article "Typology Revisited: A New Perspective" Humphrey Osmond, Miriam Siegler, and Richard Smoke. "Typology Revisited: A New Perspective," (Fall 1977), pp. 206-219, Astro Journey Services for permission to use and modify the picture of Neel Kantha – Shiva Swallowing the Poison *www.astromandir.com*. I am grateful to the International Gita society for their kind permission to use the quotes from Bhagwad Gita. All the Yantra images in this book

270   are adapted from the excellent Yantra images created by
Per Krueger at the Swedish Institute of Computer Science.
These may be previewed at *Vamakhepa's* Yantra Page -
http://www.sics.se/~piak/yoga/yantra/. I am grateful to Per
Krueger for his generous permission to use the originals
and adapt some of the Yantra art.

I am grateful to photographer Harshad Kamdar for
assisting with the Aditi photograph and modifying the
Yantra art, to Karen Higgins for graphic art rendering of the
goddess images, to my daughter Ami Bedi for her support
and guidance during several trips to India to the goddess
sites to collect stories, photographs and inspiration. I am
grateful to Mr. B. J. D. Jada, the chief general manager
of the Mahalaxmi Temple Charities (February 1999) in
Mumbai, India for giving me access to archives at the
temple, for his gracious hospitality, history of the temple
and permission to photograph the goddess icons. Many
thanks to Ms. Alyssa Otter for the author photograph.

I wish to extent gratitude to my patients whose stories
inspired the deepening of my understanding of the latent
code. The case examples in the book are composite,
disguised and often hypothetical. The biggest gift of the
latent code was the opportunity to collaborate with my
daughter Ami on the project. She visited India with me
several times to research the project and edited the book. My
son Siddhartha gave it a final revision sweep. The Ganesha
archetype manifested in my life as my grandchildren Signe
and Loki, who have ushered in my new beginnings and
inspired me to look at life, world and the future with a
sense of hope and anticipation of a peaceful world.

References

1 Carl G. Jung, Collected Works, Vol. 6, Para 708-709

2 Peter R. Breggin. Talking Back to Prozac. New York: St. Martin Press (1994).

3 Gita Metha, Karma Cola, Penguin Books, 1979

4 Preyer William, (1888/1909) The Mind of the Child, 2 parts, translated,.W.Brown: New York, Appleton and Co.

5 Haeckel, Ernst (1900) The Riddle of the Universe, Translated by J. McCabe (New York, Harper)

6 Carl G. Jung, Collected Works, Volume 5, paragraph 320.

7 Gareth S. Hill. Masculine and Feminine: The Natural Flow of Opposites in the Psyche. Boston: Shambala Publications Inc. (1992), pp. 45-46.

8 Ibid. p. 39.

9 Gareth S. Hill. Masculine and Feminine: The Natural Flow of Opposites in the Psyche. Shambala Publications Inc. (1992) pp. 45-46

10 Collected Works, C.G. Jung, Volume 6, Psychological Types: Bollengen Series, 1971

11 Humphrey Osmond, Miriam Siegler, and Richard Smoke. "Typology Revisited: A New Perspective." Psychological Perspectives, (Fall 1977), pp. 206-219.

12 Ibid.

13 Anatomy of the Psyche: Alchemical Symbolism in Psychotherapy : Edward F. Edinger Open Court Publishing Company , 1985

14 Shakti and Shâkta: Essays and Addresses on the Shâkta tantrashâstra by Arthur Avalon (Sir David Woodroffe),London: Luzac & Co., [1918], Chapter 20

15 Retire Your Family Karma, Ashok Bedi, Boris Matthews, Nicholas-Hays, Inc. 2003

16 Path to the Soul, Ashok Bedi, Weiser Books, 2000

17 This and other Yantra images in this book are adapted from the excellent Yantra images created by Per Krueger at the Swedish Institute of Computer Science. These may be previewed at Vamakhepa's Yantra Page -http://www.sics.se/~piak/yoga/yantra/

18 Bhagwad Gita, Chapter 3, Paragraph 7-8

19 http://www.biocheminfo.org/klotho/

20 Path to the Soul,: Samuel Wieiser Inc. 2000

21 Anjula Bedi. Gods and Goddesses of India. Eshwar Publications: Mumbai (1998), pp. 79-82.

22 This and other Yantra images in this book are adapted from the excellent Yantra images created by Per Krueger at the Swedish Institute of Computer Science. These may be previewed at Vamakhepa's Yantra Page -http://www.sics.se/~piak/yoga/yantra/

23 C.G. Jung. Collected Works, Vol. 13, Para. 33.

24 Shakti and Shâkta: Essays and Addresses on the Shâkta tantrashâstra by Arthur Avalon (Sir John

272   Woodroffe),London: Luzac & Co., [1918], Chapter 20

25   This and other Yantra images in this book are adapted from the excellent Yantra images created by Per Krueger at the Swedish Institute of Computer Science. These may be previewed at Vamakhepa's Yantra Page -http://www.sics.se/~piak/yoga/yantra/

26   Path to the Soul, Ashok Bedi, M.D., Samuel Weiser Inc, 2000

27   Retire Your Family Karma: Ashok Bedi, Boris Matthews, Nicholas Hayes, 2003

28   Jean Shinoda Bolen. Goddesses in Everywoman: A New Psychology of Women. San Francisco: HarperPerennial (1984).

29   Retire Your Family Karma: Ashok Bedi, Boris Matthews, Nicholas Hayes, 2003

30   This and other Yantra images in this book are adapted from the excellent Yantra images created by Per Krueger at the Swedish Institute of Computer Science. These may be previewed at Vamakhepa's Yantra Page -http://www.sics.se/~piak/yoga/yantra/

31   Path to the Soul, Ashok Bedi, Samuel Weiser, 2000

32   Retire Your Family Karma, Ashok Bedi, Boris Matthews, Nicholas Hayes, 2003

33   Adapted from -Ego Defenses: Diagnostic and Statistical Manual, Fourth Volume, American Psychiatric Association Press

34   Donald Kalsched. The Inner World of Trauma: Archetypal Defenses of the Personal Spirit. London and New York: Routledge (1996).

35   C.G. Jung. "Answer to Job." C.W. 11, para. 553-758.

36   H. Racker, Counter resistance and Interpretation in Transference and Counter transference. New York: International Universities Press (1968), pp. 186-192.

37   Gareth Hill calls this dissolving action a "watery initiation." G. Hill, The Masculine and the Feminine. Boston: Shambhala (1995).

38   Diane Wolkestein and Samuel Noah Kramer. Innana: Queen of Heaven and Earth; Her Stories and Hymns for Sumer. New York: Harper and Row Publishers (1983).

39   Edward F. Edinger. : Anatomy of the Psyche: Alchemical Symbolism in Psychotherapy. LaSalle, IL: Open Court Publishing Company (1985).

40   C. G. Jung, Collected Works, Vol. 11, Para. 98.

41   This and other Yantra images in this book are adapted from the excellent Yantra images created by Per Krueger at the Swedish Institute of Computer Science. These may be previewed at Vamakhepa's Yantra Page -http://www.sics.se/~piak/yoga/yantra/

42   Donald Kalsched. The Inner World of Trauma: Archetypal Defenses of the Personal Spirit. London and New York: Routledge (1996).

43   David H. Rosen. Transforming Depression: A Jungian Approach Using the Creative Arts. Los Angeles: Jeremy P. Tarcher/Putnam Book (1993).

44   Tracy Pintchman. The Rise of Goddess in Hindu Tradition. State University of New York Press (1994), pp. 32-34.

45   Translated with a popular commentary by Ralph T. H. Griffith. The Hymns of Atharva Veda.

2 vols. Chowkhamba Sanskrit Series, no. 66. Varanasi: Chowkhamba Sanskrit Series Office

(1968). See also Athara-Veda-Samhita. Translated by W. D. Whitney. Harvard Oriental Series, vols. 7-8. (1905). 2nd Indian reprint ed. Delhi: Motilal Banarsidasss (1971). Tracy Pintchman. The Rise of Goddess in Hindu Tradition. State University of New York Press (1994), pp. 32-34.

46 Ed. by Albrecht Weber. The Vajasaneyi- Samhita in Maadhyandina and Knave Sakha with the Commentary of Mahidhara. 2nd ed. Chowkhamba Sanskrit Series, no. 1003. Varanasi: The Chwokhamba Sanskrit Series Office (1972).

Translations:

The Yajur Veda. Edited and translated by Devi Chand. Sanskrit text with English translation. New Delhi: S Paul and Co., 1(965).

Yajurveda Samhita. Edited and enlarged by Surendra Pratap, translated by Ralph T. H. Griffith. Sanskrit text with English translation. Delhi Nag Publishers (1990).

The White Yajur Veda. Translated with a Popular Commentary. Translated by Ralph R.H. Griffith. Varanasi: R. J. J. Lazaurs and Company (1899).

47 F.Max Muller. Translations of the Vedic Hymns, Sacred books of the East, Vol. 32, and (1891) reprint: Delhi: Motilal Banarsidas (1964.) p. 241 and p.248.

48 Pupul Jayakar: Aditi; the Living Arts of India, Smithsonian Institution Press, Washington D.C., (1985), pp. 25-29

49 David Kinsley. Hindu Goddesses; Visions of the Divine Feminine in the Hindu Religious Tradition. Berkeley: University of California Press (1986), pp. 9-10.

50 Edited by F. Max Muller. Rig Veda-Samhita, together with the commentary of Sayanacharya. 1st Indian ed. 4 vols. Chowkhamba Sanskrit Series, no. 99. Varanasi: Chowkhamba Sanskrit Series Office (1966).

Translations: The Hymns of Rig Veda, Translated with a Popular Commentary. Edited by J. L. Shastri, translated by Ralph T. H. Griffith, Rev. ed. 2 vols. Delhi: Motilal Banasidass, 1973

51 Marie- Louise Von Franz. Creation Myths. Shambala, (1995), p. 52

52 Retire Your Family Karma: Ashok Bedi, M.D., Boris Matthews, Ph.D., Nicholas Hayes Inc., 2003

53 ibid. pp. 60-61

54 Ibid. pp. 264-266.

55 Ibid. p. 247.

56 Ibid. p. 260.

57 C. G. Jung, Collected Works, Vol. 16, Para 296

58 ibid. Para 313

59 Path to the Soul, Ashok Bedi, Samuel Weiser Inc., 2000

60 David Adams Lemming. The World of Myth: An Anthology. Oxford University Press (1990),

274   pp. 32, 99, 134-135.

61 Marie-Louise von Franz. Creation Myths. Boston: Shambala (1995), p. 113.

62 Ibid. pp. 126-127.

63 Ibid. pp. 128-129.

64 Ibid. pp. 130-131.

65 Diagnostic and Statistical Manual of mental disorders, Fourth edition, American Psychiatric Association press, 1994

66 Ibid. p. 211.

67 Paraphrase of E. C. Whitmont, The Symbolic Quest. Princeton: Princeton University Press (1969), p. 69.

68 Personal interview with Mr. B. J. D. Jada, the chief general manager of the Mahalaxmi Temple Charities. (February 1999).

69 C.G. Jung, Collected Works, Vol. 14, Para. 517.

70 C. G. Jung, Collected Works, Volume 10, Wotan, Para 371--399

71 Gita Mehta. Karma Cola. Penguin Books, (1979, republished 1993).

72 C. G. Jung. Collected Works, Volume 14, Para. 207.

73 Ibid. Para. 664.

74 Ibid. Para. 616.

75 Ibid. Para. 517.

76 This is not unlike the problem we have in our technological society, where we have been milking nature for its bounty but now have toxic wastes. Chernobyl, Three Mile Island, and innumerable other toxic sites are now in our midst. The problem for modern civilization is what to do with this toxicity we have created.

77 Retire Your Family Karma, Ashok Bedi, Boris Matthews, Nicholas Hayes Inc., 2003

78 Adapted from Path to the Soul–Ashok Bedi, M.D.; Samuel Weiser Inc., 2000

79 Carl G. Jung: Confrontation with the Unconscious; in Memories, Dreams and Reflections, Edited by Aniela Jaffe, Vintage Books 1989, pages 170-199

80 Michael Fordham: Exploration into the Self, Karnac Books, London, 1985, page 31-32

81 Edward F. Edinger: Anatomy of the Psyche, Alchemical Symbolism in Psychotherapy; Open Court, Chicago, 1985, page230

82 Retire Your Family Karma–Ashok Bedi, M.D., Boris Matthews, Ph.D., Nicholas Hayes, Nov. 2003

83 Internet Sacred Text Archive , International Gita Society

84 The Bhagwad Gita, International Gita Society, Chapter 2, paragraph 47-48

85 C. G. Jung, Collected Works, Volume 6, Para 814

86 C.G. Jung, Collected Works, Volume 6, Para 818

87 Bhagwad Gita – International Gita Society, Chapter 18, Paragraphs 5-6, www.gita-society.com

88 Alchemical Active Imagination: Revised Edition (C. G. Jung Foundation Books) by Marie-   275
Louise von Franz Shambhala; Rev Sub edition 1997

89 Inner Work: Using Dreams and Active Imagination for Personal Growth
by Robert A. Johnson HarperOne; New Ed edition (1989)

90 The Inner Journey: Lectures and Essays on Jungian Psychology by Barbara Hannah, Dean L.
Frantz (Editor), Inner City Books 1999

Ashok Bedi, M.D. is a Diplomat Jungian psychoanalyst and a board certified psychiatrist, a member of the Royal College of psychiatrists of Great Britain, a diplomat in Psychological Medicine at the Royal College of Physicians and Surgeons of England, a Distinguished Fellow of the American Psychiatric Association, Clinical Professor in Psychiatry at the Medical College of Wisconsin in Milwaukee, a faculty member at the Analyst Training Program at the Carl G. Jung Institute of Chicago and a Psychiatrist at the Aurora Psychiatric Hospital and the Aurora Health Care Network. He has been a psychiatric consultant to several agencies in Metro Milwaukee. Presently he is the consultant for the Sexual Assault treatment center at the Aurora Sinai Samaritan Hospital and the Pastoral Counseling Service of Greater Milwaukee.

Trained in India, Great Britain and the US, he is interested in the emerging frontiers of Spirituality and Healing and the synapses of the Mind, Body, Soul and Spirit. He is author of the book, Path to the Soul, Weiser Books, 2000, and the coauthor of Retire Your Family Karma,

Nicholas-Hays, Inc. 2003, His activities can be previewed at his website *www.pathtothesoul.com*.

Ashok Bedi has been in practice in Milwaukee for over thirty years and specializes in Adult Psychotherapy and Jungian Psychoanalysis. He regularly presents lectures and seminars in India, Great Britain, Ireland and USA on the topic of the Spiritual and analytic dimensions of treatment, healing and personal growth. Over the last several years, he has been the International Association of Analytical Psychologist's liaison person for developing Jungian training programs in India and travels annually to India to teach, train the consult with the Jungian Developing groups at several centers in India including Ahmedabad &, Bangalore. He leads the annual "In the Footsteps of Carl Jung in India" study group to several centers in India under the auspices of the New York Jung Foundation.

1120383